INTERNATIONAL ORGANIZATION IN THE AGE OF GLOBALIZATION

International Organization in the Age of Globalization

Paul Taylor

continuum
NEW YORK • LONDON

Continuum

The Tower Building, 11 York Road, London, SE1 7NX
15 East 26th Street, New York, NY 10010

First published 2003
Reprinted 2005

© Paul Taylor 2003

All rights reserved. No part of this publication may be reproduced, or transmitted in any form, or by any means, electronic or mechanical, including photocopying, recording, or any information storage or retrieval system, without permission in writing from the publishers.

British Library Cataloguing-in-Publication Data
A catalogue record for this book is available from the British Library.

ISBN 0–8264–6153–0 (hardback)

Library of Congress Cataloging-in-Publication Data
Taylor, Paul Graham.
 International organization in the age of globalization / Paul Taylor.
   p. cm.
 Includes bibliographical references and index.
 ISBN 0–8264–6153–0—ISBN 0–8264–8512–X (pbk.)
 1. International agencies. 2. International cooperation. 3. Globalization. I. Title.

JZ4850 .T39 2002
341.2—dc21   2002031092

Typeset by RefineCatch Limited, Bungay, Suffolk
Printed and bound in Great Britain by MPG Books, Bodmin, Cornwall

For Janetta
again

Contents

List of Abbreviations	ix
Introduction	1
1 The United Nations at the Millennium: Order and Sovereignty	21
2 Peacekeeping in the Age of Globalization: Kosovo and After	55
3 Globalization and Regionalization among Modern States: The Case of the EU	99
4 The Social and Economic Agenda of International Organization in the Age of Globalization	135
5 Development and Labour Welfare in the Age of Globalization: Aspects of the US International Economic Stance and International Organization	167
6 The Principle of Consonance in Global Organization: The Case of the United Nations	210
7 Conclusions: Globalization, International Organization and Regionalization	242
Notes	261
Index	273

List of Abbreviations

ACABQ	The Advisory Committee for the Administrative and Budgetary Questions
ACC	Administrative Committee on Coordination
ACP	African, Caribbean and Pacific Group of States
APEC	Asia Pacific Economic Cooperation
ASEAN	Association of South East Asian Nations
CET	Common External Tariff
CFSP	Common Foreign and Security Policy
CPC	Committee for Programme Coordination
DAF	Development Assistant Framework
DFID	Department for International Development
DHA	Department of Humanitarian Affairs
ECOSOC	Economic and Social Council
EPZ	Export Processing Zone
FAO	Food and Agriculture Organization
FDI	Foreign Direct Investment
GA	General Assembly
GASPP	Globalism and Social Policy Programme
GATT	The General Agreement on Tariffs and Trade
HIPC	Heavily Indebted Poor Countries
ICFTU	International Confederation of Free Trade Unions
IGO	Intergovernmental Organization
ILO	International Labour Organization
INGO	International Non-governmental Organization
IR	Integrated Research
MAI	Multilateral Agreement on Investment
MEI	Media Elite International
MERCOSUR	Common Market of the Southern Cone
MFN	Most-favoured Nation (in GATT)
NAFTA	North America Free Trade Agreement
NGO	Non-Governmental Organization
NIEO	New International Economic Order

OCHA	Office of the Coordinator for Humanitarian Affairs (UN)
OECD	Organization for Economic Cooperation and Development
P5	Permanent Five Members of the Security Council
TNC	Transnational Companies
UNCTAD	UN Conference on Trade and Development
UNDAF	UN Development Assistance Framework
UNDG	UN Development Group
UNDP	UN Development Programme
UNFPA	UN Fund for Population Activities
UNHCR	UN High Commission for Human Rights
UNICEF	UN Children's Fund
UNIDO	UN Industrial Development Organization
UNRWA	UN Relief and Work Administration
WFP	World Food Programme
WHO	World Health Organization
WTO	World Trade Organization

Introduction

This book looks at the way in which the process of globalization has affected the practice of, and ways of thinking about, international organization, at both global and regional levels. Globalization has increased the need for global international organization, as more global activity has demanded more global management, but it has often also strengthened the case for regional arrangements, as a way of supporting globalization rather than as an alternative. At first sight this might seem a paradox. The normal assumption has been that globalization challenged regions, defined as groupings of contiguous member states, but it is argued here that more often the opposite was the case.[1] References are made throughout to the implications for the arguments of the events of 11 September 2001.[2] The approach is deliberately eclectic, since the meaning of the key terms – globalization, international organization and regionalization – is subject to debate and disagreement. Students will need to look elsewhere for more detailed examinations of each of these concepts.[3]

The specific examples are the maintenance of international peace and security; the management of economic and social activities, especially with regard to development; and the linked area of the protection of the welfare of individuals. The latter is considered from two perspectives: that of the welfare states of Western Europe, and that reflected in the policies of the US and their interaction with those of the UN. The three areas provide telling illustrations of the changing relationship between international organizations and the member states, as well as the changing character of international society. In each case, discussion leads to the evaluation of a regional response. It is not just that there has been more, or less, regionalization in these contexts, but that thinking about global problems has usually led to the positing of regional solutions as well as global ones. This book discusses the case *for* regionalization in the context of globalization, as well as reporting its progress.

The discussions of the specific problems are preceded in Chapter 1 by an examination of the way in which the nature of international order and sovereignty has changed in the age of globalization. Indeed such changes are themselves aspects of globalization. This chapter is therefore a summary of the changes in international society in the age of globalization and the ways they are related to changes in international organization. It provides the setting for the more empirical accounts which follow. In Chapter 2 arguments about the role of international organization in the maintenance of international peace and security are considered. Chapters 3, 4 and 5 consider economic and social responses to globalization, first in a key part of the developed world (Chapter 3), and then in the developing world (Chapters 4 and 5). In Chapter 6 the implications of what has gone before for the future of the United Nations are examined, especially with regard to the interaction between regional and global arrangements. Chapter 7 proposes some conclusions about the main lines of development of the system, interactions between regional and global arrangements within it, and their implications for the transformation of international society.

An attempt is made to judge the evidence beyond the confines of any particular theory. It does not assume that international society is dominated by states that are doomed to conflict with each other, seek always to maximize their power and necessarily limit the role of international organization, in the manner of traditional realists. But neither does it assume a natural harmony or the inevitable decline of the state.[4] On the contrary the facts about states and their interactions often raise awkward questions about the limits and possibilities of international cooperation, with regard to maintaining international peace and security, or promoting the rights and interests of people, which defy a neat response in the context of any existing theory.

A danger facing anyone who wants to understand where the world is going is that of being trapped by theory, so that profound change becomes invisible. The author endorses the approach taken by John Ruggie when he concluded that two leading approaches in the early twenty-first century, neorealism and neoliberal institutionalism, both made assumptions about their universe which made it hard for them to detect changes in the nature and implications of statehood.[5] They started from assumptions which led to self-fulfilling prophecies: neorealists assumed 'that the most powerful states in the system created and shaped institutions so that they could maintain their share of world power, or even increase it. Internationally, outcomes were mainly a function of the balance of power and institutions at best were an intervening variable.'[6] And neoliberalism, despite its different empirical expectations, made comparable assumptions. It assigned 'greater scope to institutions, but their scope was similarly functionally determined'.[7] Hence the structure of the two arguments was very similar. They excluded systemic pressures towards cooperation among states from the outset, and condemned us to a world of power-hungry states which by definition could not change.

But the problem was to find a theory which did allow a better understanding of change. It might not even be possible that any such theory could be found. Ruggie quoted Quentin Skinner with approval. Understanding change required 'a willingness to emphasise the local and the contingent, a desire to underline the extent to which our own concepts and attitudes have been shaped by particular historical circumstances, and a correspondingly strong dislike ... of all overarching theories and singular schemes of explanation'.[8] Such overarching theories could be realist or idealist, assume that man was motivated by self-interest, and always quarrelsome, or that they could see the underlying condition as that of harmony, with cooperation the natural relationship. In practice, as the more perceptive and nuanced theorists have argued, such as Machiavelli and, indeed, E. H. Carr, humankind had a capacity for both. 'Morality and power, utopia and reality, altruism and self-seeking were dual elements present in every political society.'[9]

It was, in other words, important to approach the question of theorizing with humility, so that the truths of new empirical materials could be seen ahead of existing theories, and to realize that theories usually had a moral basis. This point deserves to be stressed, since too often the scholarly community adopted one moral perspective or the other without admitting it. It was the duality of humankind's moral nature which was the difficult thing to grasp, and it was often failure to understand this which led to reluctance to see change. This was because change was largely about the strengthening of the mechanisms for the maintenance of order, of using an instinct for the good to gain greater control over an inclination to the bad.

There has been a series of damning accounts of the work and mechanisms of international organizations, including the United Nations, the Specialized Agencies and the European Union's institutions, and gloomy ruminations about the society of states, which have ignored or concealed anything positive about them. Very frequently the position has been the opposite of that of Pangloss: all was for the worst in the worst of all possible worlds! The present writer, in contrast, holds that, though mistakes and inadequacies need to be acknowledged and corrected, there has been a measure of achievement in international organization and some cause for optimism about the progress of international society. After the events of 11 September the world may enter a period of danger, but, despite this, overstressing the negative could lead to as much mischief as the opposite, and produce an equal misrepresentation of reality.

An assumption which runs through this book is that if there is a choice between acting and not acting to help ameliorate extreme human suffering there should always be a presumption in favour of acting. Even if acting, despite good intentions, could clearly be shown afterwards to have had damaging effects, it was still better to have tried, with the proviso that there was a concomitant obligation to learn from mistakes. There was a moral and practical price to pay for inaction, and often the coin in which the price was paid was in terms of both condemnation on moral grounds and cost in specific terms: in the early twenty-first century the two were often bound up with each other so closely that they were hard to distinguish. This position is sharply different from the mainstream realist view that in the universe of states only their distinct interests mattered and any transcendent morality was a delusion.

The alternatives are stark: either we must decide, for instance, that peacekeeping should *never* take place, or we should set about learning how to make it more effective. For all the mistakes that have been made in other areas, be they in environmental protection or the methods of providing food relief, the lessons are the same. The fact of mistakes having been made, as they were in Kosovo and Bosnia, or of its not having happened when we think it should, as in Rwanda, mean that we should learn to do it better, not never. Those who say 'never' have usually underestimated the short- and long-term costs of that position, defined in practical terms, but interpreted in a perspective of morality, for society in general.

But this is not the same as saying that in the early twenty-first century a set of rules should now be drawn up among states which would oblige them to act in a range of prescribed circumstances, to support peacekeeping, or to act forcefully to protect human rights. The problem is that such a code would have to be negotiated between governments and that the result would be a lowest common denominator of possible action, which could easily lead to moral actions being forbidden when they could have been pursued by some states. It should be remembered that this is indeed a world of states, and that the decision to act can at best only be the product of a coincidence between their view of their interests and the perception of what was morally desirable. They could always decide not to act and would in consequence pay the appropriate price. But the preparedness to act would inevitably be the result of an admixture of motives, including interest, and would be undertaken by coalitions of states which formed in *ad hoc* ways according to the circumstances of the particular crisis. This is not to say, though, that when statespeople said they were acting for moral reasons they were being hypocritical or deceitful. It was merely to point out that what they said might not be the whole truth and usually was not.

It often happened that an *actual* political, economic or social development went along with the prescription that it *should* happen. This amounted to saying that what had transpired was a good thing, and then explaining this judgement. This was true of globalization as it was of regionalism. But there were also frequently a wide range of varying empirical references for both the description and the prescription. Globalization was seen to be about various things; about technological change and the consequent compression of time and space, about global markets and the activities of multinational companies, or about changes in values and views about order. Regionalism was about trade or development, and stable currencies. Globalization was justified because there were global problems, and the need to pool resources to tackle them, or in order to remove economic inefficiencies. Regionalism was justified because it allowed a greater say in the world to the member states of regions, or to achieve goals which they shared, like higher levels of welfare provision, and sometimes because of a mixture of practical considerations and reasons of individual identity or the character of states. Such reasons are discussed at greater length late in the volume.

But what was important was that it was not a question of choosing one or the other. Regionalization and globalization could have a symbiotic relationship, as in previous periods further internationalization had been positively linked with greater differentiation. For instance the origins of international institutions were linked with the consolidation of the state and were not intended to supersede it. The strength of the one was positively related to the strength of the other. At the turn of the twenty-first century, as is demonstrated in this book, the same thing was happening at a higher level in some areas. It remained the case that international organization was the ally not the rival of sovereignty, even when it went along with supranational regionalization. In many ways globalization was helping to consolidate groupings of what remained states. It was the same kind of relationship of the global to the local, except that by this time individual states were – with the exception of the USA – too small to assert themselves on their own, and regions became the medium for this.

In 2001 globalization was the most visible of the processes, and it was important to understand its nature and justification, but it also often actually generated stronger regions, as well as underlining the case for them. The regional response could be either because the global policy could be obtained more easily with the help of regions, or because globalization challenged a goal which states wanted to obtain, and could only get by collective regional action. Hence some tasks, particularly economic and social ones, but also, according to many, maintaining international peace and security, required global action, but through regional agencies if necessary. However there was a difference between the two kinds of tasks. With peace and security the need for successful action through global mechanisms was clear, and regional action was to help out, whereas in the area of economic and social action success with certain kinds of globalization, such as the triumph of US culture, or the neoliberal economic agenda, was often unacceptable and prompted a countervailing regional response. Within a region such as the EU globalization helped to strengthen the case for stronger organization to achieve goals such as the protection of social democracy, and this is argued in Chapter 3, while in the developing world responses to the globalizing strategy of the neoliberals was an increase in the value of regional trade, as well as the realization that development might be best approached through regional mechanisms in cooperation with global ones (Chapter 5). In this book the pattern of argument reflects the varying patterns of these interconnections. There is a strong case for globalization, though it might not be understood by different authors in the same way, but this often leads to the realization that global arrangements both generate a regional response and require effective regional cooperation.

In this Introduction it is necessary to distinguish briefly the three main variables in the argument: globalization, regionalization and international organization. Each of these is characteristic of international society in the early twenty-first century and needs to be given an identity. In this Introduction all that is needed is to indicate the essential aspects of the three variables as they are used in the following chapters. Though the stress is upon global international organization, it keeps on running into or alongside the other two, and reacts with them in peculiar ways. The company it keeps should be identified.

Globalization

What is globalization? Among its multifarious meanings in 2001 were the following:

- It referred to development in the technology of travel and communication which had led to the compression of time and space, so that the local had become indistinguishable from the global. This was illustrated by the possibility of instant communication between any one place on the earth's surface and any other. This, some argued, was the primary fact about globalization, and all other aspects and descriptions were secondary.[10]
- It referred to the increasing interconnectedness of international economic activities. Aspects of this included the emergence of a global marketplace for a large number of goods and services, the emergence of a global financial system, the possibility of transferring large sums quickly and invisibly between financial institutions in distant cities. Stock exchanges communicated between each other instantly, and what happened in one rapidly affected developments in the other. There were now global companies, which existed in most states, and followed global strategies.
- For others the central characteristic was the development of a global moral community. There was a greatly increased chance that gross breaches of human rights in one part of the world would rapidly be detected in all other parts. Global media like CNN and the BBC news channels had the capacity to convey the bad news very quickly. Linked with this was the strengthening of the idea of global obligation, the sense that where an agent could act in mitigation it was both morally and practically necessary to do so. It could be argued that this also meant that peace had become indivisible. There had been a globalization of moral concern, in consequence of the globalization of communication.

- There had also been a globalization of risk in the sense that it was impossible to escape from the consequences of failure in a number of areas. There were global problems which required global solutions.[11] Environmental catastrophe was now possible, and would have global consequences, despite the fact that those consequences might be unequal across areas and populations. The rich could reduce the impact on themselves of the new risks, which were greater for the poor, but could not avoid them. Similarly weapons of war were such that their use could damage the global population. After the events of 11 September the dangers of global terrorism became visible to every thinking person, though they had been apparent before. This represented a threat from the development of a particular kind of internationalized civil society and, as is argued in Chapter 2, could only be countered by the establishment of countermovements which would also form a part of that internationalized civil society. In the short term there could be a state response, using Great Power military forces. But in the longer term the job could only be done by having adequate links between national police forces, intelligence services, companies, a range of transnational lobbies and the banks. It was likely that this need would lead to the further enhancement of the role of the United Nations system.
- At a more trivial level globalization had also been interpreted as meaning a convergence in lifestyles, and cultural values, icons and design. Similar food was increasingly consumed by the young who increasingly wore the same clothes. More broadly put: there had been a degree of cultural homogenization. However, this has to be set beside and evaluated against the appearance of greater cultural fragmentation, as seemed to be the case after 11 September. It was too early to decide whether to favour Samuel Huntington's idea that there would inevitably be a war of civilizations, or to point out that Islam and Christo-Judaism were both so varied in their various national and cultural settings that it was foolish to talk as if they each had wills which could clash. The problem was indeed illustrated by the war in Afghanistan. There was a claim that this was a struggle on the part of Islam against the rest, but it was most obviously a struggle of Islam against Islam.

These rather basic definitions and interpretations are expanded in the chapters which follow.

Regionalization

In this book the argument proceeds from an examination of the role of global arrangements, and the way in which they enlisted regional resources in the chosen areas. It is appropriate, therefore, to consider in this Introduction why regions were a fact of life facing global organizations. They are given substance, not by listing the various regional organizations in the various parts of the world, ASEAN, NAFTA and the like, but by considering the question of why states sought membership. The detailed arrangements of each regional group are not crucial to the argument here, though establishing the fact of regionalization is.

For the states outside the Western capitalist world a key consideration was the failure of their earlier efforts to change the global economic system so that it suited them better. The global approach of the mid-1970s New International Economic Order had surely failed by the early 1980s, mainly because the developed states recovered from the shocks of the oil crises and became increasingly reluctant to grant the concessions demanded by the Group of 77, such as the setting up of a substantial Common Fund.[12] The work of the Conference on International Economic Cooperation held in Paris in 1976 was largely futile from the point of view of the Group of 77. Hence for the developing states there was a need for an alternative strategy: hence an increasing interest in regional organization in the absence of anything better.

The European Community/Union also encouraged a greater resort to regional arrangements with specific measures to encourage trade between the developing states in the Lomé Three agreements; Lomé One in particular had been criticized for discouraging such intraregional links among Group of 77 countries.[13] A further pressure in the same direction came from the Brandt Report in the early 1980s which implied that regional arrangements among developing states should be encouraged as their growth depended mainly upon increases in South–South trade.[14] Although efforts at the global level had to continue, by the mid-1980s there was a feeling among the Group of 77 that, far from radicalizing the global system, they would have to make concessions at that level. By the late 1980s these had come to include the acceptance of the right of the main contributing states to increase their control of economic and social policies in the United Nations.[15] A retreat at that level was accompanied by a greater concern with the regional one.

Another incentive was the perception that regional arrangements would help solve pressing economic problems. The main illustration of this was of course the European Community/Union which became a model for much of the rest of the world. Emulation was a very important political fact. But it was, of course, encouraged by its association with a very persuasive literature about the advantages of regional economic activities, in particular of common markets, which applied to the developed world, as with the European Community/Union, as much as to the developing world. The theories of economists, such as James Meade, Jacob Viner *et al.* do not require extended discussion in this chapter.[16] Suffice it to say that they argued the benefits of establishing freer trade within a larger area rather than a smaller one, as this would allow more efficient producers to prosper at the expense of the less efficient ones. Regional common markets were seen as the first step to global free trade. Larger producers would be able to lower unit costs and would be able to spend more on research. One implication of this was that there would be trade creation between members of the regional market and trade diversion between members and outsiders. In the late 1990s and early years of the twenty-first century regional trade concentration in the various regions continued, in part stimulated by the currency crises of the 1990s (see Chapter 5). These various factors encouraged import substitution within the region, though not necessarily the state.

Another category of incentive towards the creation of regional organization was that which was stressed by Nye.[17] The traditional realist ambitions of statesmen were reckoned to have been to do with the acquisition of possessions, especially in the form of territory. In modern times, however, it was more likely that statesmen would pursue what had been called milieu goals, such as those which were intended to change the environment in which a state operated so that it would be found more congenial. For instance governments might see participation in regional organizations as providing a context in which leadership at that level could be sought. Or the region could be seen as a way to solve particular security problems, as with the French strategy of binding Germany in an ever-closer Union. It was also probable – as much in Europe as in Africa or Asia or Latin America – that governments would seek to locate such organizations on their own territory in order to facilitate the exercising of influence, or to gain revenue. In other words the region would aid the leadership ambitions of its core members.

There was also the urge to strengthen the region to lessen vulnerability to intervention from outside. The prospect of superpower intervention sharpened the appetite for doing it locally. One illustration of this was the Indian action in support of the government of the Maldive islands after it had been attacked in November 1988 by mercenaries. The then Indian President, Rajiv Gandhi, pointed out that the success of Indian forces on this occasion confirmed the efficacy of regional arrangements. Their involvement in Sri Lanka reflected a similar interest. It not only lessened the chances of superpower involvement but also seemed – probably wrongly – to lessen the need for action by the United Nations. This was not to say, however, that the idea of alliance with outsiders had now been rejected in Africa and Asia, but rather that there had arisen an inclination to seek security more actively at the regional level. But there could be a similar reaction to economic vulnerability. Regionalization increased the power of members to defend themselves against turbulence in the international economic or financial system.

Regionalization was also related to international coalitions, alliances and spheres of influence. The experience of the European Community/Union suggested that the emergence of the region changed the dynamics of any alliance of which it was a subunit. In particular the region – even when the initial motivation was economic – undermined the sphere of influence of the most powerful state. This was because economic interests and military strategic interests were on a continuum: as governments acquired a wider range of common economic interests it was likely that incentives towards creating a common defence would also increase. Hence after the late 1970s the idea that the members of the European Community should strengthen their common defensive arrangements was more frequently proposed and discussed than had earlier been the case,[18] and in the Maastricht agreement the possibility of building a common defence in the future was spelled out. The idea that the West European Union should be reactivated – thus ensuring a link with NATO – had become current in the mid-1980s, and was incorporated in 1991 in the agreement at Maastricht – but there were other proposals for giving the Community itself a more independent defence capacity.[19] By 2001 this process had led to the proposal to set up a European Rapid Reaction Force, which, though not intended to undermine NATO, nevertheless raised this fear among Eurosceptics and some American commentators. This again was a logical outcome of the expansion of the scope of integration; it was likely that any region would be more liable to seek a stronger common defence as its range of common economic interests expanded, a thought that was surely relevant in the early twenty-first century when there was evidence of increasing economic interdependence between the members of the world's major economic regions. This was as true for East Asia and North America as for the European Union.

In 2001 there were various types of groups of states, or regions, which could be differentiated according to the number of factors which bound members and their durability. In the UN system some groups became stronger and endured, others came and went, depending upon issues and inclinations.[20] At the top of the hierarchy outside the UN were regions of a political-economic kind. These had special economic relations between members, in the sense that they had established a higher degree of trade interdependence with each other than with non-members, shared a range of common characteristics with regard to economic arrangements and circumstances and, to a lesser or greater degree, had the intention of establishing even closer economic arrangements. But, importantly, such regions were not unifunctional: the scope of their relations could be widened. There was also a political element which could derive from economic circumstances, identity, a sense of occupying the same geopolitical space and an ambition to work together in international arrangements, institutions or negotiations, or establish constitutional unity.

The European Union was the highest expression of this, and was the only region that scored high on all the indicators mentioned. But the other two important political-economic players were the North American Free Trade Area, and the Far East group, in which in 2001 China was now finding its place. These were the three primary economic regional groupings, and each showed an increasing degree of internal trade interdependence and had forms of economic organization in common. But a number of other regions were identifiable, which included Latin America, particularly the members of MERCOSUR, Russia and the states that had stayed identified with Russia after the Cold War – Ukraine, Georgia, etc. – a group of Middle Eastern Countries and, at least bound together in a situation of severe underdevelopment, the states of Africa south of the Sahara. Each of these regions possessed characteristics which could lead members to attempt resistance to the motley pressures towards uniformity which some found in globalization. A study of the three primary economic regions from the mid-1990s proposed that in each of them there were national ways of doing business which together contributed to a set of distinctive regional characteristics.[21] The way they worked was determined by national forms rather than by global forms, despite the apparent triumph of global neoliberalism.

But at issue in the early twenty-first century was whether globalizing uniformity would eventually prevail, or whether local arrangements would be sustained. Some authors detected a trend after the end of the Cold War towards the decentralization of the international security system, and concluded that 'in most global regions there is a gradual shift taking place towards cooperative defence or cooperative security arrangements ... there was a historic strengthening, rather than weakening, of multilateral and collective defence arrangements as well as international military cooperation and coordination'.[22] But the crucial qualification was that 'regionalization and globalization of military/security relations are by no means contradictory processes but may be mutually reinforcing'.[23]

There were many other instances of regionalization with regard to specific policies, or a number of related ones, which led some to conclude that this was the dominant structural change in international society.[24] But this was also frequently denied on the grounds that the EU was the only politically significant case of regionalization, and that there was no cumulative process of regional integration elsewhere.[25] Sometimes the message was that, though globalization could lead to a regional counteraction, this was bound to fail in the long term in response to globalization.[26] The arguments in this book, in contrast, are, first, that regionalization was sometimes a necessary response to globalization and was therefore likely to endure as long as globalization; and second that it was also likely that the main regions would solidify, in that they would aquire new functions and increasing political significance. The greater the degree of economic and military regionalization the more likely was this to happen.

There was no evidence against the idea of cumulation, and some indication that members of the main political-economic regions outside Europe were acquiring a stronger sense of shared values and identity. Regions were becoming harder rather than softer. There was no strong sense of common identity, but there was the emergence of a feeling of something in common, however pale for the time being, which defined the members of one region and helped to distinguish them from others. Regional frameworks helped to uphold preferred forms of governance and economic organization. They were a concomitant of globalization, and at the same time a way of rescuing the state.

The developments within regions between the 1980s and the early twenty-first century seemed to justify the conclusion that the kind of multi-bloc world discussed by Masters in the 1960s could yet emerge.[27] In the meantime in 2001 there was no denying the appearance of an increasing number of regions in North and South America, in the Far East, Europe and indeed Africa. The boundaries of such regions were sometimes contested or uncertain – there was some unhappiness in the Far East about the membership of the USA in Pacific arrangements – and there was uncertainty about the future membership of the European Union. But it was uncontestable, despite the appearance of what could appear to be rival developments – globalization and global organization – that they were an increasingly important feature of the international system. It was also uncontestable, as will be seen below, that globalization made it easier, rather than more difficult, to develop arguments to support the view that they should be developed further.

International organization in 2001

This section is intended as a brief outline of the antecedents, and main principles, of the primary element of international organization in the early twenty-first century, namely the United Nations system. At various places in the text reference is made to the way in which this system evolved and at this point these references are tied together. There are, of course, a number of excellent more detailed accounts which might be consulted.[28]

In the sense employed here a global international organization may be defined as any institution made up of the representatives of governments, having its own constitution; with a permanent headquarters. The element of global organization particularly discussed in this book is the United Nations system and it is with this body that the introductory discussion is now concerned. This is merely a shorthand way of giving an account of the way in which international organization developed, to go along with the corresponding account above of the development of regional arrangements. There were also of course the range of institutions which could still be labelled the Bretton Woods system after the New Hampshire resort where they were set up after the Second World War. These were the International Monetary Fund and the World Bank. Much later the World

Trade Organization was established. But the range of global international organization was, of course, even wider. It included a vast range of intergovernmental and non-governmental organizations – all those institutions which formed a part of what was called international governance. But the United Nations system had been the primary focus of hopes and expectations, and fears, about that governance, and in some ways had become the primary reference point for the claims and counterclaims about global intergovernmental organization in general. It was the focus of the discussion about international community, the rights and interests of peoples, and the attempts of states to manage their own realm. It is here taken as a kind of shorthand for international organization in general.

The United Nations was established at the end of the Second World War as a result of initiatives taken by the governments of the states which had led the war against Germany and Japan, namely Britain, the United States and the Soviet Union. They were determined to build upon the experience of the League of Nations from the inter-war period, but to correct the problems that had been found with the earlier organization. In this they were joined by fifty-one other states at the beginning and over the years, since then, maintained near universal membership. By the mid-1990s there were nearly 200 member states. 'By a perverse paradox, the United Nations, identified in so many minds with internationalism, presided over the global triumph of the idea of the sovereign state.'[29]

Its main purpose was to maintain international peace and security, in the sense of dissuading states from attacking each other, and to organize countermeasures if this happened. But the Charter should not be interpreted as being entirely about states, a point which is developed at various places in this book. It also referred to the needs and interests of peoples. In the Preamble it was asserted that: 'We the peoples of the United Nations [are] determined to reaffirm faith in fundamental human rights, in the dignity and worth of the human person, in the equal rights of men and women and of nations large and small . . .' And in Article 1, para 2 the founders said they were determined to develop 'friendly relations among nations based on respect for the principle of equal rights and self-determination of peoples and to take other appropriate measures to strengthen universal peace'. Peoples as well as states figured in the Charter. This was the basis of the argument that the Charter contained provisions about the rights of peoples which themselves justified the action in Kosovo, regardless of the decisions of the Security Council.

The arrangements of the United Nations could be understood as developments from those of the League of Nations. The main lines of development here were towards an increasing specification of permanent machinery to deal with crisis and, indeed, to manage an international effort, but also towards the increasing allocation of key responsibility to particular states. There was an international division of labour which was set against the principle of the democratic and equal representation of all states, which was a trend that appeared to feature in the development of most international organizations.

In the League there had been no clear division of responsibilities between the main executive committee, the League Council, and the League Assembly, in which all states were represented. In contrast in the United Nations, the Security Council, made up initially of eleven states and then, after 1965, of fifteen states, was firmly given main responsibility for maintaining international peace and security. Decisions were to be by a majority of nine out of the fifteen, and each of the five permanent members, namely the US, Britain, France, the Soviet Union (later Russia) and China, could exercise a veto. In the League there was no mechanism for coordinating military or economic actions against miscreant states, which was one reason for the League's weakness, as states feared that they would be vulnerable if they had to act individually and separately in response to League Council recommendations.

In contrast, in the United Nations, as stated in Chapter VII, there was to be an army set up by agreement between the Security Council and consenting states, to be commanded by the Military Staff Committee of Chiefs of Staff of the Permanent Members of the Security Council. And the Security Council could demand member compliance under Article 25. This was a very important development from the powers of the League as it meant that from the beginning the members accepted that they could in effect be ordered to do something by the Council. The Secretary-General explicitly referred to this at the time of the decision to impose sanctions on Southern Rhodesia in 1966 after its illegal declaration of independence.

Security was the main concern of the United Nations proper, the so-called *central system*, based in New York, and within that the Security Council. But other institutions were set up alongside the Security Council, which were also developments from the arrangements of the League. There was to be an assembly of representatives of all members, the General Assembly, which was now to agree its resolutions, in the main, by majority vote: the League Assembly had followed a rule of unanimity. Both institutions evolved more practical formulas, such as consensus and agreement without vote on the initiative of the Assembly President, which happily for some states permitted a more ambiguous commitment to some resolutions. But as the General Assembly's decisions were not necessarily unanimous, they were regarded as recommendations, rather than as binding decisions, with a small number of exceptions, such as the vote on the budget in its Fifth Committee. This was a binding decision taken by majority vote. In this way there emerged in global arrangements a broad acceptance in practice of the need for the great powers to take the lead, as the range of functions increased, alongside the requirement that the general community of states should be consulted.

In the United Nations there was a degree of differentiation between the responsibilities of the various organs which was absent from the League. The General Assembly was precluded from acting when a question was on the agenda of the Security Council, though in 1950, through the General Assembly's *Uniting for Peace* Resolution, a procedure was introduced by which an item could be transferred from the Council to the Assembly if the former had been unable to act. In addition to the Fifth Committee, the Assembly had five other Committees of the Whole which could act on specific questions, legal, economic and social, and so on.

The central system also included the Secretariat, headed by the Secretary-General, which was given responsibility for the administration of the activities of the central system, such as servicing the meetings of the Security Council and the General Assembly. It became synonymous in the uninformed mind with the United Nations as a whole. It also carried out, on the recommendation of the other bodies, a number of research functions, and some quasi-management functions, among which the support of peacekeeping activities had become especially important by the mid-1990s. But its role was primarily bureaucratic and it lacked the political power, and the right of initiative of, say, the Commission of the European Union.[30] The one exception to this was the power of the Secretary-General himself, under Article 99 of the Charter, to bring situations that were likely to lead to a breakdown of international peace and security to the attention of the Security Council. This Article, which at first sight appeared innocuous, was the legal basis for the remarkable expansion of the diplomatic role of the Secretary-General, compared with that of his League predecessors. Because of it he was empowered to become involved in a large range of areas, including economic and social problems, and humanitarian crises, which could be loosely interpreted as carrying a threat to peace. As will be seen the Secretariat became the target for a more or less continuous demand for reform from the 1970s, led by the United States.

The Secretariat and the General Assembly also had functions, alongside another institution in the central system – the *Economic and Social Council (ECOSOC)* – for overseeing the activities of a large number of other international institutions which formed what came to be called the *United Nations system*. In addition to the central system the latter was made up of two main kinds of institutions, namely the *Specialized Agencies* and the *Funds and Programmes*. The former included such well-known institutions as the World Health Organization (WHO), the International Labour Organization (ILO), and the Food and Agriculture Organization (FAO), which had their own constitutions, regularly assessed budgets, executive heads and assemblies of state representatives. They were self-contained constitutionally, financially and politically, and not subject to direct UN control. This was an important aspect of the structure of the United Nations system which is discussed in Chapter 3: it has to be accepted as one of the immutable facts of its constitution.

The Funds and Programmes were much closer to the central system, in the sense that their management arrangements were subject to direct General Assembly supervision, and could be modified by Assembly resolution, and, most importantly, were largely funded on a voluntary basis. Overall, they were a response to the failure to coordinate social and economic activities which did not fall clearly into the sphere of responsibility of any one of the Agencies, and therefore they emerged because of changes in global economic and social circumstances after the setting up of the Agencies. The most important were the United Nations Development Programme (UNDP), The United Nations Fund for Population Activities (UNFPA), The World Food Programme (WFP) and the United Nations International Children's Emergency Fund (UNICEF).

The founders of the Charter had tried to improve on the mechanisms of the League for overseeing the economic and social institutions. The League had attributed responsibility for this to its Assembly, but the founders of the UN agreed to establish a smaller body, ECOSOC (54 members), to carry out this more specialized function. This body was appointed by, and responsible to, the General Assembly. These changes in the UN, compared with the League, were a consequence of thinking in more functionalist terms, but they did not give ECOSOC the necessary powers to manage effectively.[31] It was only empowered under Articles 61–6 of the Charter to issue recommendations to the Agencies, and to receive reports from them. In consequence the history of the UN's economic and social organizations was one of searching for ways of achieving effective management. The United Nations system, therefore, became multi-centred and constantly concerned with the problems of coordination, as it was made up of a large number of constitutionally distinct institutions which had a strong urge to go their separate ways.[32]

The arrangements laid out in Chapter VII of the Charter for tackling an aggressor were never introduced, as in the late 1940s no agreement about the UN force on the terms of the Charter could be obtained. As is discussed later in the volume, there followed a series of improvisations which included, *first*, an enforcement procedure under which the Security Council agreed a mandate for an agent to act on its behalf, as in Korea in the early 1950s and the Gulf War in the early 1990s, when action was undertaken principally by the United States and its allies. *Second* was classical peacekeeping, which involved the establishment, usually by the Security Council, of a UN force under UN command to be placed between the parties to a dispute after a ceasefire. Such a force would only use force to defend itself, would be established with the consent of the host state, and would not include forces from the major powers.

And, *third*, after the late 1980s, the UN increasingly became involved in maintaining international *order* by helping to solve problems of *disorder* within states. Peacekeeping forces became more proactive and, as will be seen, began to experience a range of new problems as well as opportunities. Other parts of the United Nations system, the Specialized Agencies, and the Funds and Programmes, as well as a wide range of other intergovernmental and non-governmental organizations, got more involved in work which was seen as related to the maintenance of international order. The security function had been the primary function and it still was. But, whereas during the Cold War it was interpreted as being concerned with the interests of states in a narrow sense, resisting aggression and defending frontiers, afterwards a wider interpretation emerged. The meaning of the interests of states was broadened so that they got mixed up with the interests of peoples. This ambiguity was, of course, in the Charter, but it had been concealed by the Cold War. This is a theme that runs throughout this book.

Enough has been said now about the development and *raison d'être* of the regional and global international organization to provide the essential background for what follows. It was possible to generalize appropriately about the specific histories of the international organizations at both levels, as well as about globalization, but also to give sufficient detail to provide the specific contexts of the following discussions.

Some of the chapters have their origins in earlier work. Chapter 1 is derived from the author's contribution to the book edited by John Baylis and Steve Smith,[33] as well as a chapter in a Special Issue of the journal *Political Studies*, edited by Robert Jackson, in August 1999. Chapter 3 is a much altered version of Chapter 1 of the book edited by Gavin Boyd *et al.* on Globalizing Europe.[34] Chapter 5 is adapted from a much longer contribution to a book edited with A. J. R. Groom in December 2000.[35] The author is grateful for permission to use material from these earlier works. Needless to say all of these have been amended, updated and much rewritten so that the arguments which are proposed here emerge more clearly.

Three themes recur, but each of them ends up with a discussion of aspects of the interface between global and regional organization in the context of globalization. First is the development of new ways of maintaining international order, especially those which, after the end of the Cold war, involved a more direct involvement of the international organization within the state. Second is the problem of reconciling the granting of a wider range of competences to the United Nations, and other international institutions, with the sovereignty of states. And third is an examination of the specific problems encountered in the global international organization, especially the United Nations system, in carrying out its allotted tasks, and the proposals made for their correction, which again have regional dimensions. Each of the chapters looks at what could be called the frontier between achievement and change in the system. It will be found that such proposals are revealing about the developing character of international society.

CHAPTER I

The United Nations at the Millennium: Order and Sovereignty

Introduction

In this book there is concern with international organization, globalization and regionalization. More globalization may mean more international organization but does not exclude, and indeed may encourage more regionalization. All three may increase at the same time. But in this chapter the stress is upon globalization, particularly with regard to sovereignty, and how this is related to the greater role of international organization in the maintenance of international peace and security. Globalization is seen as the emergence of an imperfect moral community among states. In the next chapter, which is more directly focused on the security role of the UN, the regional dimension emerges more explicitly. But that is in the context of the themes of globalization that are stressed in this chapter.

According to an essay by Hedley Bull, order among states, and justice within them, were often mutually exclusive: pursuing the one tended to exclude the other.[1] But by the early twenty-first century there were changes in the relationship between these two key concepts which the practice of the UN both reflected and encouraged: there were standards which the state was expected to meet which included the provision of a minimum acceptable quality of economic and social justice as well as security.

One reason for this was an increasing objection to the classical realist argument that what went on within states was no concern of any outsider. It was entirely appropriate for the international community to make the attempt to put right violations of individual rights, since the cosmopolitan moral community was indivisible: individuals throughout the world had rights in common and owed obligations to each other. Such rights were increasingly interpreted as meaning both individual political and civil rights, as well as the right to basic means of life support. Although the efforts of the United Nations, and other international organizations, were entirely inadequate in this regard, the principle of their involvement in order to promote these rights was increasingly accepted.

What was new, however, was that it was increasingly accepted that violations of individuals' rights were a major cause of disturbances in relations between states: a lack of internal justice risked international disorder. In consequence there was challenge to the traditional injunction on the behaviour of diplomats that they should ignore the internal affairs of the states with which they dealt in order to preserve international stability. There was increasing unease with a dual standard of tolerance among states at the expense of intolerance within them. There was still some mileage in the old ways but the change in the moral climate was evident.

International organization reinforced the perception that pursuing justice for individuals was an aspect of national interest. Thus in 1996 the US administration's view that action in support of justice in Bosnia–Herzegovina was a part of US national interest was attributable in part to the actions of the UN and the expectations it generated. The organization was a constant reminder to Americans of the positive relationship between order and justice, and this was surely one reason why it was heartily disliked by American right-wing anti-internationalists.[2] If there was a clear-cut conflict between perceptions of national interest and the pursuit of justice the former had priority, but more frequently the choice could not be put in such stark terms.

In an increasing number of states, it was paradoxical that contributions to activities which might be justified on moral grounds, such as peacekeeping, or humanitarian intervention, were in fact defended in terms of national interest. The moral injunction to be involved was stronger, but so was the need to justify moral action on grounds of practical national interest: states like Canada accepted an obligation to develop their capacity for peacekeeping for moral reasons as well as national interest. Canada gained status in the international community through such contributions, and could punch above its weight in the United Nations because of that. The Japanese also responded to moral pressure as well as national interest when they contributed substantially to defraying the cost of British involvement in the Gulf War. This unusual action could only be explained in terms of the synthesis of morality and interest. Reputation in the United Nations context had become for some states an important national good. The Japanese wanted to be a good citizen because it would help their case for becoming a permanent member of the Security Council.

Moral action and its changing relationship with national interest

In the past the United Nations had helped to promote the traditional view that it was necessary to put the maintenance of order among states ahead of the goal of achieving justice for individuals. This led to a somewhat disdainful attitude among diplomats with regard to attempts put human rights high on the diplomatic agenda. President Carter attracted a torrent of abuse for seeming to advocate a more proactive policy on human rights.

But in the circumstances of the time stressing the priority of maintaining order among states seemed the right strategy. The Cold War stand-off between the East and the West alerted member states to the danger of raising questions about the conditions of the sovereignty of states. Jean Kirkpatrick's notorious essay, which recommended tolerating obnoxious dictatorships in Latin America in order to fight Communism, was at least a reasonable report of what the situation in fact was: unsavoury right-wing regimes in Latin America were tolerated by the US because they were anti-Soviet. On the other hand ending the Cold War reduced the risk that any promotion of justice could become a context of superpower rivalry. China was the chief heir to the tradition of Cold War thinking, and any return to superpower bipolarity, with China replacing the Soviet Union, would probably again lead to the downgrading of the pursuit of justice for individuals.

The UN also reflected the claims of colonies to become states, and in the General Assembly the right to statehood was promoted ahead of any of the tests of viability, such as the existence of a nation, adequate economic performance, defensibility or a prospect for achieving justice for citizens. This unconditional right to independence was enunciated in the December 1960 General Assembly Declaration on the Granting of Independence to Colonial Countries and Peoples, which was approved by a vote of 90 in favour, none against and 9 abstentions. In the subsequent phases of decolonization this often suited the ex-imperial powers, such as Britain, which became more anxious to be rid of the colonial burden.[3] There emerged an unfortunate tendency for the claims of elites in the putative states to be seen as a sufficient indication of popular enthusiasm. There were few attempts to test this through such devices as a pre-independence referendum. Again, the attitudes of the anti-colonial movement reinforced the propensity of governments in the developed and the developing world to pay little regard to the needs of individuals.

Charles Beitz was one of the first to question such insouciance on the part of the imperial states when he concluded, in defiance of political correctness in the 1970s, that statehood should not be unconditional: attention had to be given to the situation of individuals after independence, and such considerations could mean that independence in existing circumstances was unacceptable as the majority of individuals would be worse off.[4] Michael Waltzer and Terry Nardin produced arguments that led to similar conclusions: states were conditional entities in that their right to exist should be dependent on a criterion of performance with regard to the interests of their citizens.[5] Such writings surely helped to alter the moral content of diplomacy.

But this does not lead to the conclusion that the priorities of the Cold War era, and the period of decolonization, were mistaken and that promoting human rights should always come first. That view would be incompatible with the character of international society which has to be acknowledged. The best that could be done by diplomats was either to avoid having to choose between interest and moral principle or to find some way of reconciling or combining the two. The diplomat who wished to pursue a moral foreign policy could avoid situations in which a harsh choice had to be made, because it would inevitably have to be made in favour of the national interest.[6] Or a way of combining a case for moral action with a calculation of practical gain would have to be sought.

What was striking in the diplomacy in the United Nations in the 1990s and later, however, was that this was exactly what seemed to be happening. The United Nations processes revealed the moral course, but there was an increasing number of occasions when it coincided with a calculation of interest. Sometimes this was an obvious duality as with the defence of the sovereignty of Kuwait, and the Western interest in assuring its oil supplies but, more interestingly, the practical cost could now be seen more clearly in moral terms. Not acting was a demonstration of weakness, or carelessness or of bad behaviour which could prove a cost in general diplomacy. So, in the

United Nations the moment of decision increasingly became the moment of revelation: it launched the next moral crusade which states found increasingly difficult to ignore. In a sense the United Nations was expressing the dynamic of the cosmopolitan community as envisaged by Kant. Conscience needed an agent and the United Nations was it. But states that failed to acknowledge conscience lost something in real terms.

The relationship between order and justice had, therefore, been brought much closer after the end of the Cold War, and of the period of state-building. The fact that the United Nations had achieved a degree of success indicated that with more effort and more resources it could do better. The question of commitment to the UN was, therefore, not just a question of commitment to an ideal, but rather of making as sure as possible that something that had worked could work better. The world had never got to this point before. Even though the record was mixed there could be no easy return to the old standards of attainment: the world would forever have higher expectations, even if these were doomed to continuing disappointment. The Brahimi report on peacekeeping from 2000, set out in the next chapter, is an illustration of this. It proposed taking forward the existing achievement, building on it so that it worked better.

Changing versions of the meaning of sovereignty

These changing views about the relationship between moral action and the interests of states are closely related to changing views about the nature of sovereignty. Since the 1990s a considerable literature has emerged with a variety of takes on the new sovereignty. Sometimes these accounts are concerned with the implications for sovereignty of the increasing permeability of national borders, a symptom of globalization, with what are seen to be transnational systems of accountability and authority. Sometimes they apply new methodologies to a more traditionally interpreted concept.[7] This chapter is, however, more concerned with the implications for sovereignty of the greater concern to protect the basic level of standards for individuals. The author is not convinced that the new transnational systems have altered the location of sovereignty, though is impressed by the application of new methodologies.[8] As will be seen below, he is, however, convinced that the conditions of sovereignty have been greatly altered.

Until the 1990s the Charter of the United Nations was usually understood to mean that the rule of non-intervention was to be rigidly applied, and that what happened within states was no concern of outsiders. But this was not exactly what the words said. For instance in the wording of the key paragraph, Article 2, para 7, the word *essentially* was mostly overlooked as this would weaken the assertion of state exclusiveness. 'Nothing contained in the present Charter shall authorise the United Nations to intervene in matters which are *essentially* within the jurisdiction of any state or shall require the Members to submit such matters to settlement under the present Charter' (author's italics). The predominant view of governments was that sovereignty was a private world into which the outside world was not permitted to enter. The only exception was operations under Chapter VII: 'this principle [exclusive domestic jurisdiction] shall not prejudice the application of enforcement measures under Chapter VII' (Article 2, para 7). Almost always the Security Council justified intervening within a state only when there was a threat to international peace and security, even when there had been gross infringements of human rights.[9]

But there was a contrasting notion of sovereignty: that it could be envisaged as having a licence from the international community to practise as an independent government in a particular territory. Such a licence could be granted by the act of recognition of that government by other states, and a consensus among them that this should be done could be interpreted as an expression of the will of the international community. After the end of the Cold War, however, more governments were prepared to demand that those among them whose internal policies were not up to international standards should change their ways, and those accused, however defiant, had to pay a price for their defiance which was continually inflating. The standards by which they were measured were increasingly those of the liberal democratic states – a cause of complaint for those who were not of that world, but fortunate for those who were.

There were, therefore, two contrasting notions of sovereignty with regard to the rights and interests of individuals: that it referred either to a private world, with weak international authority, or to the possession of a licence to operate as an independent government, granted by the collectivity of states with a strong international authority. The argument here is that there was a discernible move to the latter after the end of the Cold War. But there is no prospect for the abandonment of sovereignty, and indeed a strong case for resisting this, but it was in the process of adaptation to new circumstances.[10]

Traditionally a 'state' was held to be sovereign when there was no authority which had precedence over it: outside actors therefore had no right to be involved in its internal affairs, and sovereignty was an absolute unaffected by the circumstances of the time. States had no role with regard to the rights and interests of individuals in other states. But what is often overlooked is that philosophers like Bodin held that there was indeed a superior authority – God. In a number of writings this notion took substantial form in the assertion of a general requirement for civilized behaviour as part of the divine order.[11] The question which follows is that of whether there was any equivalent of this in modern times. An underlying point, which will be disputed by those of a more traditional disposition, is that there was indeed something that could be called an international will. There was indeed something above the state in the form of the will of the international community, reflected in the general view, among the overwhelming majority of international actors, governmental and non-governmental, that there were general standards which should be upheld. There were also very few states that could avoid involvements with outsiders through which pressures in favour of these standards were channelled, which were becoming harder to resist. After the end of the Cold War there was, therefore, an expression in more utilitarian and secular terms of the ancient qualification of sovereignty as an absolute: a stronger form of the international community could be discerned which was a modern equivalent of the divine order.

Sovereignty cannot be considered in exclusively theoretical or philosophical terms, but always needs to be related to the current circumstances of the state, including prevailing expectations about its emerging role. The changing circumstances after the end of the Cold War included, first, developments in the way in which international organizations sought to protect international peace and security; second the further evolution of a system in which laws made outside the state required compliance within it, especially in the world of business and commerce – they imposed upon the state (in this the European Union was the most advanced illustration of a general development); third was the extension of the range of mutual involvements through which common standards, such as democratization, were promoted; fourth, a rudimentary global watch – a system of surveillance of states – to identify crisis points, linked with the development of mechanisms for more rapid response, was being set up; and, fifth, the international community had set about establishing mechanisms for rehabilitating and restoring states that had failed. There were failings in each of these mechanisms but, as is pointed out in the next chapter, the trend was definitely towards building upon their foundations, rather than changing course.

These various developments reflected and promoted moral interdependence. For instance the idea of increasing international surveillance to detect incipient crises assumed that obligations to assist extended beyond the state, and that there was moral solidarity which took precedence over a community's right to privacy. This implied that efforts to deal with failed states, Somalia, Cambodia, Bosnia, etc. were not *just* a series of special cases, reflecting the special interests of the Great Powers, but were also expressions of the evolving norms. The point needs to be stressed that promoting what appears a mechanical process through organizations like the UN, such as gathering more information relevant to security, is in fact bound up with moral considerations. It implies in itself a preparedness to act to make the world more peaceable. Otherwise it would not be necessary.

In the next section the development of the system with regard to peace and security arrangements is considered. The stress is upon both the way in which they increasingly involved intervening in the state and the changing norms which this reflected. Parallel changes were also reflected in the gradual emerging of agreed codes with regard to human rights arrangements, as well as a widening range of mechanisms to monitor their application and to bring major transgressors to trial. The latter trend reached a new height with the trial in 2002 of President Milosevic of the Federation of Yugoslavia at The Hague. In the subsequent section attention is focused upon the expanding agenda of the United Nations regarding the maintenance of international order after the Cold War. In a final section the implications of the developments for sovereignty are discussed and proposals for taking forward the arrangements to strengthen international order are set out; this illustrates the direction of evolution of the agenda.

The evolution of peace maintenance

Peacekeeping was a natural outcome of the development of globalization, interpreted as a set of related views about international order, justice for individuals and sovereignty. It should not be seen as merely one of the mechanisms of a particular international organization, the UN, and has to be understood in the wider setting. The new peacekeeping was just one manifestation of a wider range of involvements within the state, which were all part of the changing concept of order, and reflected a new concern to strengthen the state so that it was more capable of carrying out the necessary functions of statehood in modern international society. The new activism could be enhanced without compromising the traditional norms of intervention:[12] it was not directed at imposing an order founded on principles that were foreign to that state, but rather built on an inherent cosmopolitan consensus. It was, however, adding a new ingredient in implying that there was sometimes a need for an internal maturation within a framework of internal order under international supervision.

It was possible for the international community to use greater degrees of compulsion in holding the ring within a state without compromising neutrality and without constituting intervention in the sense of seeking to impose precise forms of outcome from outside. Just as a police force could remain impartial when using duress within the state – so long as the laws were generally known, and the response of the police was proportional to the scale of the offence – so an active international peacekeeping force could appear neutral as long as the rules of engagement were clear to the parties to a dispute, and no partiality was shown in applying them. Being proactive in the use of force by peacekeeping forces need not jeopardize the principle of neutrality. This was part of a more general trend towards a greater involvement of the UN system in the rescuing of failing states, as was reflected in the new mechanisms for providing assistance in humanitarian crises.

The reader needs to be disabused of the view that this is somehow a fundamental challenge to the unchanging state. The trick is to understand that the state, and the conditions of its sovereignty, has been subject to continuous evolution, and that there is something unchanging about it, in that it has sovereignty, but within that constancy there has been change. In the present circumstances, it is important to understand this. In the view of the present writer too much of the literature on sovereignty had moved too far away from the recognition of the key role of the state even in the early twenty-first century. We can think of the new forms of sovereignty without abandoning the idea of the state. The new practices can be seen as but the latest phase in the emergence of the state.

This point is reinforced by a brief examination of the phases through which the state has passed since the emergence of a primitive state system out of medieval Christendom after the Thirty Years War in the early seventeenth century. The fact of this progression was itself evidence of the impossibility of staying with the arrangements as they had emerged in the Cold War and it underlined the point that the new forms of activity were as much about evolving norms as national interests.

- Before the Treaties of Westphalia in 1648 medieval Christendom had been a system of shifting and permeable territories under a variety of princes, who continuously intervened in each other's realms and were challenged by the Church's claims to secular power.
- Between 1648 and 1815 the state in Europe gradually consolidated its internal arrangements and established internal monopolies of force, taxation and administration. At the same time elements of international society emerged, such as a distinctive system of international law, and a body of less formal rules which applied to relations between states and the practice of diplomacy in international society. This was the period of the emergence of an international society more strictly defined as a set of actors – the states – which accepted a range of conventions of behaviour in their mutual relations.
- In the period after the defeat of Napoleon until well after the Second World War, the predominant concept of the state which emerged was that of a national welfare state, with increasingly formal prohibitions on intervention internally. This was a natural corollary of the extension to the nations of sentiments of attachment which had been previously confined to relations between family members. The notion that such intervention was an infringement of a moral right to domestic privacy was reinforced: this development was linked with the positivist view of cultural relativity, sometimes called communitarianism. The right to privacy reached its high point in the period after the Second World War, and in particular in the insistence in the 1960 Declaration on Decolonization that the right to independence of peoples in states was unconditional.
- This period arguably extended into the mid-1980s and the first indications of change were the new approach by Soviet President Gorbachev and the resulting *entente* among the five

permanent members of the Security Council initiated by the British. This was the basis of a growing international intrusiveness in the internal affairs of the UN member states.[13] The relationship between the state and international order was again being altered as the idea of cosmopolitanism re-emerged. It was not that the state as the primary form of organization was challenged, but that its claim to be a moral absolute was challenged. McCorquodale pointed out that 'a commitment to applying international human rights law to the right of self-determination reinforces the acknowledgment of states that their sovereignty is not absolute at least as far as the treatment of persons and groups on their territory is concerned'.[14] The challenge to cultural relativism and the re-emergence of cosmopolitanism was associated with the view that what went on within states was indeed of general concern.

A point that needs to be stressed, however, was that accepting obligations to citizens globally had to go along with acquiring a right to judge the behaviour of those citizens, and governments which claimed to speak for them: an increasing preparedness to undertake international humanitarian actions, and the linked use of proactive peacekeeping forces, was necessarily associated with the assertion of the right to judge. The older forms of security maintenance among states were appropriate to the communitarian approach to inter-state relations: the new form, which acknowledged that security was no longer only a matter of relations between states, was a necessary adjunct of the new cosmopolitanism.

Peacekeeping forces were part of a spectrum of involvements in failing states each of which arguably reflected a degree of moral solidarity. This spectrum could be divided into four interrelated stages. First was the stage of using the forces to ensure that food was provided and disease controlled. At this stage the forces might be required to use force to get food through. Second was a stage at which the forces were involved in various kinds of pacification. Such activities had by the late 1990s been identified in a number of categories, including establishing safe areas, corridors of tranquillity, green lines and the rehabilitation and resettlement of refugees. Activities at this stage might also include restraining the availability of arms to a civilian population and collecting and guarding heavy weapons. In a third stage the forces might be required to provide back-up support for a range of activities related to the restoration of civil society. These included establishing an administration and civilian police forces, and supervising elections, activities which were becoming a regular feature of the business of the system. They might also involve helping to encourage the establishment of organizations such as forms of representation for workers and political parties – the process of democratization. A final category of activity was found throughout the spectrum and involved attempting to keep apart the armies of the parties to a conflict, and promoting negotiation.

There were of course dangers and difficulties which were typical of each of these activities. There was the risk that help might be diverted to assist the warring factions and thereby prolong the conflict. This was a serious argument against humanitarian assistance. But it could not be regarded as a fatal impediment in the way of the development of a more moral community, though every precaution needed to be taken to prevent this happening and to encourage the handing-in of weapons. There was a constant danger of the abuse of international aid by corrupt regimes – this was the theme of John Le Carré's novel, *The Constant Gardener*, published in 2000 – but the response to this had to be greater conditionality and more involvement, not less. Second, the question arose of whether such investment was worthwhile when it might lead to the hardening of the lines of division between communities as with the green line in Cyprus. The only response to this was that such a green line was very much cheaper than the prolongation of active war.

That interventions often reflected interest in the sense that the active states had specific and general gains – raw materials and security – was undeniable. But there was an admixture of moral imperative: governments could not tolerate undue suffering for a number of complex reasons, including the natural sympathy of their electors with the victims. That it occasionally had outcomes which were difficult to accept as a settlement or solution to a problem, and involved continuing commitment of money and resources by the international community, was no reason for refusing such involvement. It was part of a process of active order maintenance which was relevant to international society, as well as the individual states, which could best be described as pacific engagement.

This was entirely typical of the phase of globalization of the early twenty-first century. There were moral grounds for such activity, which were an aspect of the development of a cosmopolitan moral community, as well as more utilitarian calculations of costs and benefits.

The UN agenda after the end of the Cold War

Attention is now focused upon the evolving practices, and perceptions of new problems, in the new millennium. These are seen as reflections of the new principles of order, as well as responses to particular problems.

The new UN and crisis response

Though much more could be done to improve the work of the UN with regard to intervention, there had been improvement after the late 1980s in two main respects: information gathering and analysis and increasing capacity for speedy response. Again it is useful to place this account in the context of the overall development of the system for promoting peace and security through a global international organization.

- The first example of this was of course the League of Nations. In the original design its executive committee, the League Council, was to be convened if a crisis was reported: it was not intended to be in permanent session. And the mechanisms for gathering information were primitive: they depended on *ad hoc* procedures such as whether states had noticed a crisis and were prepared to convene the Council. It was as if the fire brigade had to be put together when someone happened to notice a fire in the neighbourhood. In the first years more peace maintaining was actually carried out by the representatives of the powers that had been victorious in the 1914–18 war, acting outside the League framework, but this was not part of the design. The League also had no machinery either for setting up or for commanding military forces on a collective basis, though a number of efforts were made without success to correct this deficiency.
- The United Nations was a development from the League in that the Security Council was indeed a permanent institution which functioned continuously and not just when called into session, with special responsibility for maintaining international peace and security. The fire brigade was now on permanent standby, and the alarm could be sounded either by the member states or by the Secretary-General. He could report the outbreak of fire anywhere in the world: the watch tower was permanently manned, and the response could be much more rapid. In order

to evaluate the increased range of information a department was created in the Secretariat for the analysis of the information available to it. This was the Department of Political Affairs which worked alongside the Department of Peacekeeping Operations.

- In the 1980s and later a third phase of development of the global institution was observable. In the preceding phase, despite the enhancement of the UN's information collection and analysis capacity, there remained a random quality to the engagement of the Secretary-General or states. In the new phase, however, the institution began what became known as a *global watch*. Its information gathering and analysing machinery was enhanced, professionalized and on permanent duty, despite the difficulties made by some states.[15] It was not, as had earlier been the case, that the organization surveyed the horizon in search of fire and then acted, but rather that increasingly a whole range of factors which were likely to encourage fire was regularly reported and analysed. Some of this was done in cooperation with the intelligence services of the Great Powers, but an increasing role was played by the UN's own machinery, and there were advantages in working this way. Proposals for the use of satellite and computer technology were put forward, though, mainly because of the US reaction, the response was limited, and information from local officers in various organizations was systematically collected. A special case of this was the creation of the arms registry, which collected data on the movement of arms around the world, of which a surprising amount was readily available in the public realm, in newspapers and specialist journals.[16] In the late 1990s the next step was to require that both governments and manufacturers should fully disclose the range of their wares and the customers they served.

This information was a help in identifying possible trouble spots. Troop movements could also be more easily spotted, and it was now more likely that a potential malefactor would be aware that his or her misdeeds would be known. The greater likelihood of being found out was likely to be itself a deterrent: the intelligence services of the world's main military powers had the capacity to do this for years but there were advantages in going beyond this to a discrete UN capacity in this area, as the Brahimi report acknowledged. Information would be less likely to be sensitive to political interest and more likely to be generally available and given credence. Information about a developing crisis would be placed firmly in the common realm. In this third phase it was as if the streets of the international neighbourhood were under constant surveillance by video cameras.

There were, however, two further difficulties in the way of using the information. The first concerned the capacity to respond quickly and to sustain that response. The second was how to bring the attention of the Security Council to a problem after the relevant information had been collected and evaluated by experts in or outside the Secretariat. With regards to the first difficulty there were a number of significant developments in the early 1990s. These included the professionalization of the Department of Peacekeeping Operations. Though still too few, in relation to the work undertaken, the number of its staff was increased, and included more specialist military and political advisers. It was closely involved in the new system for information gathering. And it was placed on 24-hours operation. A great deal had been achieved, even though more needed to be done.[17]

With regard to the second difficulty there were in the late 1990s and early twenty-first century a number of proposals. It had been noted that the Security Council had been slow to focus on the Somalia crisis in 1992, and, later, had largely ignored the crisis in Rwanda and Burundi. Some argued that the Secretary-General had deliberately contrived a row at the London Conference on Yugoslavia in London in the summer of 1992 in order to attract attention away from the first-world crisis to the worsening third-world crisis in Somalia.[18] There were many other reasons why attention might not be engaged with a crisis, including various kinds of fatigue or a shortage of resources. But the problem was that information about a developing crisis was not itself a guarantee that it would engage the Security Council's attention. One proposal was that a committee of high-level experts should be set up alongside the Security Council which would help the Secretary-General to get an item onto the agenda, and advise about the realism of the response. At the time of writing this remained, however, a problem area.[19]

Similar improvements in the mechanisms for acquiring information and generating initial evaluation of the scale of the problem, as well as getting involved, also occurred in the area of humanitarian assistance. The picture which emerged in both peacekeeping and humanitarian assistance was that the United Nations system had gone through a period of astonishing change in the 1990s with regard to information collecting and evaluating and with regard to the enhancement of its capacity to respond quickly to crisis. The machinery had become more professional despite the continuing shortage of resources and the increase in the number and type of problems with which it had to deal. It was hard to see how the emergence of an enhanced moral solidarity could be excluded from an explanation of its development; it was an aspect of changing views about the proper relationship between the international community and states which was justified primarily in terms of the welfare of individuals. Of course some target states objected, but the increasing capacity to respond and to respond quickly was generally expected and generally required. This was no special plot of the Great Powers, but rather a product of collective obligation. But – the point needs to be reiterated this was not anti-state: indeed, precisely the opposite – it was focused upon strengthening the state. The international community could now be dimly discerned as a discrete agent of change, embodying an increasing cosmopolitanism, and enlarging the area of consensus about the norms which were appropriate within states.

Confederalizing national security orders

In the 1990s it became increasingly clear that two patterns of involvement from outside were likely to interact in the state, one from legitimate and another from illegitimate agencies. The former was the increasing involvement of international organization, more evident in the third world. The latter was a threat to the security of individuals, more often in the first world, from the new dangerous non-governmental organizations of international crime and state-sponsored terrorism. This was becoming increasingly visible, and was beyond the reach of either peacekeeping forces or enforcement procedures from outside the state, and from conventional police forces from within the state. Examples included the various Mafias of the old kind, and new kinds such as those from Russia and the Far East, which were often linked with the trade in illegal substances, but were increasingly operating in a more diverse range of areas, some legitimate. Another new illustration was the appearance of private mercenary armies, such as Executive Outcomes, which in the late 1990s had been hired by some governments in Africa to deal with internal military threats which they could not handle with their own armies.[20]

But on 11 September 2001 events occurred which were of such a scale, with such horrific consequences, as to make international crime hitherto seem trivial. These events were the attacks by Osama bin Laden's al-Qaeda network at the Twin Towers in New York and the Pentagon in Washington in which nearly 4000 people lost their lives. The organization responsible for these acts was motivated by a complex of criticisms of the US, but also by its determination to change governments in the Islamic world. The failure of many governments in the Islamic world to respect what it judged to be the true faith, and to introduce the Sharia law, was as much a reason for the attacks as the direct criticisms of US policies in the Middle East. Indeed one commentator persuasively argued that the US attacks were an episode in an Islamic civil war.[21]

The response to 11 September was a coordinated attack on the organization responsible and on the government that was believed to have given it succour. This attack was led by the US and consisted of a sustained series of bombing raids on the positions of the then government of Afghanistan, the Taliban, and threats to do the same to any other government that supported terrorism. The first response was therefore very much by the state. But the question was inevitable of whether these events supported or challenged the development of international organization.

International crime and terrorism challenged the states' monopoly of force and were capable of enforcing codes of behaviour, and systems of private taxation, which were alongside or hostile to those of the state. They clearly challenged the security of individuals and threatened order within the states, and had an obvious international dimension. It was a special form of warfare: in some cases states orchestrated the use of violence in other states through groups or individuals which had been infiltrated into the territory of another state. Modern technology and sophisticated skills in evading recognition could make it very difficult for the target state to identify such individuals: all of these were features of the al-Qaeda group responsible for the 11 September attacks.

The impact of such forces on the civil order, and life and property, in the targeted state could be very serious, and for the initiating state it would have the effect of war without the need to acknowledge responsibility. Of course comparable developments had occurred in earlier periods, such as the infiltration of Soviet Communist elements into capitalist countries which actively pursued the goal of fermenting revolution and the overthrow of the government. But the new practices were different in that they involved a preparedness to use deadly force in the pursuit of private gain and influence, or particular systems of ideas and values, on a scale not seen before.

But, though the initial response of states was understandable, and, probably, necessary, in the long term the 11 September attack strengthened the case for more multinationalism and more international organization, indeed, for more and better transnational governance. The nature of these problems indicated the need for strengthening international cooperation between police forces, and setting up unified transnational command structures if the problem required this. States and their individual police forces, assuming they themselves were not a part of the scam, were likely to find dealing with them separately and individually impossible precisely because they were transnational. The organizations were capable of withdrawing from one state and regrouping in others only to be reactivated in the target state later. It was also difficult for police forces in particular states to gain access to the command and control structures of the organizations in other states without themselves transgressing the rules of exclusive national jurisdiction.

There were also some kinds of such operations, which were closely linked with government officials, or members of business or political elites in another state, which needed the weight of an extra-territorial authority to be effective. In an extreme form, when they were directly controlled by another government, as with the events of 11 September, doing something about them which was effective could lead to an escalation of violence, either because the controlling government, when found out, reacted with greater force, or because the scale of the intervention was such that it could not be coped with except by attacking the source government. This was a problem which, therefore, raised the question of the civil order within states as well as that of maintaining peace and security. It was on a continuum extending from the problems of disorder within the state, and those dealt with by new forms of peacekeeping, to those security problems of a more traditional kind.

The appropriate form of such a force would include the capacity to deploy a range of specialist forces, which could be asked to operate in more open combat or in situations where SAS-type skills were more appropriate. But the forces also needed to be linked with sophisticated investigative techniques which could work on an international basis, and which could if necessary demand answers from individuals who were close to governments. The new information techniques also demanded a greater degree of transnational penetration of the various civil societies, both those acting within the law, and those acting outside it. The new terrorism was in fact an aspect of the development of international civil society, and in order to cope with it, it was necessary to promote the appearance of adequate countervailing forces within that society. An effective arrangement for dealing with such problems therefore also assumed a range of features in the participating state. They would need to be prepared to tolerate the incursion of a transnational police force into their domestic arrangements, and to be open enough at least to accept this.

The European Union was one group of states where advanced police cooperation existed and in which a further enhancement of regional transnational capacity was being actively sought: the ability to create forces which were likely to be effective depended on the civil order within the state, but a variety of different forms of liberal domestic order could tolerate the kind of arrangement that was emerging in Europe.[22] But some states – generally those with intolerant and precarious regimes, quite probably at risk of internal humanitarian crisis – would not, and were likely to play the sovereignty card to avoid cooperation. The well-founded state sought after by the international community was, therefore, also desirable from the perspective of dealing effectively with new kinds of non-governmental threats to individual security. The problem clearly had an international dimension: it suggested the need to confederalize the mechanisms for protecting national civil orders. It was, therefore, a feature of international society after the Cold War that the range of conceivable force deployments to maintain order had been considerably broadened, compared with the earlier phases of international society, and that the earlier distinctions between instruments for national and international security, such as those between army and police, had been blurred. The events of 11 September underlined this point.

This implied in the early twenty-first century something quite startling: that the direction of development of the use of police and military was positively linked with the development of new views about the nature of order discussed above – that new peacekeeping was a step towards enhanced international civilian police capacity, and that this was only possible if the civil values of communities around the world become more similar and more liberal. The step beyond that would be a transnational cosmopolitanism linked with advanced forms of police cooperation dealing with crimes over a very wide spectrum. Like business and ideology, crime was also likely to become more transnational and to demand transnational response, and to create difficulties in deciding what kinds of crime were local, and the exclusive responsibility of national police forces, and which were transnational and therefore the proper responsibility of a higher police authority.

There were also, in the early twenty-first century, much stronger grounds to be fearful of rogue governments such as that of Saddam Hussein, or the Taliban. It had become possible for a government to adopt an effective international criminal strategy on a scale that had never before been possible. Modern technology could give them the means of global destruction for relatively modest outlay. It did not require, as al-Qaeda had shown, many resources, but it did depend upon the opportunities created for doing damage in a time of advanced technology. The technology needed to gain access to the aeroplanes that were crashed was elementary, but the advanced technology of the planes themselves created unprecedented opportunities for havoc. The dangers posed by rogue states and organizations to international society, to the citizens of the world as well as to governments, were sufficiently appalling to justify firm action against them. Such action could become an imperative if the government appeared to have nuclear, chemical or bacteriological weapons.

The scale of the problem was illustrated by the response to Saddam Hussein's attempts to evade the UN inspectors appointed to locate and destroy his more dangerous weapons. At first the international community hesitated but eventually accepted the need for a firm response, though disagreement about whether or not to use force remained. One report was that the US had been prepared to use a specialized nuclear device to penetrate and destroy bacteriological weapons bunkers and their contents. By 2001, however, the main states of the UN became increasingly divided about the need for forceful action with the US and UK remaining in favour, but France, Russia and China increasingly opposed. As never before the world could be held to ransom by irresponsible, corrupt or plain mad regimes possessed of such weapons. For the first time technology and custom had reached the point at which the removal of a dangerous government was justifiable simply because of the degree of damage which it could do. There was, of course, the need for satisfactory ways of licensing such action. But this was a revolutionary qualification of the concept of statehood, which happily coincided with the preponderance of the liberal states in the post-Cold War period. It demanded solidarity but it also supported the drive to achieve it.

Democratization and international organization

Since the late 1980s, however, the UN had become more directly involved in helping the emergence of democracy. This was also an activity which was motivated both by reasons of interest and reasons of morality. It was possible because of the fall of the Iron Curtain and the happy coincidence of power and Western liberal democracy. But it was also related to the changing concepts of order and, indeed, to the process of globalization.

A letter from the European Union to the Secretary-General picked up a theme which was increasingly visible in UN and UN-related documents, namely support for enhancing the role of the UN in helping the development of a *civil society* in states that had experienced internal crisis.[23] The use of the term civil society was striking: it was now often found in UN documents, but had rarely been found before the late 1980s. It appeared in this case in the context of support for the recovery of states in which there had been serious humanitarian crisis, but it often had a wider reference: support for a proactive strategy on the part of the international community in promoting democracy.

By the early twenty-first century an unprecedented commitment to the promotion of liberal pluralist arrangements had emerged as a condition of development on the part of the major players, the World Bank, the UN system and the EU: it encompassed the elements of a well-founded civil society and democratization as well as such changes as improved credit and insurance arrangements. The head of UNDP, Gus Speth, stated in 1998 that 40 per cent of the resources of his organization now went on activities that had an element designed to improve governance. There was increasing evidence of UN agencies, and other international organizations, helping governments to strengthen democratic forms. Cases mentioned in the mid-1990s included Niger and Guatemala, where UNDP had adopted a more political role in supporting government reform. The human rights mechanisms were also directly involved in this process, with some success in introducing liberal judicial and governmental procedures. One case was that of Bahrain. The point was made that in Latin America the UNDP was an active factor in democratization.

This was a remarkable alteration in stress and its significance should not be underestimated: for the first time in the history of the United Nations the organization was directly addressing core structures in the state and even in the difficult continent – Africa – illiberal practices were increasingly being delegitimized. The Security Council's authorization in July 1994 (SC940) of armed intervention in Haiti to restore a democratically elected government was particularly striking: there had been no credible threat to international peace and security.[24] This surely contributed to the *de facto* dilution of the concept of sovereignty as earlier understood in the Council and elsewhere. UNICEF's strategy had also been rededicated: the new approach was to be rights based, meaning that it was to be derived from the Rights of the Child Convention.

The EU urged the adoption of a comprehensive approach in respect of non-military aspects of peace operations (including tasks such as democratization, police training, institution building, capacity building and delivery of humanitarian assistance), to help with the transition from humanitarian relief to long-term planning, including in the context of support for civil society.[25] The EU had also begun to impose *multiple conditionality* in its relations with the ACP (African, Caribbean and Pacific) countries: strings were attached to economic support which included democratization.[26] This approach also became a part of the strategy towards states in central and eastern Europe which were seeking membership of the European Union. The change in this direction could be traced from the mid-1980s when Margaret Thatcher became the first European leader to attempt to build human rights conditions into provisions for European Community aid to ACP countries under the Lomé Conventions. 'Although that attempt was initially rejected by ACP leaders as an unwarranted infringement on their domestic sovereignty, by the time of the Lomé IV convention of 1990 an explicit reference to human rights in the context of EC aid could no longer be avoided.'[27] In fact the EU programme was broadened to include a requirement for a whole range of internal adjustments to promote greater transparency and efficiency in using their aid. Although the mechanisms for dealing with human rights infringements in the international legal system remained flawed it was undeniable that in a number of ways the intrusions of the international community to promote minimum acceptable standards had been extended. The start made upon the setting up of an International Criminal Court in 1998 was an aspect of this. The revolutionary proposal was to bring international criminals to account, including the leaders of states. In the meantime there was success in setting up an international court to try those accused of war crimes in ex-Yugoslavia and at the time of writing ex-President Milosevic was on trial before it.

The promotion of well-founded states was a strategy that coincided with globalization in that it created the conditions in which it was easier to deal with the problems of a stronger international civil society. Terrorism should be seen as a pathology of that society and it seems can only be dealt with in the long term by creating and using the positive agencies of that same society. In a succeeding chapter it will be shown, however, that development and democratization were not necessarily positively correlated with globalization when this is interpreted as a neoliberal process of deregulation. This kind of globalization could make it more difficult to sustain democracy since it could encourage increased disturbance, public protest and corrupt behaviour in states. It was a happy coincidence that the apparent progress of globalization up to the early twenty-first century had coincided with the choice by a number of major actors of a deliberate strategy of democratization.

By the early 2000s globalization, therefore, had paradoxical consequences for the state: on the one hand it was both a form of transnational arrangement and an agency for the development of more of the same: international crime suggested a need for transnational crime-fighting agencies, which themselves were most likely to be effective in a democratic setting. But on the other hand it led to the reinforcement of the need for an agenda of statism. Democratization was to make better states, even though it was a consequence of cosmopolitanism. And neoliberal economic globalization produced problems in the distribution of wealth which demanded correction through the state. In both cases, as is argued later, the most effective strategy was likely to work through regional groupings of states. In the age of globalization it was necessary to make the world safe for sovereignty.

Sovereignty and cosmopolitanism in the early twenty-first century: a neo-Westphalian system?

The development of mechanisms to protect international peace and security, the extension of the range of involvements to promote common standards, such as democratization, and the emergence of a global watch and more speedy response, have been discussed in their main phases. It is apparent, however, that under these headings only a selection of new interventions and involvements have been considered. Kant had proposed a strategy which stressed the importance of international discourse, commerce and hospitality.[28] By the early 2000s there had emerged countless illustrations of a modern equivalent of this strategy in the work of international institutions, including those of the UN system, of which Kant would doubtless have approved.

The point should be stressed again that the involvements and interventions were to consolidate the state, to protect its position and not to weaken or remove it. But international organizations, taken as a whole, seemed to have considerably enhanced their authority compared with the period of the Cold War. There was now a sense in which sovereign states were legitimized and sustained by such an authority to which they were in general terms accountable.[29] States were regarded as being responsible, and having a right to exclusive domestic jurisdiction, only when their performance was adequate in an expanding range of specific practical arrangements. This could be seen as a filling out, and translation into secular terms, of a feature of the Westphalian system: that even princes were subjects of a divine order. In the late twentieth century, however, such a higher authority could only exist in the context of the new cosmopolitanism, as was bound up with the active pursuit of a better government on Western lines within states.

Some reformulation of the act of creating sovereignty seemed to be indicated to reflect the expanding role of the international community in monitoring internal circumstances and rescuing failing states. Indeed in the early twenty-first century there was a case for granting the United Nations primary responsibility for conferring sovereignty through the recognition process – i.e. multilateralizing the process – and for removing that right from states to act individually and separately. If states were to be monitored and rescued multilaterally should they not also be licensed multilaterally? Sovereignty was a goal of the international community deserving recognition in its procedures as well as its constitutive principle.

Popular support of statehood had often been looked for in earlier times as a condition of recognition, but publics and other states were coming to regard this as a starting-point. The range of 'sovereignty-creating acts' was in effect being expanded from seeing that territory was controlled by a central agency, even without reference to popular support at the time of recognition, to a more comprehensive concern to establish that support, and to look at the details of internal arrangements, so that the support would endure. A new condition of sovereignty was therefore now discernible, in addition to the traditional one that a territory should be controlled by a government: that the state was well-founded in the light of the standards of the international community. The terms of the granting of the licence to practise statehood were in the process of being enlarged, and giving responsibility for awarding the accolade of recognition to the United Nations was a concomitant of this.

The failures in Yugoslavia in the 1990s are relevant. The recognition as states of the territories which had formed Yugoslavia was a fairly *ad hoc* business with unintended and disastrous consequences, driven by the interests of Germany, and imperfectly monitored by the Bartinder Commission set up under the authority of the Commission on Yugoslavia.[30] The result was a chaos of ill-constructed states fought over by fractious minorities. The conclusion followed that the recognition process should not be left to states individually and separately and, as was increasingly happening, the UN[31] being left to pick up the pieces. The obligation of states to the international community to maintain acceptable internal standards needed to be underlined as their poor performance could lead to major costs for other states; there was a straightforward utilitarian justification.

The *ad hoc* character of the recognition of states, was matched by a corresponding ad hocery about their derecognition, the removal of the acknowledgement of sovereignty. The lack of any general procedure for derecognition increased the difficulty of intervening – meaning an involvement using force – as the states which separately continued to recognize a state were more likely to argue that the sovereignty of that state should not be breached. But as the cosmopolitan moral community was strengthened, sovereignty would be weakened as an impediment in the way of intervention. Indeed the earlier relationship between intervention and sovereignty would be reversed: weight would increasingly be placed on the question of the justice of the state's claim to sovereignty rather than upon the nature of the justification for intervention. The question of which *precise* justification of intervention was proposed, be it a threat to international security under Chapter VII, or a gross infringement of human rights, (whichever happened to fit in with the prevailing interpretation of the Charter) would be of lesser significance as a liberal interpretation if either would suit the case. The logic of the situation was, however, that derecognition should also be a matter for the United Nations, with appropriate safeguard procedures, given the changing character of its role in maintaining international order. It should be done as a single multilateral act under the authority of the UN. This would clarify the point that sovereignty had a relationship with being well-founded, and that when intervention by the international community was judged necessary, a state-entity could not be sovereign as by definition it could not be judged to be well-founded.

Sovereignty could be interpreted as being ultimately responsible – the buck stops with the sovereign, though paradoxically – as was argued above – being ultimately responsible could come to be the result of an enabling act from the international community. But sovereignty also meant having the right to do certain things: it involved having a role with regard to a range of specific functions. The question was whether this role had been affected by the changing circumstances of sovereignty. New problems in the way of legitimizing states by granting them sovereignty were matched by new problems about deciding what states should be able to do in order to remain sovereign.

Having a role, and doing something, involved being granted a *competence*, and was not the same as being ultimately responsible. In recent years the analytical distinction between these two questions – who was ultimately responsible and who had competence to act – was more frequently reflected in the practice of states and international organizations: the question of which body was ultimately responsible was increasingly separated from that of which body was allowed competence.[32] The exercise of exclusive control over certain key functions, such as foreign policy and defence, used to be regarded as being central to sovereignty, and could not be allocated to other centres. The experience of the European Union was illustrative. The member states accepted that the Union should have a role in their harmonized foreign policy, and that it might increase its involvement in the common defence. There was a majority for this among the Union's citizens, even in cautious states such as the UK. The question of taking decisions in these areas by qualified majority vote had even entered the agenda. This was an astonishing development which seemed to remove the dilemma, discussed *inter alia* by Rousseau, that responsibility for maintaining the peace could not be allocated to a higher, federal authority without fatally damaging the entity which it was designed to protect, namely the state itself.

But *ultimate* responsibility remained with the sovereign states, as a condition of their sovereignty, as long as they retained reserve powers, including the power to recover the competences, even though the grant of the right to exercise that responsibility came from the international community. Public opinion and governments could accept that such a transfer of responsibility for foreign policy and defence was not an infringement of sovereignty as long as the reserve power was kept! Something remarkable had happened: sovereignty was now a condition, even a form, of participation in the larger entity. What was stressed in the role taken on by being sovereign was the right to be involved, to participate in the mechanisms of international society and to represent there the interests of the state. It was even possible to imagine states which were sovereign but which normally exercised no exclusive competences.

Outside the European Union it was unusual for issues of foreign policy or defence to involve supranational authority. But it was common for other questions, previously regarded as essential to the exercise of national sovereignty, especially in the economic, social and other technical areas, to be handled elsewhere in whole or in part. The transfer did not always go smoothly and states were sometimes surprised by what they learned they had given away. For instance in the late 1990s individuals in the US Administration and members of Congress reacted with horror to judgements against the US made by the World Trade Organization. The general trend, however, was for issues to become less sensitive with regard to sovereignty: competences were now routinely exercised by international agencies in areas which would have been sacred to sovereignty in earlier times. But paradoxically the states' survival rested on the assumption that this transfer could not be guaranteed: the competences could still be recalled in principle even if this in practice was unlikely.

Earlier in this chapter it was suggested that a successful diplomat would try to avoid situations in which a choice had to be made between acting morally and defending national interest. Successful diplomacy also involved avoiding policies which could lead to having to make a choice between national interest and courses of action indicated by the agenda of cosmopolitanism, as in this case national interest would have to come first. This was the nature of international society and the state. A policy competence would have to be renationalized if, for instance, a state's ability to provide for the welfare of its citizens was likely to be damaged. The skilled diplomat would increasingly require a sophisticated grasp of paradox. But in a community of well-founded states it would be less likely that a choice would have to be made to repatriate a competence, as the interests of all states would be informed by the cosmopolitan ideology.

Lurking behind these points was another more important one: the dialectical relationship between the state and the international community, as it had emerged by the early twenty-first century, increasingly demanded that states should be acceptable as proper participants in the international civil order. There was increasingly the perception that unless they met certain conditions of probity and internal welfare they could not be full members. One illustration of this was that members of governments which fell short were more often regarded among the community of diplomats as unsuited to the exercise of public office in the institutions of the international community. The EU member states had asserted this to bring the Austrian government of the right-winger Haider back into line. Member states were subject to a test of democratic standards as a condition of membership in their society. If this tendency-norm were to evolve into a practice-rule it would be hard to deny that in this key area states had become unequal as citizens of the international community, and that this had grave implications for the question of whether they could be regarded as equal and, therefore, sovereign.

In effect: changes in the circumstances of sovereignty suggested that it could come to depend upon being recognized as a fit member of international society. It could be ultimately responsible, exercise competences on behalf of its citizens and play a full part in the community that sanctioned this, only if it complied with the conditions of both the international and the domestic community. It was a short step to seeing the unfit as the unsovereign.

Directions of evolution

The significance of the above can be underlined by a sketch of conceivable next steps. What was on the agenda of the reform of international organization and its relation with the state in the early twenty-first century? Where was the system headed? These items give a preliminary indication of a possible direction. There were proposals which aimed at enhancing the accountability of governments to the international community; proposals for requiring qualifications of individuals and institutions as a condition of allowing them to operate international instruments (institutional development); and proposals which were aimed directly at improving the lot of individuals within states independently of the proposals aimed at national or international agencies. The proposals in roman (normal) type are those which appeared frequently in the literature at the turn of the millennium:[33] they amounted to expectations about next steps, which were as realistic a measure of what had been obtained as a list of actual attainments. They were the other side of the line represented by the word 'now'! Subsequent steps linked with the proposals might also be entering the discourse and are in *italics*: this enhances the sense of the direction of movement.

Proposals under these various headings were:

A. Government accountability

Under this heading proposals appearing on agendas included:

1. Strengthen the War Crimes Tribunal and set up an International Criminal Court. *A certificate of good housekeeping to be provided at the end of a government's period of office in all states by a designated international agency as representative of the international community, with the power to freeze and sequestrate the assets of malefactors.*
2. Tighten up the arms register arrangements and agree an international code for the supply of arms with effective policing. Make it compulsory to register and to apply an international code of manufacture and supply, *with direct access to manufacturers' inventories and production facilities for the international arms authority.*
3. A code of proper behaviour for political leaders to be agreed by the General Assembly linked with the publication of a register of corrupt governments by the UN. An index of governments rated with regard to corruption to be published by the General Assembly.
4. More liberal formal procedures for intervention – based on the interests of peoples – Chapter 1, Article 1(3) in contrast to Chapter VII. *A code for the use of force (military or economic), as in Haiti, to restore democracy in the event of military takeover.*

B. Institutional development

Items included:

1. Judicial review by the International Court of Justice of the decisions of the Security Council.

2. Enhancement of the powers of the Security Council to include more sectors reflecting a wider interpretation of sovereignty, e.g. environment and human rights. The capacity to achieve cross-sector coherence in its decisions would be enhanced. *The ICJ could then be granted power to rule on the priority of international agreements, so that coherence and consistency within and across sectors could be maintained.* That is the ICJ could be active in resolving conflicts between acts of international legislation such as that between World Trade Organization rules and Multilateral Environment Agreements. (In 1998 WTO rules required that trade liberalization codes override tighter environmental requirements in the MEAs; there was often a straight contradiction between the two with no formal process of reconciliation.)
3. A Commission of Experts to be created to bring the attention of the Security Council to new crises and recommend an appropriate response: *such a commission could also develop a role in determining the adequacy of resources with regard to SC mandates and their strategic and other implications for peacekeeping. It could be empowered to require that SC resolutions were technically efficient.*[34]
4. *Responsibility for the recognition and derecognition of states to be transferred to the UN and exercised under a special procedure.*
5. *Exclusion of governments with a low index rating, as determined in the procedure in A4. above, from executive positions in international institutions including the UN – and from voting, or new memberships in international organizations in the UN system.*

(In the Treaty of Amsterdam in the European Union states agreed that if a member was found guilty of offences against human rights it could be punished by having its voting rights in the Council of Ministers suspended.[35])

C. Cosmopolitanism and citizens

Items included:

1. All diplomatic relations and diplomacy to be linked to the promotion of human rights.
2. *All states to have formal constitutions subject to international approval by a designated agency (see C3.) which guaranteed civil rights and respect for minorities.*

3. *A Commission for Constitutionalism and Due Process to be set up. The UN Human Rights Conventions to be incorporated into all national constitutions under its supervision on the model of the European Convention of Human Rights.* In 2000 the British government accepted such incorporation.
4. States to be required to pursue a *civil rights first* strategy involving a range of obligations intended to maintain and promote civilized internal orders. These would include an obligation to avoid infringements of internationally recognized civil liberties. *The obligation could be extended to include an obligation to avoid excessive income differentials – mean income, not average – and exclude privileged access to social services, such as health, police and education. Indicators of civilized society could rate poorer societies more highly than rich countries with, for instance, wider income differentials and uneven social service access.*
5. Removal of prohibitions on direct appeal to international courts and forums by individuals against governments.
6. *Instigation of rules requiring that development and investment strategies promoted human rights, equity and environmental considerations.*
7. *The making of a list of recognized NGOs that could operate within all states as of right, i.e. without requiring the explicit permission of governments.*
8. More mixed representation in international institutions, i.e. by individual, group, region as well as governments.[36]
9. Limiting certain new collateral effects of war upon individuals: e.g. by limiting the use of land-mines, *and* damage to health from lack of proper precautions in testing, developing or storing chemical, bacteriological or nuclear weapons. An international mechanism for identifying and destroying redundant weapons.

Two kinds of implications of the changing circumstances of sovereignty were discussed in this section. First was the changes in views about the implications of being sovereign, and ways of becoming sovereign. Second was the proposals for future developments which had become conceivable because of those changes. Such proposals only acquired a veneer of credibility in the light of the changes in views about order and sovereignty.

Conclusions

The definition of sovereignty always had to take account of the circumstances of the time and of the place. It was an absolute which had to be constantly reinterpreted in the light of the actual limitations placed on state behaviour, and this produced continuous controversy and a steady stream of dissertations – which was hardly surprising in view of the logical impossibility of qualifying an absolute.

One reason for this was that the traditional discussion of sovereignty worked from the state-actor, and its claims to sovereignty, to the compromises with the principle which resulted from membership of international society. This reconciliation was always unconvincing. Changes in the work of the United Nations since the end of the Cold War, and the implications of membership in the European Union, extended the list of anomalies with regard to the traditional view to breaking point: how could a 'state' be sovereign in the traditional sense when its people could appeal to a superior court, such as the European Court of Human Rights or the European Court of Justice, against its own government and when laws made outside the state apparently prevailed over those made within, as in the European Union? One response to the difficulties, as in this chapter, was to reinterpret the principle as a reflection of the constitutive role of the international community *as well as* an acknowledgement of the innate need of people for self-determination. In the past sovereignty had been seen as being made by the subsystems, the states; a stronger appreciation was needed of the way in which the international community could constitute the state and express its sovereignty.

Developments in the work of United Nations system in the 1990s, and attitudes towards it, made it possible to identify somewhat more clearly this dialectical quality in sovereignty.

Aspects of this dialectic are brought out in the following summation.

- Sovereignty increasingly defined a unit of participation and established a right to participate in the institutions and arrangements of the international community. Having the right to participate in the management of common arrangements with other states was a much more important consideration in sovereignty than the traditional right to exclusive management of any single function, even defence and foreign policy. (Luxembourg, but not Quebec, was a sovereign state, not because the former did more alone than the latter – arguably Quebec had more functional independence in Canada than Luxembourg in the European Union. It was rather that Luxembourg had the right to participate in the range of international forums with state members, whereas Quebec did not; and Luxembourg retained the reserve powers mentioned below to limit the competence of external agencies.)

- But sovereignty increasingly came to be seen as conferring on states the obligation of being accountable to the international community. Being licensed to practise as a state carried with it the condition of its government's being prepared to demonstrate, to the satisfaction of the international community, continued adherence to the terms under which it held the licence, i.e. being well-founded in the varying senses discussed above. The sovereign was the entity which was accountable to the higher unit, and states which evaded this obligation were increasingly seen as falling short of the standards expected in the state-citizens of international society.
- Sovereignty identified a) the locus of responsibility in the state and b) the focus of popular perceptions about which authority was ultimately responsible. The rights and obligations of sovereignty were vested in a government which was the ultimate guardian of the popular interest and which could not renounce that interest because it was sovereign. It was the focus of popular hopes and expectations.
- And it was an embodiment of interest: its government, embodying the sovereignty of the state, had the right to determine a collective interest according to accepted procedures in the state.
- But, with regard to competence:
   a Sovereignty embodied a grant to the state from the international community of the right to act on its own account in international society.
   b It was also a grant of the right to extend competence to act to other entities such as international institutions, other states or private organizations, within its territory or on its behalf in international society.
   c Conversely the sovereignty of states meant that the system of which they were members necessarily left them with the right to limit that competence. By the early twenty-first century no form of majority voting in international institutions

had limited this right. This was the equivalent of the traditional right to exclusive domestic jurisdiction. It had, therefore, become less useful to see states as having exclusive domestic jurisdiction and more useful to see them as having reserved the right to limit the effects of legislation made outside. This was because of the development of an increasing capacity for making rules, with direct implications within states, in international institutions; the prime example of this, but by no means the only one, was the European Union.

- Sovereignty also carried the implication of a grant of the right to privacy for citizens. This was the perception that their behaviour among themselves was no business of others. But the limitations of this right included the requirement that practices should have general approval within the state and that they did not compromise the privacy of the citizens of other states. This right did not exclude the rights of others to argue against practices which they found abhorrent, and to promote intervention if a practice was contrary to a clear internationally held standard. But the assumption had to be made that any practice which turned one section of a community into the victims of another was necessarily abhorrent.

These perceptions of sovereignty arose in the context of the turn of the millennium. They included, in particular, extensions of the role of international institutions, especially the United Nations and the European Union, and the emergence of a more proactive cosmopolitanism which stressed an overlay on diverse cultures of universalizing values. All of this was in the process of *becoming*: it was a consequence of the happy coincidence that the end of the Cold War left the democratic liberal states in a position to push their values.

The entrenchment of cosmopolitanism, based on such liberal values, confirmed the right of outsiders to judge internal arrangements, and to act to ensure that acceptable standards were maintained. This was the essential condition of the grand underlying dialectic: the sovereignty of states obliged them to meet the norms of the international community but the norms of the international community were a product of the sovereignty of states.

CHAPTER 2

Peacekeeping in the Age of Globalization: Kosovo and After

Introduction

In this chapter the role of the United Nations in promoting security is discussed with particular reference to the action in Kosovo in 1999. It is important to locate what happened in an account of the evolution of this kind of thing, since this both helps to explain the particular episode, but is also suggestive of the future. The changes of attitude towards international order discussed in the previous chapter were the necessary context. Kosovo was the first instance of military action against a sovereign state which was justified on the grounds of a violation of the rights of individuals within that state. It was therefore a significant landmark and important lessons could be deduced.

There are lessons about the future development of the arrangements of the UN in this area of activity, about the specific role of the Security Council, but also about the respective roles of regional and global organization. The global organization was unable to find the military resources to pursue the goals it had sanctioned, and indeed on many occasions had found itself embarrassed.[1] A key question, from the point of view of what could be called the globalization of accountability, was therefore that of how far NATO, the regional organization which acted, had been sanctioned by the UN and how far the Security Council remained ultimately responsible.

But in the late 1990s and early twenty-first century the problem of resources in the global institution meant that it often worked through or with multi-purpose regional organizations for security maintenance. The relationship between the centre and the regions therefore became a complex one. It seemed vital that the global organization should protect its role as the initiator and legitimizer of all security actions: that it be the actor to which all others were accountable. This chapter argues that on the whole it succeeded in this. But the question of how far the centre could further develop its operational functions and overtake the role of the regions was by no means settled and in 2002 two avenues remained open. It could try to protect its authority but accept an increasing operational role for regional agents; or it could develop its own operational role so that regional agents were minor partners. In 2000 a very well-received study, the Brahimi Report, reported at length below, suggested the latter course. But the jury was still out.

Explanations in context

The action of NATO in Kosovo may have been carried out by the members of a regional alliance, but it can only be explained by reference to the increasing propensity of the United Nations to act in cases of human rights' abuses, and to use military force in a more focused and active way compared with the period of the Cold War. The fact was that the action in Kosovo was in a tradition of UN actions observable after the ending of the Cold War, as argued in Chapter 1, and that in this sense it was not surprising. The list of actions in the evolution of this kind of action included Somalia, Angola, Mozambique, Cambodia and Bosnia–Herzegovina. This is not to deny, however, that in the Balkans there was a special history which was also relevant.[2]

There are three levels of explanation of the action by NATO in Kosovo. These are changes in the nature of international society, which amounted to a permissive consensus about using international forces to achieve purposes agreed in the primary international forum, namely the United Nations, and within that the Security Council; specific developments in the practice of peacekeeping and enforcement; and the specific history of events in ex-Yugoslavia. Explanations in each of these contexts help understand why the action took place, though the diplomacy of the relevant Security Council Resolutions explains their application more directly.

A permissive consensus

A number of changes encouraged the more activist stance. There had been changes in views about the nature of sovereignty and international order, which were discussed in Chapter 1. The world had moved from the hard-line view of sovereignty which had been a feature of the period of the Cold War, to a view which stressed that it was conditional upon maintaining generally approved standards.

A number of changes went along with this: internal and external orders were linked together increasingly. One consequence of this was that national interest and morality were often linked together in a way which would have been surprising to those who took a more traditional view of international society. These changes were in the context of massive developments in the area of communications technology, which introduced what was often referred to as the CNN factor.

The emerging practice

The Kosovo action was the most recent expression of a series of developments in peacekeeping, taking that form of activity further towards the form of enforcement which had evolved from Chapter VII of the Charter.

Peacekeeping was the second of the two ways of actively promoting peace and security within the United Nations: Chapter VII of the Charter contained another approach which became known as *enforcement*, though it had never been practised exactly as prescribed. There remained the question of whether there was any comparable action which derived from the original form. Enforcement might be defined as the kind of UN action which involved a decision by the Security Council about the precise outcome which was to be achieved, and the provision of military means judged as sufficient to ensure its attainment. It was likely that such agreement would only be obtained among the permanent members of the Security Council, and the majority of non-permanent members, in very unusual circumstances; there would need to be a general agreement that a flagrant breach of the fundamental principles of the rules of international society had taken place.

Before Kosovo enforcement in this form had only taken place twice in the history of the United Nations, when North Korea invaded South Korea in 1950 and in the Gulf War in 1991, and on both occasions the UN failed to use the operating principles of Chapter VII.[3] In both instances the Security Council agreed that a particular group of states should act on its behalf under the leadership and control of the United States. In the case of the action against the Taliban in Aghanistan in 2002 the US government was anxious to obtain the implied consent of the Security Council for its response, but on this occasion, unlike the earlier ones, it was more difficult to find in the Security Council Resolution any indication of a claim to United Nations overview. The resolution of 12 September 2001 (Resolution 1368) unequivocally condemned the attacks but also asserted the inherent right under the Charter to individual and collective self-defence. But it is important to note that the resolution contained no explicit or implied targeting of the Taliban, though it did imply a licence to punish the guilty parties. But there had been earlier condemnations of Taliban policies, so no one could say that it was surprising to think that they might have been involved and therefore likely to attract reprisals (Resolution 1333, 19 December 2000). But it was as if the members of the Security Council realized that the UN role in the response would have to be limited to the implicit acceptance of the right of the US to decide on its own response.

The Security Council did however adopt a strong line on doing all it could to limit terrorism. It spelled out what needed to be done by member states to counter terrorism, and the principles of the required collective response, and set up a committee of the whole of the Security Council to supervise their application (Resolution 1373, 28 September 2001). In fact the measures indicated were themselves a more intrusive set of obligations on states then ever before, for instance with regard to the freezing of the assets of terrorist groups. So the conclusion has to be that the UN's response to the attacks by al-Qaeda, with the supposed support of the Taliban, were an indication of the limits of what it could do in this kind of case, rather than of any ambition to do more.

The instances of UN-approved action up to the Kosovan case reflected an ambition to do more, though these were cases which fell short of the kind of extreme assault on a major power in which the UN was bound to have a supporting role only. The earlier cases fitted into a pattern of enhancing UN supervision and involvement, even though the actions were nothing like what had been envisaged in the Charter. There was no UN command and control structure under the Military Staff Committee, as the Charter intended, and no UN budgetary procedure to pay for the military operations. The arrangements for effective UN command of military actions on this scale did not exist, either in 1950 or 1991 – or in Kosovo in 1999 – and it was unlikely that states could agree to UN command over their national armies when a hot war was on the cards. The scale of the war, and the associated risks to personnel, would lead governments to insist on retaining national control in order to minimize casualties. This was a responsibility which they could not abjure. Enforcement even in some approximation of Chapter VII of the Charter was, therefore, something unusual in the history of the United Nations and by the early twenty-first century the consensus was that it was unlikely that it would ever occur.

Peacekeeping was the form of peace maintenance that became the main practice of the United Nations. The traditional style of peacekeeping is well known and does not need to be revisited here. In the series of crises since the end of the Cold War it had become more active, and involved the use of forces from larger states under forms of UN command to achieve humanitarian goals such as providing food and medicines to those in need. These new functions were in addition to that of attempting to keep the warring parties apart and promote negotiations between them. Various problems arose because of these changes, but the new more proactive peacekeeping quickly encountered the problem of being dragged into the dispute they were intended to ameliorate. They also began to use heavier weaponry and to be more prepared to use force to achieve the goals in their mandate. In Bosnia–Herzegovina this also led to the use, in support of UN action, of NATO aircraft to impose air exclusion zones, a precedent for what was to happen later in Kosovo.[4]

In sum the new peacekeeping, in terms of its equipment and strategic purpose, became more like enforcement. An important difference, however, was that the kind of goal it sought was not explicitly and directly to do with resisting a challenge by an aggressor state to the integrity of another, the primary international sin predicated under Chapter VII. If it was agreed that such a sin had been committed the Security Council could authorize action to restore a state's independent sovereignty, as in Korea in the 1950s, or in the war against Saddam Hussein in 1991. But in Kosovo a new form of specific goal was agreed by the NATO states – that of stopping particular forms of infringement of basic human rights – in that case the ethnic cleansing of Kosovo by the forces of Serbia–Montenegro, under its President, Slobodan Milosevic, of people of Albanian origin. In addition the participating states agreed to use forms of aggressive warfare – in the first instance, air power – which they deemed necessary and appropriate. This was not an intervention in a war between two states but an action targeted at an existing sovereign state, which was deemed to be transgressing internationally agreed values on its own sovereign territory.

Kosovo was new in its combination of elements though not in any one of them. There was a specific goal of a humanitarian kind, like earlier acts of peacekeeping, justified however under Chapter VII, but it was like enforcement as experienced by the UN in that it used high levels of force and was directed against a sovereign state. It was also like earlier forms of UN enforcement action in that it did not rely upon a UN command and control structure, as foreseen in the Charter, but that of the members of NATO dominated by the United States. In sum the Kosovo action was the strongest hybrid so far of peacekeeping and enforcement as practised by the UN. But it was an unsurprising development in the sense that the way in which peacekeeping had been practised in various parts of the world, but particularly in ex-Yugoslavia, since the turn of the decade had led step by step towards that kind of thing.

Evolving trends towards the type of action found in Kosovo might be summarized as follows:

1. Enforcement had developed from the Charter, but used high levels of armaments to oppose infringements of the sovereignty of one state by another. This was the closest the practice of the UN members had got to the intentions of the founders of the UN with regard to the maintenance of international peace and security as stated in Chapter VII.
2. Peacekeeping forces had been used increasingly frequently for humanitarian purposes and after the end of the Cold War they had used heavier weaponry more proactively to achieve humanitarian ends. *But they had been used where sovereignty was uncertain or was disputed.*
3. In Kosovo the developments with regard to enforcement and peacekeeping merged. In this case, for the first time, higher levels of force were used for humanitarian purposes under Chapter VII *when sovereignty was not contested.* Indeed the NATO states which undertook the action underlined this point by stressing that they were fighting for a satisfactory arrangement for Kosovans *within* the state of Serbia–Herzegovina.

Events in ex-Yugoslavia

Yugoslavia was the unfortunate context of the appearance of a scale and purpose of the use of force by an international organization which moved outside the limits of what could reasonably be called peacekeeping, even of a new kind, but which was different in a number of ways from the earlier practice of enforcement. The turning-point came with the tragedy at Srebrenica and the Dayton agreement in 1993–4.[5] The NATO action in Kosovo in 1999, and the appearance there of what could be called the new enforcement, should be understood in the context of those earlier events and the subsequent developments.

The mismanagement of the safe areas in Bosnia–Herzegovina by the Security Council forced a painful reappraisal of the chances of achieving a satisfactory outcome with peacekeeping, which was based on the assumption that negotiation was possible. The very vulnerability of the UN at the end of the safe areas episode indicated that its leaders had expected compromise. The Serb's ruthless exploitation of that vulnerability put the Western states in the Security Council on notice that from then on enforcement was likely to be necessary. The Americans, therefore, had to be directly involved, and if this could only be done through an enhanced roll for NATO then so be it. The new peacekeeping spilled over into a new enforcement as NATO forces were now carrying out the business of the United Nations by using its air power directly and by flexing, but not using, its massive ground-force muscle. The Dayton agreement was a deal which was only accepted by the Bosnian Serbs because Milosevic had a NATO gun at his head, and the Bosnian Serb leader, Karajic, was becoming a threat to Milosevic leadership of Greater Serbia. Although it effectively created a confederal tripartite Bosnia, with the Serbian enclave having *de facto* independence, Milosevic still determined to cock a further snook at the UN negotiators after independence. The confederal architecture was often ignored in the area carved out for Serb domination, and to all intents and purposes it was added to the realm of Milosevic's Federal Yugoslavia. Milosevic's actions, and those of his Bosnian cronies, implied that the formal reunion of the enclave with Yugoslavia was only a matter of time.

By the spring of 1999 it was evident that the later history of Bosnia was a direct stepping-stone to the Kosovo crisis. There were therefore three developments, identifiable in the crisis about ex-Yugoslavia, which contributed to the NATO action.

First was Milosevic's drawing of lessons from the events, in particular that he could get away with the appearance of flexibility while getting so close to what he wanted as to make no difference. Milosevic came to believe that he could outplay the UN and those who acted for it: NATO could threaten but would fail to hold to its purpose. In one view he also learnt that: 'when intervention by outside powers is imminent, step up the ethnic cleansing, for no one will have the will or the power to change the new demographics created by war'.[6]

Second was the Western allies' increasing determination to use available force to stop Milosevic from continuing to prevent their carrying out the UN mandate, as he had in the Bosnia–Herzegovina crisis. The collective memory of the allies of the earlier episode was a powerful reason for action now. This time, negotiation was not possible, not because of *their* unwillingness, but because of the demonstrated unwillingness of Milosevic to take any product of negotiation seriously, indeed, his failure to deal with negotiating partners with anything but contempt. As the crisis developed the mere fact of involvement meant that NATO had to succeed or risk grave damage to its reputation. Kosovo also provided an opportunity for a further testing of a novel military doctrine, which strategists had regarded as unworkable. The continuing development of the technology of air attack after the Gulf War raised the question afresh of whether air power could be accurate enough to do the work of ground troops.

Third was the judgement of the main states that such grave breaches of the standards of civilized society also posed an actual threat to international peace and security in the Balkans and in the wider context in Europe, and this justified UN action. This was the first time that *a sovereign state* had been subject to UN-sanctioned violence in order to pursue a humanitarian purpose. But this was not what appeared in the relevant Security Council resolutions, SC 1160, 1199 and 1203: intervention in Serbia was justified, as it had been in Somalia, not by reference to the serious breaches of human rights, but on the grounds that it constituted a threat to international peace and security under Chapter VII. But though the events in Kosovo had obvious security implications for NATO members – for instance the danger of Greece, Turkey, Bulgaria and Romania being drawn in – the humanitarian argument was the dominant one in that the bulk of the resolutions focused on the actions of the regular and irregular Serbian forces in Kosovo, which were carrying out the brutal ethnic cleansing of the Albanian population of Kosovo.

The type of enforcement by the international organization was new. Traditionally the decision to insist upon goals and to use force to obtain them had been that of the UN. This time the UN remained prepared to negotiate as long as the outcome complied with the standards of good humanitarian practice. It was Milosevic who by now had acquired the nerve – in part encouraged by past UN hesitancy – to refuse compromise. Enforcement became the only conceivable UN response in the new context. By tolerating variations from the Dayton agreement in the Serb section of Bosnia the Allies had in a way encouraged Milosevic in his obduracy. But Milosevic's obduracy went along with his overestimation of the leverage he could apply through his purported ally, the Russians. He saw the main activists in the UN Security Council as weak and divided. He reckoned without the earlier Council Resolutions and Chapter VIII arrangements to justify their response.

The UN mandate on Kosovo

In what sense was the bombing of Serbia sanctioned by the UN in the relevant Security Council resolutions, 1160, 1199 and 1203? Although the wording of the resolutions which came before the NATO action was not explicit in authorizing the NATO action they arguably contained a large measure of justification for that action. Those who expect Security Council resolutions to be explicit about the use of force, as will be shown below, are likely to be disappointed, since mostly they are not. Indeed there are good grounds for saying that this cannot be the case.

Three points could be made about the resolutions. First that they became increasingly specific about the violations of humanitarian standards; the resolutions were about gross violations of the rules of civilized conduct, as embodied in a wide range of international conventions, and the language of the resolutions was increasingly pointed and forceful about this. Secondly, from the first SC 1160 through to the one closest to the action, SC 1203, they became increasingly focused upon the transgressions of the forces of Federal Yugoslavia. The first, SC 1160, was fairly even-handed in demanding compliance from both the Kosovo Nationalist forces, the KLA and the Serb forces, but the later resolution was focused on the transgressions of the Serbs. The appeal for help in identifying breaches of the laws of war and bringing those accused to justice was also targeted more at the Serbs than the Kosovans. Thirdly the resolutions contained an appeal to states to act, which increased in strength. A comparison of Article 12 in SC 1199 (September 1998) with Article 13 of SC 1203 (October 1998) revealed a more pressing appeal. SC 1199 '*calls upon* Member States and others concerned *to provide adequate resources* for humanitarian assistance in the region' while SC 1203 '*urges* Member States and others concerned *to provide adequate resources* for humanitarian assistance in the region'. States were asked to act in support of humanitarian assistance and, in the context of the nature of Milosevic's actions in Kosovo, and their vigorous and explicit condemnation, this could be reasonably interpreted as including the use of military force. The crisis was there: the cry was for someone to do something about it.

Demands were made for the arrest of those in Kosovo who were guilty of war crimes, for a return to negotiation with the Kosovans, and the suspension of the extreme measures used against them. The Security Council also implied in SC 1199 that what was happening within Yugoslavia constituted a war in the sense required by the terms of the legislation on the War Crimes Tribunal, and there were appeals in the resolutions for the collection of evidence of war crimes. It must be agreed that there was no explicit request for the use of NATO military, but this raises the further question of whether a measure of interpretation of UN resolutions was likely so that they could be seen as implying approval.

There are two answers to this question: one is that the history of SC resolutions is full of examples of the use of coded language about the use of force. Secondly that on 26 March 1999 the Security Council was asked by the Russians to condemn the use of force. That was two days after the action by NATO had started. But the resolution was overwhelmingly rejected by 12 votes to 3. The only three states which approved the condemnation of NATO action were Russia, China and Namibia. The reasons for the position taken by the last were obscure. Countries which opposed the Russian proposal included Brazil and Malaysia; the government of the latter overruled the advice of its own UN delegation to vote against. It could hardly be argued that the members of this coalition were lackeys of the Americans or the British!

The Russians agreed to all of these strictures in the Security Council. Yet they denied that they had foreseen the use of force in Kosovo when approving such condemnations and their implied consequences, and agreeing to urge states to provide adequate resources for humanitarian assistance. But the Russians, like the other members of the Council were used to the coded language of its resolutions: it was normal practice that they were not explicit about the use of military sanctions. The reasons for Russian behaviour are complex, but must include the idea of a two-level game. At one level there was a feeling that something had to be done in Kosovo and Milosevic restrained, but at another level there was an awareness on the part of the government that internal divisions, and popular sympathy with the Serbs, meant that this view could not be made explicit. The Russian government, in its own search for role and status, was anxious to demonstrate that it had power in the region, and in particular with regard to Serbia. One part of the Russian Foreign Office, including its very able representative in the United Nations, was, therefore, prepared to play a rather dangerous game. It thought it could hold off NATO action, as long as there was no explicit Security Council authorization, but used it as back-up for its own diplomacy with Milosevic to get him to back down and reach a deal. The latter strongly implied that they understood that the use of force was a probability.

There was also evidence to suggest that when the action started the Russian public was ill-informed about Kosovo – it attracted little attention in the Russian press – but that, as information increased, the preparedness to risk conflict with the West in order to defend Milosevic declined. The Russians were therefore likely to follow two apparently contradictory lines in the cause of their own internal stability. But there was likely to be an understanding in the Russian Foreign Office of what the wording of the resolutions meant because there was a record of the need to interpret the specific wording.

For instance they had taken the message that the formula of 'all necessary means', which had been used in SC 678 – the legal basis of the use of force against Saddam Hussein in 1991 – had meant war.[7] Similarly Resolution 770 of 13 August 1992 during the Bosnian crisis used the words 'all measures necessary' and was then interpreted by the Serbs, recalling the earlier SC 678, as a threat of the use of force. (The people of Belgrade, it was reported, thought they would be bombed that night.) Again, Resolution 688, which was interpreted as mandating the no-fly zones to protect the Kurds in Iraq asked 'Iraq to allow immediate access by international humanitarian organizations to all those in need of assistance in Iraq'. It contained no explicit request for the formal authorization of military action, but it was accepted as meaning that, and was the legal basis of the use of air attacks against Iraq up to the time of writing in 2002.

There were also at least two other contexts through which the Russians could have obtained information which would have led them to understand that NATO action was possible. The first was that of NATO procedures, of which Russia was certainly aware: as early as 24 September 1998 NATO had taken the first formal steps toward military intervention in Kosovo, approving two contingency operation plans, one for air strikes and the second for monitoring and maintaining a ceasefire agreement if one were reached. The discussions of the Contact Group, in which Russia was involved, had also given frequent indications of the possibility of military action. For instance after the breakdown of the talks with the Serbs and Kosovans on 19 March the Joint Chairman of the Contact Group said that any action would be met with the 'gravest consequences'.[8] In the Security Council itself there had also been Presidential Statements, approved by both Russia and China, which went as far as to support the presence in Kosovo of an international military force.[9]

The point became increasingly pertinent that there was a sharp disagreement between those who said that SC resolutions should be clear, immediate and precise; and those who said they were cumulative, and bases for interpretation. This was one of those occasions when two apparently contradictory positions were equally true: there had been no explicit Security Council resolution approving the NATO action; but there was a plethora of resolutions, which could be interpreted, and had been interpreted, as justifying that kind of response. The interpretation of SC 1203 as an invitation to NATO to do what it could to provide humanitarian assistance, including the use of military means, was entirely reasonable, but it was even more justifiable in that it was the kind of thing that had been done before.

What explained this characteristic of Security Council resolutions? Sometimes, as with the Russians, the explanation might be to do with internal divisions: ambiguity was the result of the wish to conceal actions from those who opposed it within the state. On other occasions the ambiguity might be explained by their wish to maintain two contradictory positions, first, the view that the exclusive domestic jurisdiction of states meant that international agencies should have no powers or rights to act within them and, second, that maintaining international order might sometimes require international intervention to correct problems in states.

China may be taken as an illustration of this tactic. For both international and domestic reasons China was determined to resist the strengthening of the *general* principle that the sovereignty of states was conditional upon maintaining acceptable standards of human rights within their frontiers, as the current writer has argued, but accepted that action might be required in particular instances. The trick was to find a way of allowing action, without conceding the precedent. There were two ways of achieving this. One was to abstain; another was to insist upon a form of words which was not explicit in granting powers to act. China insisted on both of these in the Gulf War resolutions.[10] Explicitness was more likely to reinforce precedent, to strengthen the view that the normal practice was to intervene. A coded message was more likely to allow approval for action in the particular instance with a lesser risk that this act of intervention, however cautious and conditional, would contribute to the strengthening of the norm.

If necessary, conservative states could argue later that they had not understood the coded message, and that the states which acted had opportunistically exploited a lack of clarity in the resolution. For those states which had the veto the ideal would be to have a lack of explicitness combined with abstention, but other members could have reasons for favouring the coded message. This tactic was symbolic of the current phase in the evolution of international society: short of a secure international authority but moving beyond the traditional, realist view of sovereignty. But the use of the tactic by the conservative states in fact conceded the point that the norm of intervention, and international authority, was becoming stronger.

This kind of *ad hoc* approach to intervention was also a characteristic of this phase of the development of international society. It was arguable that all Security Council Resolutions should be explicit and agreed in the light of the rule governing intervention which had been agreed beforehand. There were a number of difficulties with this position. It would have been very difficult to agree the rules between the states: there would be departures from them as particular states calculated that action in that instance did not suit their interests; and they would have reflected the lowest common denominater, the least activist position. It was natural therefore that decisions to act should be *ad hoc*, as they were as yet based on a mixture of national interest and morality, as proposed in the preceding chapter. Action had to be taken when it was possible and desirable, and not just when it was desirable.

But this still does not answer the question of whether NATO could be seen as having been authorized to act under the Charter, in particular Chapter VIII on regional organizations' role in maintaining peace and security. In one sense that answer is simple: states had been asked to do something and NATO was an available group of states which had the equipment and the expertise. It could equally have been any grouping of states, but NATO was there and prepared to do it. There were, however, two uncertainties, each of which could be interpreted in Nato's favour. First, Chapter VIII could be interpreted as applying only to breaches of the peace *between members* of a regional organization; the action in Kosovo was outside the territory of NATO and, if this interpretation was correct, the alliance should not have acted. But there is a counter-argument: that the troubled area was immediately adjacent and posed a real threat to relations between NATO members, especially Greece and Turkey. Second, the crisis had not been returned to the Security Council, as required by Chapter VIII, because of the Russian opposition. But Chapter VIII did not state the time period in which regional actions should be returned to Security Council supervision, and that could be when the crisis was moving towards a settlement – as long as the delay was not unreasonably protracted – when Russia would be anxious to be involved and welcome to do so. At that point the Security Council's role, whether or not it was under the terms of Chapter VIII, could be resumed. But it was important that in the course of the action the special responsibility of the Security Council was acknowledged and respected. That was confirmed by the fact that the Security Council was regularly, and according to a British Foreign Office official, comprehensively informed about the progress of the war.[11] This reflected compliance, though it is hard to confirm its extent, with the requirement in Chapter VIII that the Security Council should be kept fully informed.

There were therefore grounds for saying that the NATO action in Kosovo had indeed received a degree of justification in Security Council resolutions, as well as in the general support in the Charter for state action in cases of gross violations of human rights. But events since the end of the Cold War, and especially events in the late phases of the crisis in Bosnia–Herzegovina, are key in explaining the crisis, and themselves also constituted justifications for the action. The differences between the pattern of UN involvement in cases of peacekeeping up to the Kosovan action, and that against Afghanistan, are striking. The latter lies outside the trajectory of the development of the former.

The Security Council put itself in the position of acting alongside the main active state, the US, rather than implying a moral and practical supervision. There was to be an attempt to deal with a general, and very serious, problem, namely international terrorism, but not close engagement with the specifics of the response, either with regard to the target – the Taliban was not mentioned in the

12 September Resolution – or the means – there was no indication of the acceptability of all necessary means, and merely an acceptance of the right to act. This is not to say that developments up to Kosovo can now be ignored as having no implications for the trajectory of future developments, but merely to point out that 11 September lies outside that trajectory. Indeed 11 September could be seen as a marker of the limits for the time being of the involvement of the United Nations in the maintenance of international peace and security.

Kosovo and the future of the United Nations

Turn the clock back?

The above are reasons why the UN acquired the habit of peacekeeping, of which Kosovo was a natural evolution. But one reaction to increased UN activity of this kind was that peacekeeping had done more harm than good, and that it would be less costly in terms of life and resources if warring groups within states were allowed to fight it out, until one side or the other had prevailed or there was mutual exhaustion. Intervention by the United Nations had only served to create a series of interludes in which the parties to a dispute could rearm and prepare themselves for further onslaught. It was as if a boxer were continually revived, when near defeat, in order to receive more punishment. An example of this depressing argument was that put forward in an article in *Foreign Affairs* in the summer of 1999 by Edward Luttwak.[12]

It is a view that needs a reasoned response. What follows is a set of arguments to challenge the views put forward by Luttwak, taking his position as illustrative of this position.

The arguments against the opt-out view are as follows:

- It was morally objectionable for those who were in a position to alleviate human suffering to do nothing. The point could be made against this that there could be less suffering in the longer term if the stronger side were not prevented from winning, and that propping up the weak extended their suffering. But human beings could not know the longer term: the opt-out argument only seemed valid in hindsight but could give no clue as to what should be done next. Human beings had no means of knowing whether the consequences of moral action now were more or less costly in the medium or long term. Indeed it was irresponsible to claim to be acting morally on the basis of foresight which of necessity could not be validated. The safer course must always be to strive to reduce suffering, as it could not be known how much suffering there would be otherwise. The moral basis of the opt-out argument as a guide to action rested on a false view of the individual's relationship with history.

- An argument against the opt-out position was that the record was mixed, not clearly always successful, but not clearly always disastrous either. It was also relevant that the reasons for things sometimes going wrong had not always been the same. In Cambodia there was a high degree of success. In Cyprus there was success in the sense that the UN forces seemed to have succeeded in keeping the warring Greeks and Turks apart, although by 2002 there had been no success in reuniting the island. In Somalia there had been a period in which things seemed to be moving the right way but then a new descent into chaos with very mixed results. In the series of crises involving Croatia, Bosnia and Kosovo there were phases of appalling failure and some degree of success. The new state of Croatia emerged from the turmoil reasonably well founded, and the Dayton Agreement appeared to give Bosnia–Herzegovina a deal which, though flawed, had potential for success.

Serious mistakes were made. But overall the UN actions in ex-Yugoslavia, pre-Kosovo, seemed at least to have given some cause for pause to the Serbs who would surely have killed far more people in the absence of an international presence. In Angola it looked as if the intervention by the UN had achieved considerable success until the resumption of action by the forces of Jonas Savimbi.

The important point, though, was that all the various outcomes did not demonstrate the total failure of the actions of the international community through the UN. Rather they indicated some success and some failure. The further crucial point followed: the lesson of all of this could not be that it had to stop, but rather that there were lessons to be learned about how to improve the process. A measure of success was enough to demonstrate the possibility of learning to do it better.

The list of ways of going on to do better was easy to construct but difficult to implement. But one key variable was of course the question of how much time was needed to judge the effectiveness of UN action. This was a much more profound question than appeared at first sight. It was however likely that one assumption made by those critical of UN peacekeeping performance needed to be examined critically. The habit developed, especially in the US, of requiring that success be rapid and the intervention be of a specified and limited duration. It was, however, in contrast, likely that UN peacekeeping needed a greater degree of endurance, which of course was also likely to require greater resources. The argument that complex crises needed to be solved in the short term was to misunderstand the nature of social crises. It was a characteristically American prejudice: that profound crises in human relations, problems of ethnicity, contrasting values and the like, could be fixed with a short-term input of resources and a little skilled public relations.

The assumption that United Nations intervention would have affected the consolidation of states adversely, had it happened, for instance in the US or British civil wars, was also hard to substantiate. The UN could not intervene directly, then or now, in crises where there were large, organized armies involved in war, though it might have helped to ameliorate the associated misery of non-combatants. The 11 September attacks and the response to them indicated another limit on the UN's capacity. The attacks were against a superpower, which could be guided but restrained with difficulty, and the attacks came from a source that was very hard to identify with certainty. The UN did however take on the task, which could be more important in the long run, of pushing for general systems of response to the organizations that sponsored and carried out terrorist attacks. There were some crises between warring parties which were, and always had been, not liable to action from the international community through the UN, and although UN intervention affected the process of state creation in some cases, the experience was that there were very few cases where the UN had been decisive in determining the ethnic mix within a state or the extent of its territory on being set up.

- The same point might be approached from a more theoretical perspective. The question was about how conflicts ended. Was it the case that long-term settlement was always the result of the subjugation of one side or of exhaustion? Were there changes in the conditions of settlement in the modern world which suggested other possibilities? It has to be accepted that settlement was possible by subjugation and the exercise of extreme force, backed by ruthlessness. But Machiavelli recognized the need for the Prince, in applying his rule, to attract the fear of his enemies but also their respect. It was extremely difficult, if not impossible in practice, for a conqueror to remove all vestiges of opposition and to sow no seeds of future uprising. Indeed many of the crises of the 1990s were themselves the descendants of failed attempts to do this in the past. The more practical course was to seek compromise, but to back that up with the manifestation of power, in the hope that enough benefit could be given to the defeated entities to start a process of transforming that power into a legitimized authority. The lesson of wise government over peoples which had been defeated was to grant what could be granted but to back settlement with power. This gave the best chance of gradually strengthening the bases of order.

How does this relate to the possible role of international forces in conflict situations, such as those between peoples within states? The international forces had two advantages in the modern world. First they were better placed than earlier forces to combine the ability to promote compromise, and the appearance of benefit, while at the same time manifesting power impartially so that offers made were less likely to be lightly rejected. But international forces were also more capable of promoting alternative frameworks of settlement: they were able to legitimize such proposals as the setting up of autonomous regions within states, as in Kosovo, a proposal which a victorious army from an individual state, or coalition of interested parties outside the global authority, would have found hard to sell.

In the modern world, however, this mixed bag of compromise seeking, power manifesting and alternative framework initiating would be insufficient within the framework of the existing state. At this point a further innovation might be necessary which only an international authority could legitimize: the setting up of an alternative state. In modern international society the strengthening of common governance, regional or global, of which the UN was a key element, had enabled a much less fundamentalist attitude towards state creation and state change. The European Union's experience suggested that it was easier to bring about devolution, and degrees of regional autonomy when there was a stronger transcendant organizational framework. There had been devolution in the UK and considerable regions in Spain and Italy, which were easier to accept in the common framework. Similarly in the UN: a stronger organization could be conducive to a more flexible attitude to state-building as a solution to the problems of minorities in existing states. In a common framework of stronger international governance strong minorities could be more readily permitted to look for solutions to their perceived problems, and to remedy their perceived grievances, in an autonomous region or even a new state.

Stronger common governance and the existence of an international authority to police the action and legitimize it were capable of easing this process, which was impossible in a period or area of weak governance. This was one reason why arguments about statehood were likely to be more bitter and more viciously contested in more primitive and less developed parts of the world. That reflected a duality of modernism and primitivism: modernism with regard to valuing the state, but primitivism in insisting on its absolute character and unchangeability. In modern international society, which of necessity included stronger international authority and greater interventionism, the state could be regarded as being more malleable though it remained indispensable. The new medievalism, which some had announced, included a respect for the state but a preparedness to give ground for good reason with regard to its frontiers.

- The opt-out argument depended on a version of the realist approach to international relations, and in many ways revealed its inadequacy when proposed in this extreme form. It rested on the assumption that the primary actors in the world remained states, but, more than that, that individuals within states owed no moral obligation to those in other states. In fact the view was tainted by a certain ethnic supremacism: that those in other states, or without states, could be treated as if they were inferior creatures, which need not be treated as if they were individuals in pain. In his article Luttwak remarked that the natural sympathy of observers with the suffering of others was a 'frivolous' reason for government action to help! (p. 38). In terms of the opt-out argument a difficulty was knowing where to draw the line between a carelessness about the plight of outsiders, and caring about the plight of insiders within the commentators' own state. One difficulty was knowing exactly what was an insider. Was it any fellow citizen or was it sometimes to do with family links or other forms of mutual identity?

If the latter then the Luttwak argument faced an increasing problem in that there were more and more extended diasporas around the world within which individuals rated very highly loyalty to their fellows in other countries. The increasing movement of refugees, economic or political, was likely to make this problem increasingly difficult in the future. The paradox of the Luttwak argument here was that stopping the kind of UN action which he disliked was likely to increase the flow of such refugees. In consequence feelings of obligation to kith and kin in the crisis area were likely to be increased and – to square the circle – strengthened the feeling that intervention should take place.

But the citizenship argument against involvement also looked rather thin. It was to be assumed that those in favour would not advocate that the police in Los Angeles should have stood back while rioting blacks rampaged in the streets of Watts. But what would be said if the rioting was in Windsor, Canada, just across the border from neighbouring Detroit, USA, or in a Mexican border town like Tijuana? Surely no one would wish the police to ignore civil commotion in her/his own backyard? But the difficulty was to decide the extent of the backyard: in various parts of the world by the early twenty-first century integrated regions cutting across borders were increasingly common. But realists had difficulty in recognizing a trans-state territoriality because their theory disposed them to see states as having hard frontiers. That this was increasingly not the case was something their theory disposed them not to see.

This point revealed another linked realist assumption: a negative circularity of argument in the observation that there was no effective international police force, and that this must be the case because there was no international community. Hard realists, like neorealists could not afford to concede the view that international community could be developing and that therefore it might be worth working at making the international police force more effective, a development which was certainly observable in the European Union. The problem was a trivial intellectual one of paradigm enclosure, though the conclusions which flowed from this banal impediment were morally repugnant. They were increasingly faced with an anxiety about the evidence and a willingness to stretch the meaning of history to keep their parcel intact.

- The strategy of not intervening in cases of war between groups within other states was also one that was not straightforward in terms of the policies of those states which opposed intervention. What conclusions followed when internal war had clear risks for peace between states adjacent to the conflict, as in Bosnia–Herzegovina and Kosovo? Was the conclusion to be that international institutions should do nothing about those causes of international war which flowed from conflicts within neighbouring – or even distant – states? Here was another problematic trade-off between short-term and long-term cost: resources could be saved in the short term but at what cost in the longer term? Was the risk that international war could follow from internal war always to be ignored, a conclusion that followed from the opt-out thesis?

A further problem went back to the classical arguments about intervention proposed by John Stuart Mill, which was a body of advanced international relations literature completely ignored by Luttwak. Mill did not exclude intervention completely, but did argue that it should be an exceptional activity only undertaken in certain carefully defined circumstances. The Mill view was that if one side was being helped by an outsider, then states would be justified in helping the other side, and if such intervention did not take place intervention in effect amounted to support for the stronger side. The remarks attributed to Talleyrand were apposite: 'non-intervention is a strange policy which means exactly the same as intervention'. This was precisely what the Western liberal states failed to do during the Spanish Civil war, and the result was that the forces of General Franco had massive assistance from the Fascist powers to defeat his leftist opponents in Spain. Would Luttwak really claim that this strategy was the correct one?

But the view propounded by him led to an even more extreme and unpleasant dilemma for the international community. Were the conflicting elements in the state to be prevented from receiving arms impartially – i.e. was there to be an international boycott of the provision of arms? In this case there was almost always the problem that one side happened to have the better forces when the conflict started, by accident or design, or was more likely to be better placed to make deals with those providers of arms who were prepared to run the international gauntlet. The technology of war had developed so that the world had become more interdependent with regard to the provision of war materials. There was an imperative in modern warfare to improve military forces to that of the best available and for all but the superpowers that meant seeking outside suppliers of arms. The idea that conflicts could be separated from the international arms bazaar was a naïve illusion for all but the strongest and most developed states. The paradox was that the biggest divider of states, war, also contained a powerful incentive to interdependence in the provision of the means to conduct it. This was itself a powerful argument in favour of maximizing the chances of enlightened intervention, if only to negate the inevitable resulting forms of interdependence.

The logic of the opt-out position suggested a much simpler and less problematic course of action by the outside states which Jonathan Swift might have savoured: that they should be encouraged to supply both sides equally with as much military material as possible so that the war would be fought to a standstill in the shortest possible time. Perhaps the international community could find a way of offering credit to the warring parties to facilitate this process, and, of course, low-cost export-guarantee coverage for arms exporters!

- A particularly damning criticism of the opt-out position was revealed by subjecting it to a little constructivist examination. It had been made in a particular political context in the USA in 1999. That context included the persistent theme of the anti-internationalism of right-wing Republicans, who fancied they had a chance of beating the Democrats in the upcoming Presidential elections in 2000, and who often 'cared less about making foreign policy than arguing about why the United States should have even have one'.[13] The mood of the times helped to give voice to the view that the US should have nothing to do with peacekeeping. The strangeness of this position is all too evident after 11 September.

There were also likely to be influences which related to the special responsibilities of the US in the international system. It had become the single most important world power after the breakup of the Soviet Union, and was therefore increasingly expected to take the lead in intervention, and to bear the major proportion of the costs. The position of the US was bound to lead to a certain arrogance on the part of elements in its political elite when asked to act with responsibility in its external relations as well as in its internal ones. For instance there was an increasing number of breaches of international law committed by the US within its own frontiers, such as the refusal to allow the German government to obtain the transfer to Germany of a German citizen found guilty of murder in the US, as international law prescribed. There was an arrogance in denying the right of any outsider to point out that things were not all they should be in US internal arrangements, especially with regard to the rule of law. US commentators pointed out that the US frequently fell short in its own territory of the high standards it demanded of foreigners in theirs.

And there was irritation on the right of the political spectrum at the tendency of foreigners in the UN and elsewhere to recommend actions to the US, such as playing a full role in cases of humanitarian intervention, which would lead to their incurring costs and risking the lives of US servicemen. One cynical observer, commenting on the move of feeling against the UN after the killing of US soldiers in 1993 in Mogadishu, said there was a strange situation in the US: 'military life is more valuable than civilian life. You're safer in the US army than walking the streets of Washington!' Determining not to be involved was a perverse but natural reaction to the expectations of others that as the strongest state the US had a special responsibility to accept the costs of international activism, and do something.

The position in which the US found itself in the early twenty-first century encouraged irresponsibility. The opt-out argument was likely to find favour in a context of sensitivities generated by the arrogance of overwhelming power, which as Karl Deutsch pointed out was often expressed in the capacity of a state to do nothing. Its power was to do something but also to insulate it from the costs of doing nothing. Conversely anxiety about being in the game, and understanding its rules, would be greater if others were clearly prepared to play. After the election of President Bush, the world waited to see the direction in which the US would move.

Kosovo and the role of the UN

The role of the UN included the crucial function of acting as a trigger to set in train the processes appropriate to the upholding of the rules of the system. Over the previous half century or so these rules had become increasingly numerous and specific, covering an increasing range of the activities of relations between states. Not only were they concerned with commerce, and the protection of the rights of states, but also with the rights of individuals. The biggest change of all was probably the last one, with a number of conventions defining transgressions against the individual person, and beginning to set up remedies if they were demonstrated.

But obtaining the agreement of governments to the principles of individual rights was but the first step. It was necessary to find ways of instituting the remedies and of triggering the actions of the relevant instruments. As within states, this was not merely a legal matter: it was also necessary to have an instrument to trigger action when a law had been transgressed. There was in this process an absolute need for an instrument which appeared to embody in some sense the collective will – as with police acting in the name of the collectivity in a stable democracy – and which achieved consistency, and was impartial and reliable.

The closest to that in the international system in the early twenty-first century remained the executive committee of the UN, the Security Council, and it was striking that even the largest states tended to prefer to get its authorization for any action they proposed, as with the US intervention in Haiti. With regard to Kosovo, the active states were all concerned to demonstrate that they were acting justly according to the Charter and the relevant Security Council resolutions. After the attacks on the Twin Towers and the Pentagon the US was anxious for rapid expression of support for action from the Security Council. Even though some disputed the legitimacy of the action in Kosovo under UN Security Council resolutions there was no denying that the governments of the active states were concerned to demonstrate this.

A number of adjustments to increase the authority of the Council in this context had been discussed in the literature, and had been proposed by governments: special procedures might be needed to reinforce the impression that the decisions taken represented the collective will. These included stronger qualified majorities in the Council, and a concurrent vote by a qualified or simple majority in the General Assembly. But the normal pattern was for Security Council involvement and it was to that body that even the more powerful states had come to seek authorization. In the early twenty-first century the US still saw the need for collective approval, with the Security Council the preferred agent, as desirable, even though it might reserve the right to go it alone. In practice, however, it was always looked for. The one state it was feared might not do so was China.

Other ways of establishing the value of the UN stressed the role of this context in what could be called the evolving civil society of governments. It had become the legitimizer of international agreements, including that SC 1244 which marked the end of the NATO bombing of the Serb military. Its function in this kind of role had become the equivalent in the international system of that of the registrar or notary in civil society. There was, however, a debate about the limits of the role of the UN which served to distinguish between a range of system functions on the one hand, and their institutional location on the other. The United States had tried to get support for a new strategic concept for NATO in 1998–9: US Secretary of State Madeleine Albright, proposed that NATO should act in lieu of the UN as an agent for global stability, partly because of the unpopularity of the global organization with some Americans – mainly elite Republicans – partly because NATO was an effective organization which was in search of a role for itself at the end of the Cold War, and partly because in 1996 Congress approved an act requiring the Administration to get its approval for each and every future US involvement in UN peacekeeping operations.

The consequence of this was that the US Administration was pushed into a preference for the action through NATO rather than the UN, as NATO spending was covered by the regular Defence budget and dealing with the top people of the UN – who could easily find themselves demonized by the American right wing – could be avoided. The advantage of working through NATO would be that the Adminstration could avoid the requirement for Congressional approval. One cynical observer claimed that the real reason was that Albright got on better with generals than UN officials![14] But the US preference was rebuffed. At the NATO Council meeting in March 1999 the US was greatly disappointed by the refusal of other NATO members to accept the new US view of the NATO role. They asserted that the UN should have priority, and that NATO should not have a general sweeper role.

This US initiative should, however, be seen as a forlorn and ill-thought-out attempt to relocate a function of the international community, namely the executing of the various tasks linked with the maintenance of international peace and security, rather than an attempt to deny the UN a role. It went along with a number of other developments that were also noticeable in the mid to late 1990s, such as the increasing use of local or regional organizations to carry out that function in some parts of the world, in particular in Africa, and indeed an increasing preparedness to work with non-governmental organizations to achieve UN-approved goals. But it was important to note that those goals were UN approved. US officials and the military wanted the approval of a significant coalition, and the UN mandate was an acceptable even desirable example.

There were obvious dangers in accepting the two linked principles of using a regional organization like NATO to act, even under licence, outside its own area, and of contracting out the job of maintaining international peace and security to a state or an organization. Where did the field of NATO action stop? Could it act anywhere in the world? In the Middle East, the Far East, or just where the interests of members were directly affected? How was this to be decided? Was it merely a hired gun? On contracting out: was there not the risk that this would reinforce the older spheres of interest idea, with local powers asserting their primary responsibility to the exclusion of the global authority? It seemed to this writer that the way forward had to be to support the enhancement of the authority of the UN and the contracting-out option discredited the global organization and licensed local bullies.

It could be argued therefore – though it was too early to be sure – that different functions were being distinguished and attempts made to relocate some of them. An operational function was being located more frequently in other organizations, as with the cooption of regional organizations to perform a task mandated from the centre; but the function of overseeing and approving stayed with the UN Security Council, and it was the latter which also legitimized ensuing accords, and was the primary forum of their negotiation. After the 11 September events the role of the UN with regard to building international civil society was also given a new importance: it was seen as necessary to build a counterterrorism element into international civil society, as indicated in the previous chapter, and the UN was the appropriate framework for this. As pointed out, there was no doubt among governments about the need to use the UN machinery to look at the details of the settlement at the end of the Kosovo action. The authority of the UN and the key position of the Security Council as the generator of mandates, the overseer of security maintenance operations and the granter of legitimacy, was defended.

The context of the UN was also one in which governments acquired status in the system. They had come to regard success in that context as a criterion of success as states. Being accepted as a candidate for high office in the UN, for instance by membership of its key committees and the performing of key roles in the system, had come to be regarded as legitimizing their autonomy.

There had been a qualitative change in the international civil society of governments which had two related elements. First was the gradual accumulation of institutional contexts in which governments were involved, and second was the gradual identification of an international moral order to which governments were under continuous pressure to react, as was argued in Chapter 1. Indeed it was now, for the first time, possible to construct a typology of the characters of governments in relation to this moral order.

There were governments which were conformist; there were those which were missionary; which were creational, or vocational; and, of course, there were those which were reformist or revolutionary. For those governments which were positive about the international moral order, regardless of their orientation, the United Nations system was a key element in legitimizing that order. But this disposition was reinforced by the increasingly dense institutional context. Involvement through diplomats in that context was routine and increasingly it was the mechanism through which governments derived their self-esteem.

There had indeed been a switch in the balance between internal resources and external performance. Increasingly the external performance and pattern of involvement generated added value to the internal resources. That British performance and status in the United Nations was a multiplier not a consumer of British diplomatic leverage was an obvious example, but the increasing density of the international institutional context meant that was likely to be true to a greater or lesser degree for all states. Diplomats had become not merely the instruments of state policy, and consumers of national power resources, but also actual generators of national merit. How they stood in the dense institutional context was a key element in a government's judgement of itself and in the way it was judged by others in the system. Hence office-holding, initiative-taking, providing personnel, norm policing, etc., were seen as having value because they added to the self-esteem – in traditional terms, power – of the state. The UN was a natural beneficiary of this and developments in peacekeeping including the Kosovo experience did not damage this role.

In this way the development of the international civil society had generated in governments ways of seeing their own worth and the worth of others which were like the ways in which individuals evaluated themselves, and were evaluated, in stable national orders. Measures of achievement and of status were socially determined: without the roles ascribed by society the state would lose its worth. This was a consequence of the two developments mentioned: reaching a particular stage in the increasing density of the institutional context, and a degree of consensus about the appropriate international moral order, or international community. In these two contexts the United Nations system was key, and that was one reason why states were overwhelmingly agreed that, although the reform of the United Nations might be appropriate, no risks should be taken with regard to its survival. They agreed that the Charter should not be renegotiated, and the essential character of the system of agencies, funds and programmes should not, and indeed, could not be altered. The Kosovo experience had by no means undermined this view, or damaged the view that the UN performed an essential system role in international society.

Peacekeeping in the UN at the millennium

Having established the general need for peacekeeping, and located it in its appropriate institutional home, the United Nations, it is necessary to look in rather more specific terms at its mechanisms and at its problems. What had been achieved with regard to the use of UN forces for humanitarian ends by the late 1990s, what difficulties had arisen and what should be done to improve matters? These questions can be discussed in three contexts: that of the setting up of humanitarian intervention forces, that of managing them in the field during the crisis and that of scaling down the presence and getting out.[15] Each of these questions could produce a separate volume in response, but in this discussion the most important issues under each heading are touched upon. The discussion in the previous section did, however, indicate the ideal general direction of its evolution detected by this writer. As in the last chapter a set of ideas about what happens next is now set out.

In the late 1990s peacekeeping was an occasional, if more frequent, activity linked with the perception that international and domestic orders had become more closely linked than realists were prepared to admit; there had been change in international society. What was needed was that it should become a routine activity characteristic of a more highly integrated international civil society. One of the key tests of this would be the appearance of the habit of explicitness in relevant Security Council resolutions, though this was unlikely for the foreseeable future. As indicated above, the Kosovo resolutions, like the others from the 1990s, contained at most an implied authorization of the NATO bombing. This implicit quality was a characteristic of the stage reached in the evolution of the relationship between the sovereign state and the international community.

Getting in

It was necessary to have adequate resources and mechanisms for ensuring that crises had the attention of the Security Council. Too often particular instances of gross violations of human rights were ignored or for various reasons given less attention than others. This was a matter of making intervention a matter of routine, rather than of chance and selectivity. Obviously this would mean a considerable increase in the scale of available resources, and the reform of the present funding system. Moving in this direction was desirable, in that international arrangements would become more like a stable internal order, where the public authority was exercised reliably and impartially. But it was also in line with the apparent emergence of stronger common norms and forms of international authority. This would be the maximalist goal.

But falling short should not lead to overlooking the range of achievement with regard to peacekeeping by the early twenty-first century. These included: greatly improving the effectiveness of the Department of Peacekeeping Operations in New York; greatly increasing the range and analysis of information relevant to the detection of danger spots; the setting up of supply centres such as the one at Pisa; the training of increasing numbers of military and civilian personnel for use in complex emergencies; the entering into agreements with national forces by the Security Council for the supply of troops in emergency situations – as foreseen for enforcement operations in Chapter VII of the Charter; and the drawing up of contingency plans and rules of engagement for peacekeepers, such as the Dodie guidelines in Britain. More needed to be done in each of these contexts, and more governments involved, but there had been real qualitative and quantitative improvement in the last decade of the century.

Being there

Luttwak pointed out a set of problems, each of which could be taken as containing a lesson for improvement, rather than a reason for stopping humanitarian intervention. It was important that the intervening forces should not, as had happened in Sarajevo between 1992 and 1994, seek to prevent the departure of civilians who were anxious to leave the combat zone. It was essential that refugee centres should not be so constructed and resourced that they became permanent residences for the aggrieved. In this case, as with UNRWA in the Middle East, Luttwak argued, the camps were likely to become long-term centres for the training and recruitment of terrorists. Luttwak wrote 'UNRWA has contributed to a half-century of Arab–Israeli violence, and still retards the advent of peace' (p. 42). He added that, if this had been done in Europe 'Europe would have remained a mosaic of warring tribes, undigested and unreconciled in their separate feeding camps'.

It was also necessary that the intervening troops should not appease the stronger groups or be passive spectators to outrages and massacres, as had happened in Bosnia and Rwanda. The forces should be altogether more robust, resolute and equipped to hit back at any malefactor. In Bosnia the forces too often backed down from direct engagement with military elements, usually Serb, which attempted to block the delivery of food. They had acted like traditional interpositional forces, rather than the proactive enforcers of a UN mandate. The one force that had acted robustly in response to being fired upon in Bosnia had been the Danes. This reluctance to be proactive was partly a consequence of the restrictions placed upon them by their own national governments – Italian peacekeepers had on occasion asked their own government whether they should obey UN commanders – but was also to do with the lack of a clear mandate, so that the permission of the UN Representative was required for action in particular instances. In Yugoslavia the UN representative, Mr Akashi, had tended to be cautious, an argument in favour of having in this kind of position someone with greater preparedness to use initiative and be proactive. The overcaution of forces was also illustrated by their toleration of the passage of known war criminals after the setting up of the Court and appeals for their arrest. This was presumably done to avoid provoking a violent response by one or other of the warring groups.

Another lesson of Kosovo taken by Luttwak was that it was unacceptable to take no risks with the lives of intervening forces. They should not be committed to perfect safety, a strategy that meant that low-flying Apache helicopters, Warthog planes and Harrier jets were not used against the marauding Serbian troops in Kosovo who, acting under cloud cover, perpetrated atrocities against the Albanian population. The NATO countries wrongly judged that 'saving thousands of Albanians from massacre was not worth the lives of a few pilots' (Luttwak, p. 41). NGOs, according to Luttwak, should also be more careful about supplying active combatants. Too frequently they made deals with criminal elements, as when paying protection money to local warlords in Somalia. And too often they fed and effectively re-equipped combatants who were in retreat from battle zones, thus facilitating their re-entry into battle. Luttwak argued that too often 'humanitarian intervention [by NGOs] has worsened the chances of a stable, long-term resolution of the tensions in Rwanda. Many NGOs that operate in an odour of sanctity routinely supply active combatants' (Luttwak, p. 43).

Other areas where there was scope for reform was with regard to the actual procedures of the Security Council. In particular it was necessary to avoid mission creep, which led to a mandate being expanded gradually without sufficient attention to the provision of necessary resources, or to consistent and effective strategy. For instance the setting up of the safe areas in Bosnia was a disaster because the areas were not adequately defended. (Bosnians were given an entirely unfounded feeling of security; militant Bosnians were not disarmed and therefore used the safe areas as a base from which to attack the Serbs; and UN personnel were left scattered and vulnerable to capture and use as hostages by Serbs.) It was in this context that Dutch troops went through the dreadful experience of having to help the Serbs isolate Bosnian men for execution. To avoid such gross errors in Security Council mandates it might be sensible to set up a technical supervision committee to check on the technical feasibility of Security Council mandates, but clearly ground commanders needed to be more resolute in deciding what could or could not be done.

Getting out

Getting out was obviously related to the correction of the problems identified in the previous sections. But the point might be reinforced that the scale of the new interventionism, as a routine of the operation of international civil society, would need to have much greater endurance than was the case in the 1990s. The idea was proposed in connection with Kosovo that the United Nations might have to take on a kind of neo-trusteeship role at the end of the conflict. It might well be necessary for a presence to be maintained in the long term, and this could well include a military presence, as a civilized alternative to the Luttwak solution of letting wars burn. This was not, however, to deny the achievement in this area of the UN, with a widening range of activities in states which had experienced crisis. The UN took on a number of functions to legitimize settlements and consolidate acceptable regimes, such as: training administrators and civilian police forces; monitoring elections as in East Timor in August 1999; and promoting the setting up of the machinery of a civil society within the state, such as legal systems and employer–worker contacts of various kinds. But an important point was that the UN needed what in some contexts was called 'legs'. It needed the capacity and the will to endure in difficult situations. This was the opposite of the view of the US Administration, which continued with the Bush regime: that the UN should get in and get out.

Conclusions

This chapter has looked at the development of peacekeeping up to and beyond the Kosovo crisis, and has located that in the context of the development of what has been called the new interventionism in the United Nations. The crisis was the context in which a number of questions were raised about the future of peacekeeping, and it was apparent that this writer judged that the appropriate stance in the early twenty-first century was to consider the ways of reform, but to move forward. Too much had changed for the new arrangements to be abandoned. The context was as discussed in the previous chapter, which stressed that the practice of peacekeeping reflected an emerging international community, and to go back was simply incompatible with that emerging character. This was not to assert that the problems identified in the last section could be solved easily: what could be done would emerge pragmatically in the course of negotiations between governments. But an image of the place of peacekeeping in international society in the future was a sensible start.

The pattern of evolution of the UN mechanism which was illustrated by the Kosovo crisis was therefore that when it came to the need for a more proactive use of military force it was likely that a coalition of states, under UN sanction, would be authorized to act for the global organization. In some parts of the world, as in West Africa, that was also the course of action, though in that case authorizing regional actions was more because of the reluctance of the five veto-holding powers to get involved. There was a clear intimation of the need for greater involvement of regional mechanisms, which had been proposed by Secretary-General Boutros-Ghali, especially in his revised version of Agenda for Peace.[16] This was partly a response to the belief that the UN was unlikely to get the resources to do what it might be asked to do. There was a need to scale down as well as to coopt regions. From the latter side too there was a greater preparedness to take on a measure of responsibility, at least in the EU, as economic integration led to a greater preparedness among members to think of collective military action.

But there was also a clear alternative pattern which was represented in the report produced by a Panel of Experts in 2000, named after its Chairman, the Brahimi Report.[17] This was the product of a committee of experts commissioned by the Secretary-General and completed in 2000. Its specific proposals follow naturally in this discussion from the arguments about reform of the arrangements of the global organization outlined above. The essential point about the report was that it sought to build upon the achievements of the global organization; indeed, its implication was that the UN could be put right to the extent that regional arrangements in the area of peace and security could become very junior partners, if not redundant.

The proposals covered a wide range of issues and the executive summary captures them with succinctness and style. Hence they are reproduced in full below, as they form a natural conclusion to this chapter. As pointed out, they built upon what had already been started. They did not represent an attempt to create a new apparatus. The response of the member states at the time of writing was unclear. But what was striking was that unlike the second edition of Agenda for Peace, the report has little to say about regional agents. Rather it suggested that in the area of peace and security the UN could develop its operational role as well as its role as ultimate authority. It would have to be concluded therefore that the jury was still out on whether the model for the future would be an enhancement of the role of the regions, under UN supervision, or whether the UN would take the lead in operations with the regions as minor partners.

Appendix: The Brahimi Report: Executive Summary[18]

The United Nations was founded, in the words of its Charter, in order 'to save succeeding generations from the scourge of war'. Meeting this challenge is the most important function of the Organization, and to a very significant degree it is the yardstick with which the Organization is judged by the peoples it exists to serve. Over the last decade, the United Nations has repeatedly failed to meet the challenge, and it can do no better today. Without renewed commitment on the part of Member States, significant institutional change and increased financial support, the United Nations will not be capable of executing the critical peacekeeping and peacebuilding tasks that the Member States assign to it in coming months and years.

There are many tasks which United Nations peacekeeping forces should not be asked to undertake and many places they should not go. But when the United Nations does send its forces to uphold the peace, they must be prepared to confront the lingering forces of war and violence, with the ability and determination to defeat them.

The Secretary-General has asked the Panel on United Nations Peace Operations, composed of individuals experienced in various aspects of conflict prevention, peacekeeping and peacebuilding, to assess the shortcomings of the existing system and to make frank, specific and realistic recommendations for change. Our recommendations focus not only on politics and strategy but also and perhaps even more so on operational and organizational areas of need.

For preventive initiatives to succeed in reducing tension and averting conflict, the Secretary-General needs clear, strong and sustained political support from Member States. Furthermore, as the United Nations has bitterly and repeatedly discovered over the last decade, no amount of good intentions can substitute for the fundamental ability to project credible force if complex peacekeeping, in particular, is to succeed. But force alone cannot create peace; it can only create the space in which peace may be built. Moreover, the changes that the Panel recommends will have no lasting impact unless Member States summon the political will to support the United Nations politically, financially and operationally to enable the United Nations to be truly credible as a force for peace.

Each of the recommendations contained in the present report is designed to remedy a serious problem in strategic direction, decision-making, rapid deployment, operational planning and support, and the use of modern information technology. Key assessments and recommendations are highlighted below, largely in the order in which they appear in the body of the text (the numbers of the relevant paragraphs in the main text are provided in parentheses). In addition, a summary of recommendations is contained in annex III.

Experience of the past

It should have come as no surprise to anyone that some of the missions of the past decade would be particularly hard to accomplish: they tended to deploy where conflict had not resulted in victory for any side, where a military stalemate or international pressure or both had brought fighting to a halt but at least some of the parties to the conflict were not seriously committed to ending the confrontation. United Nations operations thus did not *deploy into* post-conflict situations but tried *to create* them. In such complex operations, peacekeepers work to maintain a secure local environment while peacebuilders work to make that environment self-sustaining. Only such an environment offers a ready exit to peacekeeping forces, making peacekeepers and peacebuilders inseparable partners.

Implications for preventive action and peacebuilding: the need for strategy and support

The United Nations and its members face a pressing need to establish more effective strategies for conflict prevention, in both the long and short terms. In this context, the Panel endorses the recommendations of the Secretary-General with respect to conflict prevention contained in the Millennium Report (A/54/2000) and in his remarks before the Security Council's second open meeting on conflict prevention in July 2000. It also encourages the Secretary-General's more frequent use of fact-finding missions to areas of tension in support of short-term crisis-preventive action.

Furthermore, the Security Council and the General Assembly's Special Committee on Peacekeeping Operations, conscious that the United Nations will continue to face the prospect of having to assist communities and nations in making the transition from war to peace, have each recognized and acknowledged the key role of peacebuilding in complex peace operations. This will require that the United Nations system address what has hitherto been a fundamental deficiency in the way it has conceived of, funded and implemented peacebuilding strategies and activities. Thus, the Panel recommends that the Executive Committee on Peace and Security (ECPS) present to the Secretary-General a plan to strengthen the permanent capacity of the United Nations to develop peacebuilding strategies and to implement programmes in support of those strategies.

Among the changes that the Panel supports are: a doctrinal shift in the use of civilian police and related rule of law elements in peace operations that emphasizes a team approach to upholding the rule of law and respect for human rights and helping communities coming out of a conflict to achieve national reconciliation; consolidation of disarmament, demobilization and reintegration programmes into the assessed budgets of complex peace operations in their first phase; flexibility for heads of United Nations peace operations to fund 'quick impact projects' that make a real difference in the lives of people in the mission area; and better integration of electoral assistance into a broader strategy for the support of governance institutions.

Implications for peacekeeping: the need for robust doctrine and realistic mandates

The Panel concurs that consent of the local parties, impartiality and the use of force only in self-defence should remain the bedrock principles of peacekeeping. Experience shows, however, that in the context of intra-state/transnational conflicts, consent may be manipulated in many ways. Impartiality for United Nations operations must therefore mean adherence to the principles of the Charter: where one party to a peace agreement clearly and incontrovertibly is violating its terms, continued equal treatment of all parties by the United Nations can in the best case result in ineffectiveness and in the worst may amount to complicity with evil. No failure did more to damage the standing and credibility of United Nations peacekeeping in the 1990s than its reluctance to distinguish victim from aggressor.

In the past, the United Nations has often found itself unable to respond effectively to such challenges. It is a fundamental premise of the present report, however, that it must be able to do so. Once deployed, United Nations peacekeepers must be able to carry out their mandate professionally and successfully. This means that United Nations military units must be capable of defending themselves, other mission components and the mission's mandate. Rules of engagement should be sufficiently robust and not force United Nations contingents to cede the initiative to their attackers.

This means, in turn, that the Secretariat must not apply best-case planning assumptions to situations where the local actors have historically exhibited worst-case behaviour. It means that mandates should specify an operation's authority to use force. It means bigger forces, better equipped and more costly but able to be a credible deterrent. In particular, United Nations forces for complex operations should be afforded the field intelligence and other capabilities needed to mount an effective defence against violent challengers.

Moreover, United Nations peacekeepers – troops or police – who witness violence against civilians should be presumed to be authorized to stop it, within their means, in support of basic United Nations principles. However, operations given a broad and explicit mandate for civilian protection must be given the specific resources needed to carry out that mandate.

The Secretariat must tell the Security Council what it needs to know, not what it wants to hear, when recommending force and other resource levels for a new mission, and it must set those levels according to realistic scenarios that take into account likely challenges to implementation. Security Council mandates, in turn, should reflect the clarity that peacekeeping operations require for unity of effort when they deploy into potentially dangerous situations.

The current practice is for the Secretary-General to be given a Security Council resolution specifying troop levels on paper, not knowing whether he will be given the troops and other personnel that the mission needs to function effectively, or whether they will be properly equipped. The Panel is of the view that, once realistic mission requirements have been set and agreed to, the Council should leave its authorizing resolution in draft form until the Secretary-General confirms that he has received troop and other commitments from Member States sufficient to meet those requirements.

Member States that do commit formed military units to an operation should be invited to consult with the members of the Security Council during mandate formulation; such advice might usefully be institutionalized via the establishment of *ad hoc* subsidiary organs of the Council, as provided for in Article 29 of the Charter. Troop contributors should also be invited to attend Secretariat briefings of the Security Council pertaining to crises that affect the safety and security of mission personnel or to a change or reinterpretation of the mandate regarding the use of force.

New headquarters capacity for information management and strategic analysis

The Panel recommends that a new information-gathering and analysis entity be created to support the informational and analytical needs of the Secretary-General and the members of the Executive Committee on Peace and Security (ECPS). Without such capacity, the Secretariat will remain a reactive institution, unable to get ahead of daily events, and the ECPS will not be able to fulfil the role for which it was created.

The Panel's proposed ECPS Information and Strategic Analysis Secretariat (EISAS) would create and maintain integrated databases on peace and security issues, distribute that knowledge efficiently within the United Nations system, generate policy analyses, formulate long-term strategies for ECPS and bring budding crises to the attention of the ECPS leadership. It could also propose and manage the agenda of ECPS itself, helping to transform it into the decision-making body anticipated in the Secretary-General's initial reforms.

The Panel proposes that EISAS be created by consolidating the existing Situation Centre of the Department of Peacekeeping Operations (DPKO) with a number of small, scattered policy planning offices, and adding a small team of military analysts, experts in international criminal networks and information systems specialists. EISAS should serve the needs of all members of ECPS.

Improved mission guidance and leadership

The Panel believes it is essential to assemble the leadership of a new mission as early as possible at United Nations Headquarters, to participate in shaping a mission's concept of operations, support plan, budget, staffing and Headquarters mission guidance. To that end, the Panel recommends that the Secretary-General compile, in a systematic fashion and with input from Member States, a comprehensive list of potential special representatives of the Secretary-General (SRSGs), force commanders, civilian police commissioners, their potential deputies and potential heads of other components of a mission, representing a broad geographic and equitable gender distribution.

Rapid deployment standards and 'on-call' expertise

The first 6 to 12 weeks following a ceasefire or peace accord are often the most critical ones for establishing both a stable peace and the credibility of a new operation. Opportunities lost during that period are hard to regain. The Panel recommends that the United Nations define 'rapid and effective deployment capacity' as the ability to fully deploy traditional peacekeeping operations within 30 days of the adoption of a Security Council resolution establishing such an operation, and within 90 days in the case of complex peacekeeping operations.

The Panel recommends that the United Nations' standby arrangements system (UNSAS) be developed further to include several coherent, multinational, brigade-size forces and the necessary enabling forces, created by Member States working in partnership, in order better to meet the need for the robust peacekeeping forces that the Panel has advocated. The Panel also recommends that the Secretariat send a team to confirm the readiness of each potential troop contributor to meet the requisite United Nations training and equipment requirements for peacekeeping operations, prior to deployment. Units that do not meet the requirements must not be deployed.

To support such rapid and effective deployment, the Panel recommends that a revolving 'on-call list' of about 100 experienced, well-qualified military officers, carefully vetted and accepted by DPKO, be created within UNSAS. Teams drawn from this list and available for duty on seven days' notice would translate broad, strategic-level mission concepts developed at Headquarters into concrete operational and tactical plans in advance of the deployment of troop contingents, and would augment a core element from DPKO to serve as part of a mission start-up team. Parallel on-call lists of civilian police, international judicial experts, penal experts and human rights specialists must be available in sufficient numbers to strengthen rule of law institutions, as needed, and should also be part of UNSAS. Pre-trained teams could then be drawn from this list to precede the main body of civilian police and related specialists into a new mission area, facilitating the rapid and effective deployment of the law and order component into the mission. The Panel also calls upon Member States to establish enhanced national 'pools' of police officers and related experts, earmarked for deployment to United Nations peace operations, to help meet the high demand for civilian police and related criminal justice/rule of law expertise in peace operations dealing with intra-state conflict.

The Panel also urges Member States to consider forming joint regional partnerships and programmes for the purpose of training members of the respective national pools to United Nations civilian police doctrine and standards. The Secretariat should also address, on an urgent basis, the needs: to put in place a transparent and decentralized recruitment mechanism for civilian field personnel; to improve the retention of the civilian specialists that are needed in every complex peace operation; and to create standby arrangements for their rapid deployment.

Finally, the Panel recommends that the Secretariat radically alter the systems and procedures in place for peacekeeping procurement in order to facilitate rapid deployment. It recommends that responsibilities for peacekeeping budgeting and procurement be moved out of the Department of Management and placed in DPKO. The Panel proposes the creation of a new and distinct body of streamlined field procurement policies and procedures; increased delegation of procurement authority to the field; and greater flexibility for field missions in the management of their budgets. The Panel also urges that the Secretary-General formulate and submit to the General Assembly, for its approval, a global logistics support strategy governing the stockpiling of equipment reserves and standing contracts with the private sector for common goods and services. In the interim, the Panel recommends that additional 'start-up kits' of essential equipment be maintained at the United Nations Logistics Base (UNLB) in Brindisi, Italy.

The Panel also recommends that the Secretary-General be given authority, with the approval of the Advisory Committee on Administrative and Budgetary Questions (ACABQ), to commit up to $50 million well in advance of the adoption of a Security Council resolution establishing a new operation once it becomes clear that an operation is likely to be established.

Enhance Headquarters capacity to plan and support peace operations

The Panel recommends that Headquarters support for peacekeeping be treated as a core activity of the United Nations, and as such the majority of its resource requirements should be funded through the regular budget of the Organization. DPKO and other offices that plan and support peacekeeping are currently primarily funded by the Support Account, which is renewed each year and funds only temporary posts. That approach to funding and staff seems to confuse the temporary nature of specific operations with the evident permanence of peacekeeping and other peace operations activities as core functions of the United Nations, which is obviously an untenable state of affairs.

The total cost of DPKO and related Headquarters support offices for peacekeeping does not exceed $50 million per annum, or roughly 2 per cent of total peacekeeping costs. Additional resources for those offices are urgently needed to ensure that more than $2 billion spent on peacekeeping in 2001 are well spent. The Panel therefore recommends that the Secretary-General submit a proposal to the General Assembly outlining the Organization's requirements in full. The Panel believes that a methodical management review of DPKO should be conducted but also believes that staff shortages in certain areas are plainly obvious. For example, it is clearly not enough to have 32 officers providing military planning and guidance to 27,000 troops in the field, 9 civilian police staff to identify, vet and provide guidance for up to 8600 police, and 15 political desk officers for 14 current operations and 2 new ones, or to allocate just 1.25 per cent of the total costs of peacekeeping to Headquarters' administrative and logistics support.

Establish Integrated Mission Task Forces for mission planning and support

The Panel recommends that Integrated Mission Task Forces (IMTFs) be created, with staff from throughout the United Nations' system seconded to them, to plan new missions and help them reach full deployment, significantly enhancing the support that

Headquarters provides to the field. There is currently no integrated planning or support cell in the Secretariat that brings together those responsible for political analysis, military operations, civilian police, electoral assistance, human rights, development, humanitarian assistance, refugees and displaced persons, public information, logistics, finance and recruitment.

Structural adjustments are also required in other elements of DPKO, in particular to the Military and Civilian Police Division, which should be reorganized into two separate divisions, and the Field Administration and Logistics Division (FALD), which should be split into two divisions. The Lessons Learned Unit should be strengthened and moved into the DPKO Office of Operations. Public information planning and support at Headquarters also needs strengthening, as do elements in the Department of Political Affairs (DPA), particularly the electoral unit. Outside the Secretariat, the ability of the Office of the United Nations High Commissioner for Human Rights to plan and support the human rights components of peace operations needs to be reinforced.

Consideration should be given to allocating a third Assistant Secretary-General to DPKO and designating one of them as 'Principal Assistant Secretary-General', functioning as the deputy to the Under-Secretary-General.

Adapting peace operations to the information age

Modern, well-utilized information technology (IT) is a key enabler of many of the above-mentioned objectives, but gaps in strategy, policy and practice impede its effective use. In particular, Headquarters lacks a sufficiently strong responsibility centre for user-level IT strategy and policy in peace operations. A senior official with such responsibility in the peace and security arena should be appointed and located within EISAS, with counterparts in the offices of the SRSG in every United Nations peace operation. Headquarters and the field missions alike also need a substantive, global, Peace Operations Extranet (POE), through which missions would have access to, among other things, EISAS databases and analyses and lessons learned.

Challenges to implementation

The Panel believes that the above recommendations fall well within the bounds of what can be reasonably demanded of the

Organization's Member States. Implementing some of them will require additional resources for the Organization, but we do not mean to suggest that the best way to solve the problems of the United Nations is merely to throw additional resources at them. Indeed, no amount of money or resources can substitute for the significant changes that are urgently needed in the culture of the Organization.

The Panel calls on the Secretariat to heed the Secretary-General's initiatives to reach out to the institutions of civil society; to constantly keep in mind that the United Nations they serve is *the* universal organization. People everywhere are fully entitled to consider that it is *their* organization, and as such to pass judgement on its activities and the people who serve in it.

Furthermore, wide disparities in staff quality exist and those in the system are the first to acknowledge it; better performers are given unreasonable workloads to compensate for those who are less capable. Unless the United Nations takes steps to become a true meritocracy, it will not be able to reverse the alarming trend of qualified personnel, the young among them in particular, leaving the Organization. Moreover, qualified people will have no incentive to join it. Unless managers at all levels, beginning with the Secretary-General and his senior staff, seriously address this problem on a priority basis, reward excellence and remove incompetence, additional resources will be wasted and lasting reform will become impossible. Member States also acknowledge that they need to reflect on their working culture and methods. It is incumbent upon Security Council members, for example, and the membership at large to breathe life into the words that they produce, as did, for instance, the Security Council delegation that flew to Jakarta and Dili in the wake of the East Timor crisis in 1999, an example of effective Council *action* at its best: *res, non verba*.

We – the members of the Panel on United Nations Peace Operations – call on the leaders of the world assembled at the Millennium Summit, as they renew their commitment to the ideals of the United Nations, to commit as well to strengthen the capacity of the United Nations to fully accomplish the mission which is, indeed, its very *raison d'être*: to help communities engulfed in strife and to maintain or restore peace.

While building consensus for the recommendations in the present report, we have also come to a shared vision of a *United* Nations, extending a strong helping hand to a community, country or region to avert conflict or to end violence. We see an SRSG ending a mission well accomplished, having given the people of a country the opportunity to do for themselves what they could not do before: to build and hold on to peace, to find reconciliation, to strengthen democracy, to secure human rights. We see, above all, a United Nations that has not only the will but also the ability to fulfil its great promise, and to justify the confidence and trust placed in it by the overwhelming majority of humankind.

CHAPTER 3

Globalization and Regionalization among Modern States: The Case of the EU

In this chapter the development of the European Union is discussed particularly in its response to globalization. It illustrates a response of modern states to economic globalization. In the next two chapters the role of international organization in the developing states is the focus. The argument is about how the structure of the Union could change in response to the global economy, and stresses the case against the view that in the era of globalization social democracy, a prized value in the older member states, was bound to fail. There were pressures from globalization, which some members wished to resist – and could resist – because they resented the way in which the character of their states was challenged. The chapter illustrates the way in which globalization could promote regionalization as an adaptation and as a way of holding off its undesirable aspects.

In the first section some differences between the member states, relevant to enlargement and globalization, are considered. In the second section different scenarios of the future of the EU are sketched. And in a third section some key issues concerning globalization and the social democratic states are examined.

Diversity in European political economies

Economic diversity

The heterogeneity of the member states of the Union is a key variable in its emerging structure. There were social democratic states, there were states which felt they had to compromise with the

Anglo-American model of light regulation and low levels of taxation, particularly for companies, in response to globalization; and there were differences between the level of economic performance of states, the extent to which their structures had been reformed, and indeed where they stood in the business cycle. The most Anglo-American of all was the United Kingdom, and what follows assumes a broad distinction between the Anglo-American states and the social democratic core. There were a number of states that had started on reform of their welfare and regulatory systems, in the direction of the Anglo-American model, which could easily halt that process and move back to an unambiguous commitment to social democracy.

Four groups of states may be distinguished:

1. The first included Germany, France and Italy, which might be regarded as the core social democratic states, though by 2002 the new Berlusconi regime in Italy was raising questions about the future of the Italian welfare system. They had a high per capita income (Table 1), and a pattern of taxation which took significantly more than the others in the form of social-security payments from business, which formed a significant proportion of the total tax take (see Table 2). These were also economies that were relatively slow growing, and in need of the lower interest rates made possible by the moderate recent level of wage settlements and, with the exception of oil, falling commodity prices.[1] OECD figures in 1997 also showed that higher than mean benefits could be obtained for total GDP in these states from deregulation, though at 4.9 per cent for Germany this was not high in absolute terms (see Table 3).

2. The second type was also high on the ranking of per capita GDP, but had a different taxation pattern, tending to put less stress on the social security payments from business, and more on taxation on goods and services and income tax. It included Denmark, Austria and Ireland, with the lightest social burden placed directly on business (Table 2), and Finland, Sweden, Luxembourg, the Netherlands and Belgium, which had a somewhat larger burden. The indications were also that these states would gain rather less from regulatory reform than those in the first group: the evidence for the Netherlands was that a gain of 3.5 per cent was likely, the same as for the United Kingdom which had already allegedly undertaken significant reform

Table 1 EU Gross Domestic Product 1999

	Using current PPPs US$	Using current PPPs OECD = 100	Using current exchange rates US$
Austria	24,600	110	20,700
Belgium	24,300	109	24,200
Denmark	26,300	118	32,600
Finland	22,800	102	24,900
France	21,900	98	23,600
Germany	23,600	106	25,700
Greece	14,800	66	11,800
Ireland	25,200	113	24,200
Italy	21,800	98	20,100
Luxembourg	39,300	176	43,100
Netherlands	25,100	112	25,000
Portugal	16,500	74	11,100
Spain	18,100	81	15,000
Sweden	23,000	103	27,000
UK	22,300	100	23,900
EU 15	22,000	99	22,400
Eurozone	22,100	99	22,100
US	33,900	152	33,900

Note: Purchasing Power Parties (PPPs) are the rate of currency conversion which eliminates the differences in price levels between countries. They are used to compare the volume of GDP in different countries. PPPs are obtained by evaluating the costs of a basket of goods and services between countries for all components of GDP; PPPs are given in national currency units per US dollar.

Sources: Main Economic Indicators, OECD, Paris, April 2000; National Accounts Division, STD.

(Table 3). This group of states were generally those that had begun to reform their welfare systems, in the sense that there had been a degree of deregulation and some lessening of welfare expenditure. But this was politically difficult and these states remained potentially members of the first group. They were reluctant welfare reformers, with a significant support among the electorates and political elites for social democracy.

3. A third group included those states which were the lowest ranking in the Union in terms of per capita GDP. They were also the states which were growing most rapidly. It included, in ascending order of per capita GDP, Greece, Portugal and Spain (Table 1).

Table 2 Taxation in EU countries, 1997

	Total tax receipts % of GDP	Personal income tax	Corporate income tax	Social security contributions Employees	Social security contributions Employers	Taxes on goods and services	Other taxes	Highest rates of income tax Personal income tax	Highest rates of income tax Corporate income tax
Austria	44.3	22.1	4.7	14.2	16.8	28.2	14.0	50.0	34.0
Belgium	46.0	31.0	7.5	9.5	19.5	26.7	5.8	61.0	40.2
Denmark	48.5	52.4	5.2	2.5	0.7	33.0	6.2	58.7	34.0
Finland	46.5	33.3	8.1	4.3	19.9	30.9	3.5	57.5	28.0
France	45.1	14.0	5.8	12.2	25.2	27.8	15.0	54.0	41.7
Germany	37.2	23.9	4.0	18.1	20.9	27.7	5.4	55.9	58.2
Greece	33.7	13.2	6.4	17.2	14.3	41.0	7.9	*	*
Ireland	32.8	31.4	10.0	3.9	8.2	39.7	6.8	48.0	32.0
Italy	44.4	25.3	9.5	6.6	23.5	25.9	9.2	46.0	37.0
Luxembourg	46.5	20.4	18.5	10.6	11.5	27.0	12.0	46.6	39.6
Netherlands	41.9	15.6	10.5	26.5	6.2	28.0	13.2	60.0	35.0
Portugal	34.2	17.7	10.9	9.6	14.6	42.0	5.2	40.0	37.4
Spain	33.7	21.9	7.8	5.6	24.6	28.9	11.2	56.0	35.8
Sweden	51.9	35.0	6.1	5.0	23.8	22.3	7.8	59.6	28.0
UK	35.4	24.8	12.1	7.5	9.6	35.0	11.0	40.0	31.0
USA	29.7	39.0	9.4	10.4	12.5	16.7	12.0	46.6	39.5
EU Average	41.5	25.5	8.5	15.9	15.9	30.9	9.0	49.7	36.3

Note: * Not available.

Source: Revenue Statistics, 1965–1998, OECD, Paris, 1999.

Table 3 Estimated effects of regulatory reform: summary (percentage change relative to baseline)

	United States	Japan	Germany	France	United Kingdom	Netherlands	Spain	Sweden
ParWal effects[1]								
Labour productivity	0.5	2.6	3.5	2.3	2.0	1.3	3.1	1.7
Capital productivity	0.5	4.3	1.3	3.3	1.4	2.9	3.1	1.3
Total factor productivity	0.5	3.0	2.8	2.7	1.8	1.8	3.1	1.5
Business sector employment	0.0	−1.0	−0.4	−0.4	−0.5	0.6[2]	−0.7	−0.6
Wages	0.0	0.0	−0.1	0.0	0.0	−0.2	−0.1	0.0
GDP price level	−0.3	−2.1	−1.3	−1.4	−1.2	n.a.	n.a.	n.a.
Economy-wide effects[3]								
GDP	0.9	5.6	4.9	4.8	3.5	3.5	5.6	3.1
Unemployment	0.0	0.0	0.0	0.0	0.0	0.0	0.0	0.0
Employment	0.1	0.0	0.0	0.0	0.0	0.0	0.0	0.0
Real wages	0.8	3.4	4.1	3.9	2.5	2.8	4.2	2.1

Notes:
[1] These effects are based on an aggregation of estimated sector-specific effects. They cover the business sector only.
[2] For Spain the estimates are based on 1990 cost structures, and subsequent reforms may have affected them to some degree.
[3] These effects include long-term and dynamic interactions in the economy as a whole and are based on simulations with a simplified macroeconomic model (see Section 4). The simulations for the Netherlands, Spain and Sweden are preliminary but the estimates nevertheless include some dynamic effects.

Source: OECD: G7 Countries, 7 November 1997.

Spain and Portugal had rather low levels of taxation for both corporate income tax and for employer's social security payments. Spain had a higher level of employer's social security contributions, but a low level of corporate income tax.

4. Fourth was the state that was allegedly closest to the Anglo-American model, the United Kingdom. This was a state which the OECD argued was likely to benefit in terms of GDP relatively little from further regulatory reform: an increase of 3.5 per cent was anticipated, little more than the next lowest, which was the Netherlands. The UK was also the smallest gainer in terms of GDP price level, at −1.2 per cent (Table 3). The UK was also a low-cost country for business in terms of employers' social security contributions. In 1999 it was among the middle ranking states in terms of per capita GDP (defined in terms of Purchasing Parity Prices), at tenth in the EU league table, grouped at the bottom end of the middle rankers, which included France,

Table 4 Form of governance in selected countries

	1960s–1970s	1980s	Most recent	Trend
Austria	Centralized, strong corporatist	Centralized, strong corporatist	Centralized, strong corporatist	Relatively unchanging
Sweden	Centralized, strong corporatist	Centralized, strong corporatist	Intermediate corporatist	Decline of corporatism, extension of markets
Netherlands	Strong corporatist	Intermediate corporatist	Intermediate corporatist	Move to supply-side corporatism and markets
Germany	Intermediate corporatist	Intermediate corporatist	Weak corporatist	Decline of corporatism/consensus
UK	Weak corporatist	Market-oriented	Market-oriented	Rejection of corporatism
France	Statist	Statist	Statist	Relatively unchanging
Italy	Weak corporatist	Weak corporatist	Experimenting with pacts	Experimenting with pacts
Spain	Authoritarian corporatist	Experimenting with pacts	Experimenting with pacts	Experimenting with pacts
Ireland	Market-oriented	Experimenting with pacts	Intermediate corporatist	Embracing neo-corporatism
USA	Market-oriented	Market-oriented	Market-oriented	Unchanged

Note: 'Centralized' means that a high score was given by the OECD for the prevailing wage bargaining level/degree of coordination of collective bargaining.

Source: Bernard Casey and Michael Gold, *Social Partnership and Economic Performance*, Cheltenham, Edward Elgar, 2000, p. 14.

Germany, Sweden and Italy (Table 1). In terms of the level of taxation defined as a percentage of GDP, the UK was among the lowest payers, at 35.4 per cent. The only countries which paid marginally less in these terms were Portugal, Spain and Greece (Table 2).

Member states of the EU could also be differentiated in terms of their style of government and their trend with regard to social welfare provision. Changes in these areas were broadly in line with the groups. On style of government the range moved from unchanging corporatism in Austria to the rejection of corporatism and reliance on the market in the UK (Table 4).[2] A number of other states had shown some movement away from corporatism. Those which had moved furthest included Sweden and the Netherlands, but Germany, Italy and Spain had a modified corporatist position. Germany had tried to reduce the role of the major social partners, particularly in the late Kohl period, and Italy and Spain had adopted a system whereby bargains were struck – pacts – between the social partners, unions, management and government, on specific social-economic questions. The broad conclusion is obvious from Table 4: corporatism had retained a clear presence in the member states of the EU, but there had been some retreat in most members, with Austria remaining unchanged, and the UK entirely opposed. France remained unique in having retained a system which gave pride of place to the state and central government. The trend of social welfare provision broadly reflected the trends in governance (see Table 5). By 2000 Austria had made few welfare system retrenchments. The level of retrenchment was greater in Sweden and the Netherlands, where there had been an increased role for the private sector.[3] In Germany and France there had been small retrenchments. But all systems, *except* Ireland and the UK, were described as generous. The conclusion on welfare provision was therefore broadly in line with that on governance. It was being somewhat reduced overall, with an increased private contribution, but, with the exception of Ireland and the UK, the systems remained generous. The social-democratic model remained strong though it was in modest retreat.

The pattern of direct investment flows, according to the OECD figures, appeared not to be correlated with total levels of taxation or with income tax and indirect taxation (Table 6). There was greater correlation with total company taxation, and particularly with employer social security contributions. In 1998 the only countries

Table 5 Principal features of social protection in selected EU countries

Country	Past provision	Current provision	Trend
Austria CC	Proportional insurance-based Generous	Proportional insurance-based Generous	Minor retrenchments
Sweden SDU	Proportional insurance-based Redistributive underpin Generous	Proportional insurance-based Redistributive underpin Generous	Retrenchments
Netherlands CC/SDU	Proportional insurance-based Generous	Proportional insurance-based Redistributive underpin Generous Private complements	Retrenchments Increased importance placed on private complements
UK LR	Redistributive (flat rate) Ungenerous (need for means-tested supplements for many receiving only basic payments) Substantial private complements	Redistributive (flat rate) Ungenerous (need for means-tested supplements for many receiving only basic payments) Substantial private complements	Substantial retrenchments Increased importance placed on private complements
Germany CC	Proportional insurance-based Generous	Proportional insurance-based Generous	Small retrenchments
France CC	Proportional insurance-based Generous	Proportional insurance-based Generous Extension of means-tested backups	Small retrenchments of insurance system, extension of means-tested backups

			Retrenchments
Italy CC/LR	Insurance-based Generous Limited unemployment benefit except in case of redundancy Reliance on family support as well as means-tested benefits as backup Proportional insurance-based Reliance on family support as well as means-tested benefits as backup Transition from pre-democratic/authoritarian corporatist structure	Insurance-based Generous Limited unemployment benefit except in case of redundancy Reliance on family support as well as means-tested benefits as backup	
Spain CC/LR		Proportional insurance-based Reliance on family support as well as means-tested benefits as backup	Construction of structures appropriate to democratic, industrialized society Adjustments including minor retrenchments
Ireland LR	Redistributive (flat rate) Ungenerous Limited private complements Construction of structures appropriate to industrialized society	Redistributive (flat rate) Ungenerous Limited private complements	Increased importance placed on private complements
USA LR	Proportional insurance-based Reasonably generous redistributive underpin Substantial private complements No universal health insurance Limited means-tested assistance	Proportional insurance-based Reasonably generous redistributive underpin Substantial private complements No universal health insurance Restricted means-tested assistance	Retrenchments of means-tested assistance

Note: CC Conservative-corporatist; SDU = Social democratic-universalist; LR = Liberal-residual (based upon Esping-Anderson, 1990 typology); R = Latin rim (based upon Ferrara, 1996 typology).

Source: Bernard Casey and Michael Gold, *Social Partnership and Economic Performance: The Case of Europe*, Cheltenham, Edward Elgar, p. 16.

Table 6 Direct investment in the EU

	Flows 1998, million $US					Positions 1997, million $US		
	a. inward	% GDP	b. outward	% GDP	a/b %	a. inward	b. outward	a/b %
Austria	6,494	2.79	671	1.42	967.0	17,510	57,212	30.61
Belg/Lux.	20,887	8.34	23,111	9.23	90.73	*	*	*
Denmark	6,452	3.69	3,868	2.21	166.80	*	*	*
Finland	12,141	9.73	18,643	14.90	65.12	9,530	20,297	46.95
France	28,033	1.96	40,578	2.83	69.08	141,136	189,681	74.40
Germany	19,888	0.93	86,641	4.06	22.95	185,980	280,779	66.23
Greece	3,709	3.08	*	*	*	*	*	*
Ireland	2,236	2.69	*	*	*	*	*	*
Italy	1,212	0.10	15,591	0.66	7.77	81,082	81,082	64.87
Netherlands	22,491	5.96	35,942	9.52	62.57	127,434	209,594	60.80
Portugal	1,773	1.67	2,923	2.76	60.65	18,555	5,933	312.74
Spain	8,680	1.57	15,427	2.79	56.26	100,684	47,606	211.49
Sweden	18,900	8.33	21,231	9.36	89.02	41,767	75,283	55.47
UK	63,545	4.68	114,947	8.47	55.27	259,595	371,119	60.94
US	188,960	2.30	121,644	1.48	155.30	693,207	865,531	*

Note: * Figures not available.
Source: International Direct Investment Statistics Yearbook, 1999, Paris, OECD, 2000.

which had a positive position on direct investment flows defined as a percentage of GDP were Austria, Denmark and – though the OECD lacked the relevant figures at the time of writing – probably Ireland. Denmark and Austria both had higher levels of total taxation in EU terms, with Ireland towards the lower end of the range. Denmark (figures not here, but compare with Sweden) and Austria had generous social protection systems. All the rest, including the United Kingdom had a negative position. Close to balance, though still in deficit, were Sweden and Belgium/Luxembourg. The UK's negative balance, with inward flows at 55 per cent of outward flows, was at the lower end of a group which formed the majority of member states with the corresponding figure at around 60 per cent. The figures were somewhat confused by the increase in inward investment into the UK after the setting up of the currency system. It seemed though that the inward movement was either concentrated in the so-called dot.com sector, i.e. Internet businesses, or was a consequence of decisions made before Euroland's establishment. In any case, movement out greatly exceeded movement in.

This evidence suggested that the doubts cast on the viability of the Social Democratic states in the context of the debate about the euro in 2000, and of globalization, were exaggerated. Investment movements into, and out of, European states were more closely correlated with something much more basic and much simpler, namely the level of specific taxes on companies, like company income tax and employer social security contributions, rather than with the overall level of taxation and the level of spending on welfare. It was impossible to demonstrate, on this evidence, that high overall taxation, and generous public welfare provision, made states less attractive to international capital. Denmark had a clear significant net inflow of direct investment with income tax at 52.4 per cent, and there appeared to be no correlation there between the balance of direct investment and the other economic indicators. The balance of inward and outward flows, and of positions, was not greatly different between states with a range of total tax takes and levels of welfare provision. France had a balance of flows of investment which was about the same as that of the UK, and the positions on investment showed that the French had not much less capital investment abroad than the British, yet had a much more generous level of social provision. Two countries had a significant excess outflow of investment funds compared with the others, namely Germany and Italy, but with regard to the balance of total sums abroad and at home they were not that different from the UK in 1997. These two cases would appear to support the contention that high levels of social spending discouraged investment and encouraged flows abroad, but overall the pattern was much more mixed. Indeed the case of Germany could be a special one in that the flows of investment to Eastern Europe, the primary direction of German investment flows, was as much a reassertion of traditional links as a reflection of economic pressures. In 2002 it was reported that some of the direct investment in Central Europe, including Poland, had returned to Germany. The varied experience of the EU states indicated that the idea of social democracy had to be detached from the broader agenda of structural and supply-side reform, which might proceed a long way without any necessary threat to welfare.

The concept of the Anglo-American model was questionable with regard to a number of its prescriptions about low public welfare provision, low taxation and deregulation. Even the United States fitted this bill somewhat awkwardly. Total tax level there in 1997 was well below that of any European state, but levels of tax on companies were higher than in a number of EU states. All this fitted the general conclusion, developed below, that the main explanation of the weakness of the euro in its early days was the mismatching of European and US business cycles. Whether or not European states had a greater or lesser degree of welfare provision – whether or not they were social democracies – was not clearly the key issue. The questions which were crucial, however, were those of whether generous welfare systems could survive in the period of neoliberal economic globalization and, equally important, whether attempts to protect welfare arrangements would cause structural changes in international society.

Political diversity

In the context of this argument it is necessary to rehearse some of the commonplace insights into the emergence of the European Community/Union and the character of its institutional arrangements. The European Community had developed by the 1970s into a unique international organization, which combined two features which had usually been seen as mutually contradictory: a high degree of common management together with a system of states which retained their sovereignty. The reconciliation of these two features was achieved by the splitting of the idea of competence and the idea of ultimate responsibility. Governments learned that their sovereignty could survive, if altered, even if they extended competences over key areas like currency to a central set of institutions – those in Brussels – as long as they remained ultimately responsible. If things went wrong they retained the legal and constitutional right to take back the competences they had extended, and in any case they were accountable to their domestic constituencies for the protection of their interests in the common framework.

The cautious governments, such as Britain, were under pressure to extend competences to the centre, but had to have the confidence that they retained ultimate responsibility. This was a trick which had largely been learned by the original six member states. It involved being reconciled to the possibilities of sovereignty for small or middle-sized states in the modern world, understanding how circumstances had changed, so that an absolutist view of sovereignty was no longer sustainable, and being careful to protect the reserve powers inherent in the national constitutions on which the legality of the whole Community legal system rested. Sometimes the language used by leaders of the more ambitious countries, such as Germany, alarmed the British. For instance in May 2000 the German Foreign

Minister, Joshka Fischer, said that a federal outcome should be sought. A reading of the text, reported in Britain as a plan for a European Superstate led by Germany[4] revealed a more modest appeal for a clearer division of responsibilities between the centre and the states, and an assertion, yet again, of the primary role of the nation states. By 2002 this had led to the setting up of a convention to consider the form of the future constitution of the European Union, but by this time the UK had decided that the right strategy was to accept the process but to defeat the end. Hence the British proposals to the Convention of February 2002 were a transparent ruse to defeat supranational ambitions by marginalizing the Commission and multiplying the centres of intergovernmental control. One British idea was to have a chair from a different state for each Council. The argument for Federalism, usually intepreted in the cautious states as a plan for centralization, usually, on closer inspection, turned into a plea for greater clarity about the location of competences, or a conclusive reckoning of the balance, and was irrelevant to the question of sovereignty.

But in Britain many failed to make the distinction between competences and powers, and many in government and the media, who came to be called the Eurosceptics, could not get beyond the view that granting a competence to Brussels was the same thing as abdicating ultimate responsibility and sovereignty. This view was a key part of the primitive sentimental nationalism that was a feature of Mrs Thatcher's ideology, but, in the context of the later debate about membership of the single currency system, it was a perspective that became more common.

The reconciliation of a high degree of shared management in the EU with the retention of sovereignty also depended on a range of characteristics of the Union's decision-making. The whole system rested on a Treaty, the Treaty of Rome, which had been legitimized through national constitutions. It was the latter and not the former which gave legitimacy to the Union. It followed that states could withdraw if they wished. It also followed that as long as they followed their own constitutional procedures – that is that they acted legally according to the terms of their own system, they could individually and separately reject Community legislation.

The chances were, however, that this would not happen because the member states shared economic and political interests in staying together – the British remained convinced that they were better in than out. It was also unlikely to happen because the way in which legislation was made in the main EU institutions rested on the principle of consensus. In many areas there was by the turn of the millennium the formal possibility of qualified majority voting. But the reality was that no states could or would be regularly outvoted on matters about which they cared deeply. All participants understood that it was better to avoid breaking the consensus: to do so would be dangerous. Whenever majority voting was used it was in effect with the consent of the dissenting states in each case, which were conceding that they were prepared to be outvoted, and was most often used on more technical questions in support of a policy that had been agreed earlier, on the basis of unanimity. The new major initiatives were always determined in meetings of the heads of states and governments, called the European Council, on the basis of unanimity.

The correct image of the Union's institutions was that they were not something outside of, or apart from, the states, an outside actor which could threaten or impose on states. Even the Commission, the Union's executive body, had a representative quality despite its formal task of administering the Union's rules – acting as guardian of the treaty – and proposing European policies. Even though members of the Commission were strictly forbidden from seeking or receiving instructions from their national governments, governments were always anxious to get their people into key positions where they felt their interest could best be served. The Eurosceptics in Britain and elsewhere wilfully misunderstood the situation – they talked of the Commission as if, to quote Charles de Gaulle, it was 'a foreign bureaucracy' with opposing interests. The fact was that all the Commission's actions were in pursuit of policies which the states had approved. If they did not like those policies they had no one but themselves, or earlier governments in their state, to blame, and they could not lay blame on the expropriation of sovereignty by Brussels institutions. But usually the statements of the sceptics revealed ignorance about the tight linkages between the national and collective systems. In Britain a press dominated by deracinated individuals, such as Rupert Murdoch, were all too willing to promote anti-European views, and if the cause was best served by misinformation then so be it.[5]

By the mid-1980s the terms of the diplomatic relationship between the British, and the other cautious states, and the more ambitious core states in the European Community, led by France and Germany, had turned against the former. This remained the case till the time of writing in the early months of the twenty-first century. The nature of the problem could be summed up as follows: initiatives to extend integration, such as those pushed by the French and the Germans after the mid-1980s, posed the threat of the emergence of a powerful political actor on the continent which could potentially dominate the reluctant integrators. There was a kind of diplomatic trap: either the British, and the other non-core states, had to stay with the negotiations on the new proposals to deepen integration, and make whatever concessions that had to be made to stay in the convoy, or she could withdraw and risk being isolated. This was in effect a replay of the diplomacy of the late 1950s when the Conservative government in Britain had decided that the proposal to set up the European Economic Community was not for them, and in any case would probably not work. It did work, however, despite the British-led setting up, strongly opposed by the USA, of the rival European Free Trade Area. They, therefore, had to seek admission later on less favourable terms than those they could probably have obtained earlier. After the 1980s, up to the time of writing in 2002, British governments, a Conservative one until 1997, and then New Labour, were determined to avoid making this mistake again.

Scenarios of future development

The account in the previous section is an indication of the European inheritance in terms of procedures and attitudes at the time of writing. It leads naturally to the next question: what conclusions may be drawn in 2002 from this account of the European Union? One view, though this was not supported by Eurosceptics, was that State and Community could have a positive relationship with each other.[6] The positive states did not see their sovereignty as threatened. This was not surprising. States, such as Spain, Portugal, Greece and Germany had joined the Community in order to rediscover themselves as states, indeed in order to consolidate their national arrangements. There was a sufficient identity with the common values to allow this to be recognized as a possibility by anyone who was not actually in the grip of Europhobia. The history of the Community reflected the idea of Europe as a unity in diversity. But the European Union level had also acquired its own integrity and a degree of self-containment. It was not just a matter of providing a mechanism to help the state, though this was a limitation on which successive British governments tried to insist.

In 2002 there were three scenarios about the future of the European Union. All three assumed that there would be enlargement to include most of the states of central and eastern Europe, stopping short of Russia. All three also involved a response to globalization, interpreted as the process of liberalizing the international movement of capital and goods.

1. The first accepted the dilution of the existing arrangements of the EU by granting derogations and exceptions to all members in the enlarged community. This implied the immersion of the whole in the global economy, and the triumph throughout of the Anglo-American model of economic management and of the pure 'neoliberal' agenda. This meant the further liberalization of trade, and low levels of government intervention and spending on welfare throughout. The neoliberal agenda would triumph. This was very much the agenda of the British Eurosceptics, since it removed the challenge of supranationalism to which they had strongly objected. It would also fit with the social and political agendas of the sceptics, who tended to be Thatcherite in the UK, with regard to internal policy, since very low tariffs, adopted within the framework of multilateral free trade negotiations, meant that the costs of adaptation were more likely to be placed on labour, while the advantages of free trade accrued to companies and richer individuals. There were a number of reasons why this seemed less likely in 2002 than it had in, say, 1997. One was the to do with responses to the financial crises in the Far East and Latin America in the mid to late 1990s. There seemed a new case for a development state which ran in parallel with the case for the social democratic state.

2. There were however other scenarios. The second was the successful adjustment of the Union's arrangements to accommodate all members in a higher level of integration, comparable with that which existed at the millennium. This would involve the careful working out of transitional arrangements with new members, on the assumption that their accommodation was possible, and the least possible dilution of existing cooperative arrangements. The institutions would also be adjusted so as to protect the powers of the centre and to find a generally acceptable compromise between national independence and supranationalism. There would be a measure of adjustment of welfare spending but the principle of state responsibility for individual welfare would be acknowledged throughout the Union. In this

way the Union would continue much as before, but with a considerably increased membership, and a lowering of ambitions for future integration, combined with a measure of compromise with the forces of globalization. This would be a kind of halfway house between the first and third scenarios.[7] This was also unlikely, particularly because of the problems of enlargement beyond the first five, which it was probable would not be solved on the basis of the EU's conditions of entry. It was likely that as negotiations with the candidate countries proceeded it would be found that deadlines had been reached without full compliance with the conditions for membership agreed by the member states in a series of meetings, such as the Copenhagen meeting in 1996 and Helsinki in 1999. It would be difficult to refuse admitting such states, despite their falling short of the acceptance and application in full of the *acquis communitaire*.

3. The third scenario was the most challenging both with regard to the continuing liberalization of global economic arrangements and with regard to non-core states' participation in the core activities of the Union. It was also the most probable. In this model there would be differentiation between the core states of the existing Union and the peripheral states, which included Britain and the newly admitted states from Central Europe.

The basis of the differentiation would be:

- First, the preference of the core states for protecting their higher levels of integration and making continuing progress towards a confederal union with a formal settlement of powers between the centre and the member states, as was proposed, mentioned above, by German Foreign Minister Joschka Fischer on 12 May 2000 in a lecture at the Humboldt University in Berlin. President Chirac of France echoed this proposal in a speech in Dresden on 3 October 2000. He called for Germany and France to lead a core of countries towards deeper integration within an enlarged European Union.[8] In the Treaty of Amsterdam, and later at Nice, this theme was reflected in the notion of flexibility or enhanced cooperation, intended to allow states that wished to go ahead of the others the right to do so – if all agreed to this. But flexibility, as already pointed out, became a contested concept in the sense that the more cautious states, and those sceptical about integration, were fearful about the prospect of a more integrated core.

- The second basis of differentiation would be the wish of the core states to protect their ability to pursue a social purpose in the face of perceived difficulties in the way of this resulting from globalization and the implied triumph of the Anglo-American model. They would be anxious to protect their social democratic approach – sometimes described as Alliance Capitalism – in the face of the pressures to reduce the costs of labour and welfare support resulting from more open economies. This was not surprising: the core states had consistently pushed for a more advanced social agenda than the British would accept, and were convinced that there could not be a successful integrated market without further development of social welfare measures. Labour had to benefit as much as capital. The strength of the commitment of the core states to this position was usually not fully taken on board by those outside the core, even New Labour in Britain. This was not to suggest that there was root and branch opposition to any reform of labour and welfare arrangements, but rather that it was a question of appropriate adjustment.[9] Unlike with doctrinaire neoliberalism there could be a compromise between welfare and competitiveness.

The core states could move ahead by signing a separate treaty among themselves, or by exploiting the new flexibility arrangements of the Amsterdam and Nice Treaties. The former strategy had been proposed by the leading core states on several occasions in the 1980s and 1990s in the face of the reluctance of the cautious states, led by the British, to accept stronger powers for the central institutions. They would also move towards a greater degree of harmonization of welfare in the core and maintain higher levels of spending on welfare: they would need to calculate carefully the level of costs which they could impose on capital without driving it out of the Union. This case is argued in more detail below.

- The third basis of the differentiation would be the strengthening of the perception of serious practical difficulties in the way of adjusting the existing arrangements of the Union to include all of the Central and Eastern European states, in particular difficulties which would lead to greatly increased demands on the European budget and the implication of higher contributions by the richer member states. It was likely that the EU would be unable to continue with the movement towards more federal budgetary arrangements, with significant redistribution to poorer regions, in view of the sheer scale of the sums that would be involved. The attempt to accommodate all the new states to higher levels of integration would fail in this scenario. The scenario which looked most likely in 2002 was the admittance to membership of the central European states on terms which satisfied the conditions laid down by the European Union at Copenhagen and Helsinki. But a number of states, especially those from further east, would fall short of compliance and would not fully accept the *acquis communitaire*. In this context the core states would lose their reluctance to go ahead without the British. The outer group would be members of the common market, but would not be included in the more integrative arrangements.[10]

The problems of Britain as a spoiler and scavenger in the Union would reach a threshold at which demotion to the second rank of membership would be preferred by the core states to making adjustments to keep Britain fully in the convoy. Indeed the emergence of the new problem candidate states would make it easier to limit British involvement since the UK could then be placed in the large company of states with problem credentials. The core states would be much more prepared than Britain to resist opening up to the global economic pressures, because of their implications for the responsibilities of governments for welfare. The calculation would be that such a market would be large enough, and successful enough to persuade mobile capital to pay the required price of access. The calculation of this would always be a difficult question: it would become a major item on the agenda of economic management in the core countries. The close scrutiny of OECD economic and social indicators in the late 1990s, undertaken in a preceding section, did not provide any hard evidence of the vulnerability of the social democratic model in the European Union, despite the claims of the British. With regard to the wide range of indicators the social democratic states were either performing better than the British, or were doing as well.

The group of states identified as the core would have to be amended in 2002 to reflect an increase in suspicion of the EU in France and some outright hostility under the Berlusconi regime in Italy. But it seemed to this commentator that the chances were good that the political elite in France would hold the line against active anti-Europeanism and would continue to side with Germany, for traditional reasons, on the issue of promoting integration. The Italians were also likely, though this was less certain, to move against Berlusconi when the implications of his policies, on internal matters as well as on Europe, became clear.

Developments in these two countries were therefore not likely to be decisive with regard to the emerging structure of the European Union, and the decisive considerations remained the implications of enlargement and of neoliberal economic globalization. A consequence of the former, which was an anticipation of the debilitating effects on integration of enlargement, was the mechanism for enhanced cooperation as formulated in the Amsterdam and Nice Treaties. These were arrangements whereby a group of eight members could decide to move ahead of the others, though there was the possibility of a European Council decision to veto the proposal.

Various patterns in the emerging structure of the Union could be placed within these parameters. It is proposed:

- That the eight could be made up of a core of the willing – the Six with or without Italy – and a changing supporting coalition on different issues to make up the required number. The willing outside the core would be likely to be responding to the fear of marginalization, the traditional motivation of the older cautious states. There would be other states, particularly the more recently admitted states in Central and Eastern Europe, that would be less persuaded by the fear of marginalization. For them any kind of membership would be markedly better than what went before. The dynamics of core–periphery relations would be altered by enlargement in that the periphery would not care as much about not being clearly in the core.
- That the possibility of preventing the eight willing states from going ahead, contained in the potential European Council veto allowed in the Nice Treaty, was unreal. It was likely to be evaded, if only by the option of reaching agreements outside the framework of the Treaty of Rome.
- That the other states, after enlargement, would be subject to increasingly complex negotiations among themselves about how to respond to the coalition of the willing. In the European Union as a whole it would be more difficult, and much slower, to reach the consensus which would still be necessary to make progress on any matters of importance, regardless of the possibilities of qualified majority voting.

- That the structure of the EU would, therefore, be likely to be made up of a core of states, as indicated above, which were prepared to go ahead of the others. But the core, which could itself increase or decrease marginally – depending in particular on the positions of Italy and France and would be a partner in cumbersome and complex negotiations with the others, which would still depend overall on reaching consensus. Votes in the Councils of Ministers would be the focus of such politics, and these votes would be determined by extended and complex negotiations between states which would be less concerned with the value of the community than before, and more concerned with the pursuit of narrow national interest. The nature of the alliances among the others, and whether or not they would be flexible or inflexible, would be hard to predict.
- That the overall pattern of European politics would be one reminiscent of the period of *lourdeur*, as described by the Committee of Three Wise Men in the late 1970s, but within that pattern would be a group of more willing states which were prepared to go ahead of the others, even if that meant making agreements among themselves outside the framework of the treaties. Progress to a higher level of general integration would be slow, and patchy, with a varying degree of support for the policies of the core. For the time being the achievement in the *acquis communitaire* would be safe but progress beyond that would be slow. It would take a longer time for the *lourdeur* to lighten than had been the case in the 1970s–1980s. Unlike the later 1970s there would be systemic factors which would make it difficult to restart the integration process. One of those factors would be the freeing of the willing from the restraints of the sceptical.

The importance of this third scenario derived from its proposing of reasons for both resisting the pressures of globalization, and for greater integration of a core ahead of the peripheral states. These derived from economic, political and ideological factors, and in the light of these Britain and the core states would be likely to be divided. But it was a challenge to the inevitability of globalization, previously intimated very rarely. It raised an important question: how would such a differentiation affect the economic organization of the Union and its relations with the world economy? In the next section aspects of this relationship are explored. Arguments which support the view that the social democratic states could succeed are explored. A case is argued that will be reconsidered at various points later in this book.

The social democratic states and the globalizing economies

The location of capital

The question arises of how the *acquis communitaire*, in particular the common market, could survive in such a system. At this point the account is less concerned with historical analysis and more with the logic of the situation. The calculation of costs and benefits concerning the location of capital in the European Union must take account of the different arguments about the core compared with the periphery. This is a two-stage calculation, the first being the calculation of the advantage of being inside the Common External Tariff (CET), and the second about where to locate within the EU. If the core states were to succeed in defending their higher level of welfare spending within the common market, against peripheral or Anglo-American member states with cheaper welfare costs, there must be additional benefits for capital in the core compared with the periphery. The benefit of access to the common market would be equally available in both locations, since both would be within the CET. The conclusions were likely to vary with the sector, but for most manufacturers the core was likely to possess benefits, such as the proximity of suppliers of components and support infrastructure, and a more prosperous local market, as well as greater specific and general skills of workers, and a range of attractions for managers and their families. As already argued peripheries would have the advantage of a cheaper and more flexible workforce, of weaker unions, of greenfield sites and of lower welfare costs, but these advantages would have to be set against a deficiency in the assets normally found in the core.

In these circumstances three areas of policy disagreement between the core states and the peripheral states in the European Union suggested themselves: about taxation, about the level of protection and its implications for globalization, and about the new social democracy.

- On taxation the disagreement about levels of social spending would be bound to lead to short-term differences of interest which would be hard to reconcile. The states with a higher social wage would recognize the short-term competitive disadvantage of that and prefer to have a generally agreed scale of taxation at a level necessary to achieve higher social standards throughout the Union. They would seek to equalize taxation costs upwards. The Anglo-American states in contrast would seek to protect their competitive advantage in this regard and resist attempts to harmonize taxation upward: indeed they would prefer no harmonization at all as the higher social spending of the core could be seen as a benefit for themselves. This was exactly the position of the British in 2002.

- On protection, the social democratic states had an interest in maintaining around the Union, probably through the common external tariff, a level which offset the competitive advantages of lower-cost producers in third countries. The interest would be to induce inward investment by making the costs of supplying the European market from outside exceed the costs of establishment inside the Union. The assumption would be that there could be an optimum level of protection to support the social democratic agenda within the Union, but which minimized the risk of tariff wars, or mecantilist strategies. This strategy could however only work on the basis of the European market, and hence it required integration. No individual state in Europe could present an attractive enough market to persuade multinational enterprises to pay the entrance fee demanded. The Anglo-American and peripheral states, in contrast, would be happier with lower levels of protection, deep tariff cuts, because they would be less anxious to protect their ability to afford more costly welfare, and more prepared to indulge in the 'race to the bottom' to attract inward investment.
- But the kind of social democracy was also key in this argument. The assumption of the right-wing advocates of flexible labour was that it should be easy to hire and fire, meaning low employment protection, little attempt to build a communality of interest between labour and management, through co-determination arrangements, workers' councils and the like – which were a feature of German labour relations – low levels of unionization and low levels of pension provision. The last was key in welfare provision and is discussed separately below. But there was an alternative model which involved a reconciliation of traditional social democracy with the needs of global capital. The case for

even a reformed welfare system was less likely to appeal to the poorer states, as they would be more in thrall to short-term interests and anxious to maximize their ability to attract capital, even at the risk in the short term of a higher social cost.

A high social wage could be devoted to developing effective arrangements for a more flexible labour force, by providing retraining, support for relocation and a guaranteed trans-employment income, by the action of the state.[11] The social wage would reflect the change in the structure of employment, being used to support enhanced flexibility, with economic success being a primary target of policy, but nested firmly in policies for maintaining civilized standards for employees. The aim would be to protect the right to employment, but to recognize that the concept of employment had to be detached from the right to stay in a particular job. Indeed the aim would be to generate a labour force that was unlike that of previous generations, in that, while traditionally flexibility was greater for the least skilled, now it would be greater for those with the highest levels of technical training. It should be stressed, however, that such employment strategies, which would seem ideally suited to the new capitalism, were social democratic rather than Anglo-American. Done properly they required higher, rather than lower, levels of social policy spending.

The arguments were also the context in which the weakness of the strategy of relying on cheap labour and low associated costs in anything but the short term were revealed. Three problems arose. First in the Anglo-American model a low level of labour protection was a fair-weather asset in that it was only of benefit as an attraction to mobile capital in a period of economic expansion. In economic decline the areas of cheap labour were the first to suffer because it was cheaper, and easier, for companies to fire labour there than in areas where the worker had more protection. The history of the links between the Rover car company and the German car manufacturer BMW in the UK illustrated this point very well in 2000: facing the need to restructure production BMW determined to abandon Rover and British workers partly because it was cheaper than reducing its German workforce. In 2002 German capital began to return to Germany from Poland. This indicates that in a period of decline having a low social wage was likely to make things worse rather than better for the less successful economies in that it facilitated the building up of larger pools of unemployed with all the economic, social and political burdens this implied. It was also much riskier from the point of view of political stability.

Secondly, as a low social wage usually meant inadequacy in training and other support for re-employment and resettlement, it was also likely to lead to a further deskilling of labour and a further reduction of the attractiveness of that area to mobile capital. In this situation cheap labour was part of a strategy for further economic decline rather than recovery, unless there were powerful countervailing economic and social pressures – compulsion – of a kind not usually found in liberal Western democracies. Thirdly was the problem that the lesson that cheap labour was an asset was not one that was capable of being generalized or universalized, and was therefore revealed as profoundly flawed as a global concept. Capital that relied on universal cheap labour was capital that was strangling its own market. Even when production benefited from cheap labour, in the mass-market sectors – which remained crucial – there had to be somewhere a pool of well-rewarded high-spending labour to provide their market. The cheaper the labour in an enclosed market the smaller the market for a wide range of goods: this was a lesson that was well known to economists such as Hobson, and was a key factor in his critique of imperialism.

These arguments obviously had implications for the institutional development of the European Union which were in flat opposition to those developed hitherto by Eurosceptics with regard to the Social Charter in Maastricht, Amsterdam and later. The traditional argument rested on the conviction in the Anglo-American states that a greater degree of social spending, and a degree of obligation to that in the common institutions, was likely to be a handicap with regard to their capacity to attract capital and their level of economic performance. In contrast this argument suggested that a higher level of social spending could be part of a strategy for maintaining a greater range of benefits which were attractive to mobile global capital, as long as, as argued above, the costs of such programmes were not placed too directly and obviously on companies. Such policies would mean that the wise economic move would be to opt in, and to have a higher degree of common decision-making on welfare questions, and for the less successful economies to work for welfare policies that were well funded but rethought to suit modern employment needs. In this welfare provision the central theme would be having arrangements which guaranteed a continuing supply of flexible and highly trained labour, which must involve governments' collective responsibility – the public sector – as it was difficult to see how individual companies could remain immune to the temptations to freeload. Capital-friendly welfare provision was not a difficult concept, but it did need at least medium-term thinking about the convergence of the interests of labour and capital in the context of a well-developed market.

The arguments above did not need quantification. They were sufficient as they stood to suggest that the social democracies in the Union had at their disposal policies which could increase the advantage for capital of establishing within them to a level which exceeded the advantages of establishment in the low welfare spending countries. The arguments also suggested that public action at the level of the European Union would be useful, but not essential, in that it would reduce the chances of irrational action by the low-welfare countries in a competition for capital which they could not win in anything but the short term. The appropriate level of welfare spending could be agreed and legitimized through the Union, and, as with all stable regimes, fair play refereed and cheating identified. There were also important implications for multinational corporations. The argument suggested that the commitment to social democracy on the part of developed market states, as in the European Union, was likely to generate costs which they could not avoid. Costs and benefits could be manipulated so that they preferred to stay within rather than to exit from the Union. The idea that capital would inevitably flee from welfare provision, as was claimed by neoliberals, was challenged.

The movement of investment funds

The movement of investment funds was thought to be the primary reason for the decline of the euro against the dollar in 2000. The explanation for this, commentators alleged, was that investment managers judged that the US economy would grow faster than that of Europe because the latter was over-regulated and the level of government spending on welfare was excessive. Frequently the main reason for the latter was said to be the high level of pensions brought about by the population structure – too many old people – and too few taxpayers, who were being called upon to shoulder an increasing burden of taxation (discussed below). Business was also said to be subject to too many rules and regulations concerning a wide range of matters, from environmental to health and safety standards. The solution, therefore, was to cut back on pension provision, to stop being what was described as tax-and-spend economies, to reduce the level of taxation, and to deregulate the economies. This was essentially a neoliberal logic and it often clothed arguments about social welfare with a prejudicial terminology. Higher levels of taxation were described as 'tax and spend', employment protection was seen as 'excessive regulation', and the reduction of pension payments, and welfare payments generally, was seen as 'reform'. Welfare provision was also often categorized by neoliberal moral crusaders as an instrument for the creation of a dependency subculture of workshy frauds.[12] Bonoli *et al.* demolish this argument, and make it look like the shallow dogma it is, simply by referring to the current research. The remedy, in the eyes of those who favoured the Anglo-American model, was for the guilty governments to stop these unhappy practices, and thereby persuade investors to move their money back into Europe.

In September 2000 the economic adviser to the International Monetary Fund, Michael Mussa, recommended an international rescue operation for the euro by collective intervention in the money market. The IMF Director supported this on the following day. The point had come, he alleged, at which the weakness of the euro was in danger of becoming a threat to the stability of the international economy. In the following days the central banks of the main global economies did in fact intervene in the market to buy euros in an attempt to halt its decline against the dollar, and at the time of writing there was evidence to suggest that this had achieved some short-term success. But according to many commentators the pressures to reform the 'bad' economies was now overwhelming.[13]

But in the view of the present writer the neoliberal explanation of the weakness of the euro in 2000 was relevant but insufficient. The major cause was almost certainly to do with a mismatch of the business cycles in the United States and Europe. But, as importantly, abandoning social democracy could only have a modest short-term positive impact on the underlying difficulty, regardless of the reasons for the weakness of the euro. A key aspect of the business-cycle argument was the timing of reductions in budgetary deficits. The US had entered the recession of the early 1990s with a low deficit, which permitted more expansionist policies, while the Europeans had a higher level of deficit which they were then required to reduce according to the convergence criteria applicable to monetary union. They therefore had to follow tighter monetary and fiscal policies through the 1990s.[14] As Sarah Hogg put it: 'the euro's launch coincided not merely with cyclical strength in the US economy but with serious re-rating of its economic potential. Euroland actually managed a quite respectable 3.8 per cent growth over the past year (to midsummer 2000) but the supposedly exhausted US economy managed a stunning 6 per cent.'[15] But it was hardly surprising that funds were sucked in from Europe when US interest rates were almost twice those in Europe (on 21 September at 9.5 per cent (Prime) and 5.5 per cent (ECB O/N Marginal, respectively), and when US companies were growing much faster, in part because of the self-fulfilling prophecy generated by the inflow of capital. Arguably the introduction of the euro should have been timed to coincide with the business cycles, not only of the members, but also of the main rival economies, but that would have been impossible and was excluded from the discussion. The managers of funds were also bound to be rather cautious with regard to the new multinational currency – this was an arrangement which had never been tried before – and the dice were therefore loaded in favour of US investment from the outset.

If these factors – the business cycle and the fear of the unknown – were important and arguably dominant, the abandonment of the marks of a civilized society, a well-founded welfare system, for dubious short-term benefit would seem a price not worth paying. Indeed the price only seemed right in the context of an ideology which made social as well as economic claims, namely, neoliberalism. This is not to say that intervention in the money markets, as recommended by the IMF, could not be helpful, but only if such intervention was timed to coincide with a turning in the tide of the business cycle. By late 2000 the assumption that the US economy had discovered the secret of eternal youth, in defiance of all the arguments about the inevitability of a downwards turn in the business cycle, was looking increasingly suspect. There were warnings of the falling away of profit margins, and the selling of industrial shares in the US stock markets.[16] Both the Dow Jones and NASDAQ had entered a period of decline. The US trade deficit was also causing concern as it soared to a new peak of $31.89 billion in July 2000.

IMF action could nudge in the right direction and give positive psychological signals, but without the crucial background of a change in views about the future of the US economy this would achieve nothing but the depletion of central bank reserves. The question was whether this point had been reached; at the time of writing this question could not be answered. But the point emerged very strongly that the lack of harmony in the business cycles of the US and European economies at the launch of the euro was a crucial variable in explaining the latter's subsequent difficulties at that time, and it was probably the most important one. In retrospect it was highly likely that funds would be drawn to the US, and that this would set in train a self-fulfilling prophecy of euro decline and dollar ascendancy. But this was caused more by judgements about the US economy than about the failures of the core social democratic states of Euroland. And the market being the fairly dim creature that it is, once the prophecy had been made it was difficult to make it not self-fulfilling.

It was also likely that the rules of the structure of the international economic system would prevail. Given the mismatch of the business cycles the correction of this situation would have to wait until there was a downturn in the US economy. But a further point lies behind these observations. The difficulties of the euro may have been an indication that there was a major structural problem in the international monetary system in the early years of the twenty-first century that arose from the reduction of the number of players in the system and the absence of any dominant player. In the new system there were at most three main players – the dollar, the yen and the euro – and, in a world of floating exchange rates, no fixed yardstick of monetary value. In this situation the chances of an uncontrolled oscillation in the value of currencies was a real possibility. The money was likely to flow one way or another, and was likely to flow in great volume and at great speed. It was hard to see what stabilizing measures could prove effective, given the nature of the system and the way it tended to amplify the problem as manifest in the volume and speed of movement.[17]

In this situation the question could be put of whether the move to the euro had itself created a context in which it would be hard for it to defend itself. Unless deliberate measures were taken the danger was that business cycles in different economic areas would become increasingly disharmonious, as the movement of funds to the better-performing economy would act as an amplifier of its success. The problem of the euro was revealed as an aspect of a major structural problem in the international monetary system, and an increased tendency to disequilibrium, rather than of any modest overspending by European governments.

The further point could also be made that the neoliberal argument could be reversed: if social democracy was the cause of Europe's failure then Europeans had the right to argue that the US should have more of it. The fact was that globalization also meant that Europeans had an interest in the proper resourcing of the US welfare system. The development of an increasing cosmopolitanism, in which there was a mutual responsibility for maintaining standards, meant they had the right to say so. Why should they accept the demolition of their social democracy as a consequence of low social standards and cheap energy in the US? In the US in 2000 44 million people had no medical insurance and therefore had inadequate medical support.[18] Similarly much of US labour had little or no unemployment protection. This was no doubt a plus for American capital in the short term, but it amounted to a penalty for European business. In September 2000, a time of fuel strikes in a number of European states as a result of high levels of energy taxation, it also became clear that everyone was paying a price for the low cost of US energy: in effect Europeans were paying for a global energy strategy on behalf of the Americans.[19]

The conclusion had to be that in the early twenty-first century the US was the happy beneficiary of a neoliberal orthodoxy which made it appear that maintaining civilized welfare standards was suspect, and that low standards were beneficial. The economic playing field could however be made level by equalizing upwards as well as downwards. There was a strong argument for doing this if this meant a more effective reconciliation of the principles of a civilized society and the long-term needs of industry.

Policy response to pension costs

Excessive pension payments to the elderly in social democracies were often a central concern of those seeking reform of welfare systems. As pointed out above the problem arose, it was alleged, because of long-term changes in the age structure of populations: the number of elderly pensioners was increasing and the number of taxpayers, the main providers of funding, was declining. This was a problem in most of the developed world, and affected both the social democratic states and the Anglo-Americans, including the USA. In the US it had been calculated that, if payments continued at the present level, current surpluses in the Social Security Fund would have to be tapped after 2015 and they would be exhausted by 2037. There would then only be two workers to support each beneficiary, as opposed to 3.4 in 2000.[20] The question of the future financing of the Fund was brought up in the 2000 Presidential election with the Republican and Democratic candidates both accepting the need for an increased role for the private sector. Their main difference was that the Democrat wanted to maintain matching federal government funding. In Germany the issue was also a particularly important one because of the generous level of pension provision, and, as mentioned, reducing this expenditure was regularly identified by neoliberals as the main plank of the required 'reform' of the German welfare system. The fact that Germany and the US had the same problem would however cast doubts on the view that in the former it was a special problem.

The privatization of pension provision was the preferred policy option in the discussion. There was little reference to alternatives, though privatization was itself not without serious problems in the way of implementation and operation. Not least was the question of social justice, and the implication that the obligation of the state to its citizens, after a lifetime of work, could be evaded. The irritation was fuelled in Britain by the allegation that the government had on a number of occasions, after the introduction of the National Insurance system, taken money out of funds which had been intended for pensions, in order to boost the short-term tax take; they promised that provision would be made up as required out of future general taxation, but then faced the awkward problem that the money they had promised was not available. In Britain in 2002 it seemed impossible that only a short time earlier, in the 1980s and 1990s, companies were seeking to drain off alleged surpluses from pension funds for new investment. In 2002, in contrast, there was a general clamour that companies could no longer afford final-salary-related schemes and there was general concern about future pension provision. The future problem was in large part a consequence of past government risk-taking and company carelessness, rather than of any inherent problem.

The obvious course was to focus on the root problem: would it be possible to increase the supply of workers and through that hold the necessary ratio of worker to pensioner? One way of doing this would involve having more flexible retirement arrangements with those who wished to continue in work being allowed, indeed, encouraged, to do so, and thus increase the worker stock. This policy proposal looked more sensible when the need, discussed above, to have a high level of worker training to produce a more flexible workforce for the new industrial age was recalled. Why throw away such investment in labour by encouraging, even insisting on, early retirement?

The British authority on pensions, Frank Field, argued that many retirees had sufficient savings and entitlements to finance the early years of retirement themselves and only required full pension provision when these resources began to run out, which, in Britain was at around 70 years old.[21] Given the increase in life expectancy it indeed seemed odd to stay with the expectation that retirement would normally take place at 65 or earlier, and that there should be a general guarantee of a pension at that date. Why not have a later date of retirement, and entitlement to a non-means-tested pension, with those unable to work until then supported out of unemployment protection resources? Individuals who wished to retire earlier could do so, though the level of their pension would be lower.

One response could be that the older workers had to give way to create jobs, and careers, for younger ones. But this then became a problem of the overall size of the economy, or of working hours, not of retirement: a larger economy and more civilized working hours – and years! – would create the necessary number of taxpayers. In the Union there was however a need to standardize these arrangements and to accept a common, and sensible retirement age. In some countries, such as Italy, the retirement age had been brought down to 55 in flat defiance of demographic trends! This could not be sustained. But the underlying problem was not as profound as neoliberals claimed. The problem of the cost of pensions was in reality a problem of adjustment to the new realities of demography and/or of economic growth, rather than of an inherent economic impasse. The fact that there were more elderly need not be either a problem for particular countries or a general drag on economic development. And it was hard to see how the total charge to an economy could be reduced by moving its cost from the state to the private sector, assuming that the aim of reform was not to reduce the total level of pension provision.

Beneath the pro-privatization argument there was frequently another assumption which derived from neoliberalism: that the private sector was necessarily more efficient than the public one. Anyone who has dealt with a large US health insurance company knows that this is not the case! But if the level of pension was to be maintained, payment would have to be made from the national product at the same rate, be it out of the wages of those in employment, company taxation or general taxation. Private provision would not be without public costs since a greater degree of reliance on the individual's private pension plans would also have the effect of driving wage/salary bills upwards, which in turn would create inflationary pressures. It might of course be politically easier for governments to do this as the cost would only appear in the medium and long term. But any form of provision had to be paid for, and any level of welfare could be supported by the individual if salaries were high enough!

Conclusions

By the first years of the new millennium there was the real prospect of a change of tactics by the more ambitious states in the European Union. The problem was that the old dynamics were likely to be less successful in a European Union which was in prospect of being increased to 25 or 30 members, including most of Central and Eastern Europe, as well as Turkey and island states such as Malta and Cyprus. This prospect of enlargement made it seem much less likely that the integration process could continue in its present form as the new states were simply so diverse and numerous. The stark alternatives as perceived by increasing numbers of social democrats were either succumbing to the pressures of economic globalization – which were driven by the ideology of neoliberalism and a partially concealed agenda for protecting American hegemony – or of pursuing policies of relative enclosure.

There was in consequence a slow realization by the Germans, French and pro-European Italians – the lead continental core states – that they may have to work out a new strategy, to which they would not need the agreement, however reluctantly given, of the reluctant states, including the British. Hitherto, they could believe in keeping the convoy together because the British, Danes and Greeks could be pushed to keep up despite themselves. There were no specific problems of a technical, policy-related kind in the way of this. The difficulty was more to do with will. But in the new Europe there were real technical problems in keeping the convoy together, so it was tempting to find a strategy which allowed them to opt out, for real reasons, and those which simply lacked the will could be left with them. The problems with the negotiations on enlargement also suggested that a future Europe was more likely to be à la carte than in convoy. The route of flexibility was one way in which they could achieve this, but at the time of writing that concept was still highly contested and the sceptics were unlikely to accept a more advanced core without protest.[22]

This chapter has also argued however that the core states could also protect their social democracy against the forces of globalization in the European Union. They could compete against the lower-cost states within, though there were optimal taxation and tariff strategies. There was no evidence to suggest that the problem with the euro was to do with the costs of social democracy, though adaptation was necessary, as the primary cause appeared to be the mismatch of the business cycles in the US and in Europe. There was evidence to suggest that the total level of *company* taxation played a role in company decisions to invest, but even countries with lower levels of *overall* taxation had net outflows of investment funding, and countries with high levels of *overall* taxation had significant net inflows. The main indicators of high levels of welfare spending had little correlation with low levels of direct investment funding.

There was no reason on grounds of competition for investment for social democracies to adopt low social wage strategies, though they would be well advised to adopt policies which combined civilized employment strategies with training for flexibility in the workplace. All this added up to support, in circumstances and in logic, for the core states adopting more advanced integration in the EU without abandoning their social democracy. That they would seek higher levels of integration, regardless of the wishes of the British and the other cautious states, seemed highly likely. But it was also probable that they would link this with the defence of their social democracy, thereby acting as a pole of attraction for the more hesitant states, and confounding the neoliberal forces of globalization. Such a strategy for the core states would not only push integration forward, but would put pressure on the reluctant states, including the Anglo-Americans, to maintain the necessary level of welfare spending.

One key element of the new strategy had been contemplated before, and used as a threat to keep Britain in line. That was to proceed by negotiating a new Treaty between the more ambitious states, rather than seeking amendments of the Treaty of Rome. The reluctant states could not veto such a Treaty, precisely because it was negotiated according to the principles of international law, between sovereign states. The amendment process of the Treaty of Rome allowed a veto by a dissenting state, which negotiating a new treaty avoided.

The British were approaching a period of historic choice if the third scenario was realized. The problems of their hesitations would become increasingly apparent. Now they would either have to place themselves fully with the ambitious states, or resign themselves to a period of continuing and possibly accelerating decline in a semi-detached relationship with Europe. It remained to be seen what the response of New Labour in Britain to this would be. For all the optimism of the early period of New Labour there was a gradual sinking into an apparent Euro-pessimism. It was not until late November 2000 that the first signs of a more proactive pro-European policy began to emerge. Prime Minister Blair vigorously attacked the anti-Europeans for their dishonesty and publicly rebuked Mrs Thatcher for her insular mentality. He seemed to have decided that the anti-Europeans now had to be tackled head on. The alternative was marginalization and decline.

What of the future of the European Union in the Atlantic and global context? This has to be a matter of judgement. The two major variables in the equation were the future of the US economy and of the euro. On both those counts there were some grounds for Euro-optimism. The rules of business cycles suggested that the growth in the US economy would slow down sooner rather than later. In 2000 there had been indications of increasing difficulties with the US stock market, and this was happening particularly in the so-called high-tech stocks, though by 2002 there were some signs of American recovery. At the same time the US negative balance of trade was becoming a greater problem. The relatively greater propensity of the US public to invest in the stock market, as compared with Europe,[23] would suggest that this would lead to a falling away of consumer demand and a move into recession. For the European Union, however, the position was on balance more positive. The question was whether sufficient adjustments in the structure of the European economy had been made to support a period of economic take-off, but there was an increasing determination to tackle these problems.

The Europeans were continuing to increase the proportion of trade between themselves. Trade with the rest of the world had declined steadily since the 1960s: they were becoming more interdependent with each other and less dependent on external markets for economic growth.[24] At the same time the arrangements for managing the euro were steadily improving, and in any case there were advantages as well as costs in the decline in its value.[25] The jury was still out among economists about how far the euro could fall before it became a problem for Europe. The case pressed by the IMF and the US authorities was that it was a problem for the international system – this did not mean a balance of short-term costs for the Union. Europe was becoming less vulnerable, though not insensitive, to turbulence in the international monetary and trading systems. The one exception to this was the supply of oil.

Somewhat surprisingly therefore the social democratic states of Europe could find that the cards they held became stronger in the future and that their apparent vulnerability in the very early twenty-first century was a product of short-term adverse factors, rather than any underlying problem with the way they dealt with the global economy. This did not mean, however, that they need not proactively pursue policies conducive to the development of a form of social democracy that was indeed capital-friendly. They had to resist efforts and trends which diluted the core of the Union, both because, if they failed, they could be obliterated by the social and economic forces of neoliberalism, and because of the need to strengthen their institutional and policy coherence. In particular they needed to develop a capacity to resist the aggressive stance which often characterized American policy.[26]

American aggression and insouciance about the rest of the world was most likely to be countered by a swing of the economic and political pendulum towards Europe. This would bring two major advantages. It would protect social democracy in Europe – a key value in itself – and it would make the Americans more likely to contemplate stronger multilateral arrangements in building stronger monetary and trading global structures. But on the other hand if the new Republican regime in the US became more quaintly isolationist it was important that Europe should be capable of taking charge of its own destiny.

However, it was necessary to find appropriate compromises with the need for economic efficiency and the need to protect a civilized society. Trade was not for its own sake – it was for people. The situation in Europe suggested, however, that globalization was not an unstoppable force, incapable of halt or modification. It could solicit a counter-response in the form of an adaptation to regional circumstances, when governments objected to the challenges to national characteristics which they wished to defend. Regional arrangements could be a mediator of globalizing forces and a defender of their members' interests and inclinations. Chapter 7 takes this argument further.

CHAPTER 4

The Social and Economic Agenda of International Organization in the Age of Globalization[1]

Introduction

In the 1990s the United Nations went through a bewildering succession of phases of hope and disappointment. Intimations of a new world order in the aftermath of the Gulf War in 1991 quickly gave way to despondency with what were seen as failures in Somalia, other parts of Africa, and ex-Yugoslavia.[2] On the economic and social side the main contributor states were giving less and less – mostly well below the 0.7 per cent of Gross Domestic Product (GDP) promised as part of the UN's Development Decades' agenda – and there was a crippling financial crisis in the regular Assessed Budget, and in the budget for peacekeeping operations.[3] But, paradoxically, changes proposed for the machinery of the United Nations during this same period, and into the twenty-first century, seemed promising.

This chapter discusses these with reference to the *mechanisms* for developing what could be called the global agenda and applying it to the economic and social work of the UN system; it does not deal with the impact of that system in the field.

In the main discussion the argument in favour of linking globalization with regionalization is not made explicit. This comes in the concluding section. The point made is essentially that, as the mechanisms for defining the elements of a global agenda in social and economic matters improve, and it becomes more widely accepted, so the case for regionalization is necessarily strengthened.[4] This is because the stress is placed on practical, technical and specific achievements, though they may have important consequences, and therefore, if they are that important, they must be given priority over national autonomy. The question must always be asked of the extent of the territory in which such goals can be best achieved. This follows from the argument that goals are indeed increasingly being globalized and that there is a link between them and local integrated programmes. Demonstrating this has to come first.

The point is reinforced by the fact that development requires integrated programmes. The need is for an extent of territory in which a set of interrelated goals can be best achieved. That immediately invites the consideration of spaces for some of these programmes which extend beyond the territory of individual states, and includes groups of contiguous states. There is no other way in which integrated programmes, derived from global agendas can be achieved. In the next chapter a different kind of case for the regional approach to development, which reinforces that in this chapter, is considered. That is derived from the response to the neoliberal agenda.

The evolving agenda

What was often referred to as the United Nations Organization had, in reality, always been a stubbornly polycentric system. Historically there had been no organization or agent within it which was capable of defining a coherent overall agenda or coordinating and managing the wide range of economic and social activities which were carried out beneath its umbrella. The Specialized Agencies, such as the Food and Agriculture Organization or the International Labour Office, were constitutionally independent of each other, and from the centre, and were obliged only to report to the Economic and Social Council, as laid down in Article 64 of the UN Charter. There was no central institution with legal authority over them. The *Administrative Committee for Coordination* (ACC) which was intended to function as the main coordinating mechanism had generally failed, as its members, the Agency heads, used it to defend their territories rather than agree its management. It was said that in practice: 'There exists no means of harmonising the thinking of executive heads and the senior staff of organs concerned with central policy issues, such as UNCTAD, UNIDO, UNDP, and directing it towards problems facing the international community and towards possible initiatives that the UN might usefully take.'[5]

The Economic and Social Council of the UN (ECOSOC) was intended to manage the system but it failed to live up to the expectations of its founders. In particular it failed, despite various institutional reforms, such as the setting up and subsequent reinforcement of its *Committee on Programme Coordination* in 1969, to coordinate the activities of the Specialized Agencies, because it could not direct them, or require them to carry out their operations in concert with each other. The General Assembly, too, lacked the authority to instruct the Agencies and, though it could give advice and address recommendations to them, it lacked the means of effectively monitoring their performance. It had no way of checking the relationship between the Agencies' budgets and their programmes: it was said that the General Assembly checked budgets in a vacuum. Its main watchdogs over the Agencies, the *Advisory Committee on Administrative and Budgetary Questions* (ACABQ), and the *Joint Inspection Unit* (JIU), though capable of providing good, hard-hitting reports, were essentially advisory and for much of their life were weak players. They did become more important with the reform of the budgetary mechanisms of the late 1980s, and by the early twenty-first century were important enough for the Chairman of the US Foreign Relations Committee, Jesse Helms, to demand permament US membership of the ACABQ!

Another route to effective management and policy coordination was sought when in 1977 it was recommended that a new Director-General for Development and International Economic Cooperation (DGDIEC) should be appointed, within the Secretariat, to ensure 'the coherence, coordination and efficient management of all activities in the economic and social fields' (General Assembly, A32/197, 127, para 64). The post was established but proved to be largely ineffectual, and it was eventually absorbed in the major reorganization made by Secretary-General Boutros-Ghali early in 1991. The DGDIEC found it difficult to exercise his coordinating function with regard to the Agencies, which in practice refused to recognize his authority. That he was not an elected officer, but was appointed by the Secretary-General, placed him below the Agency heads in the pecking order. This partly explained their refusal to accept the Director-General as Chairman of the ACC in the absence of the Secretary-General himself, as had been envisaged.

This experience was to a great extent repeated in that of the post of Under-Secretary which was created in 1992 to coordinate humanitarian assistance through the *Department of Humanitarian Affairs* (DHA). The first head of DHA Jan Eliason was suspected of wishing to impose a common framework of cooperation, but this role was disputed by other organizations. There was resistance in the United Nations High Commission for Refugees (UNHCR) and the World Food Programme (WFP) to allowing the DHA head to take primary responsibility in crises such as that in Angola.

Jan Eliason seemed himself to be uncertain about how far the DHA should develop its own strong coordinating, as opposed to facilitating, role, but he strongly opposed the idea that one of the other organizations, such as UNHCR, should be the lead organization, because that would pre-empt a stronger role for the DHA. What was left for the DHA was the more modest role of encouraging coordination by providing high-quality information and analysis, and a reasoned set of proposals for the differentiation of responsibilities, and this role was accepted by Eliason's successor Akashi. By 1997, however, the challenge to DHA had succeeded to the extent that it was proposed by Secretary-General Kofi Annan[6] that its operational responsibilities be transferred to other appropriate entities and that yet another attempt to 'intensify' inter-agency coordination should be made through a steering committee. What was left was taken over by a new Emergency Relief Coordinator and DHA was abolished.

There were some characteristic bureaucratic pathologies which accounted for the failure of these various efforts at coherent agenda creation and coordination. There was an inherent tendency within the UN towards *duplication*, which was reflected in the existence within the system of a number of entities, such as ECOSOC, and the ACC, which claimed to act as system managers and coordinators. Relatedly, there was what might be described as a *reservation of roles*, a tendency to resist the concentration in the system of key functions, and there remained unresolved claims and counterclaims about where such functions should be performed. So, for example, the Administrative Committee for Coordination generally took an unhelpful attitude towards strengthening central control, reflected in its unenthusiastic view of joint planning. There were numerous reports of squabbling between the ACC and another GA management committee, the Committee on Programme Coordination (CPC) – reported as a sort of 'dialogue of the deaf' by Bertrand,[7] because neither had been willing to concede status to the other – and of only half-hearted attempts at improving matters.

The duplication and reservation of roles resulted in *fragmentation*, and they were, of course, a reflection both of the play of 'normal' bureaucratic politics – bureaucratic 'turf wars' – and also of the failure of the member states of the UN to counter the 'anti-rational' tendencies which inhered in its bureaucracy. The governments had themselves been divided, so – for example – UNCTAD survived and competed with ECOSOC, the former favoured by developing states and the latter by the developed. By the late 1990s the former had emerged in a relatively favourable light, but there remained continuing doubts about its future among the main developed states. The interplay of bureaucratic politics and intergovernmental disagreement also explained the apparent increase in another form of duplication – the repetition of discussions about the same issues at various levels in the same institution, and in different institutions. Agendas remained disjointed and overlapping. ECOSOC too often covered the ground already traversed in its own committees, and the General Assembly repeated the debates already conducted in main committees. A US government official complained, acidly: 'Should we accept the continuation and repetition of the experience of the last eight months, for example, during which the issues discussed at UNCTAD Six were reopened and repeated on at least three occasions?'[8] Such duplication arose because of the mistrust of governments towards each other: rationalization and specialization were seen as increasing the risk that a key function in the system would be 'captured' by a state or group of states of the 'wrong' persuasion.

The range of difficulties in the system were symptoms of the barriers in the way of change, and to improved effectiveness through better coordination, which were found in the interplay between bureaucratic politics and the interests of states. The constraints were reinforced by fierce disagreements between governments on some matters, which led them actively to oppose change except on their own terms, and by hostility on the part of a majority of international officials to anything which might weaken their particular organization or their role within it. These difficulties were an aspect of the multicentred character of the system.[9]

Approaches to reform

An important part of the background to the following discussion was inevitably that a number of changes had taken place in the context of reform over the previous decade or so which reinforced determination to get something done. There had been a number of Global Conferences called to discuss the pressing problems of the age: most recently environmental questions in Rio de Janeiro (1992), human rights in Vienna (1993), women's questions in Beijing (1995) and population questions in Cairo (1994). Follow-up conferences were planned for the early years of the twenty-first century ten years after the last. These conferences had each spawned a Commission – discussed later – to carry forward the programme agreed at the conference itself. Such conferences represented a growing sense of the interdependence of the globe and the globalization of its problems and human concerns, and stimulated a renewed interest in translating such concerns – called by some a collective intentionality[10] – into more specific and more manageable programmes.

Were the reforms likely to be successful in doing this? This is the question which is discussed in what follows. But there was also a more realist consideration, namely that the shortage of funds, which resulted from the increasing parsimony of states, especially reflected in the reluctance of the US to pay its dues, itself placed the barons of the big agencies under a lot of pressure to undertake reforms and to get their acts together in a way which had not been true earlier. The ending of the Cold War also created an attention space previously occupied by the threat of nuclear war between the superpowers. The economic and social work of the United Nations system had always been important but it now moved up the agenda, especially as the increasing number of failing states threatened new kinds of international disorder.

Although work on the improvement of the machinery was given a new impetus in the 1990s, the European Union states remained of the view in October 1996 that 'many UN Programmes and operations in the field were too often undermined by lack of adequate coordination, overlapping responsibilities and fragmentation of activities' (European Union Presidency letter to the Secretary-General, Permanent Mission of Ireland to the United Nations, 16 October 1996, para 12). One of the reasons for the new energy behind the reform process, however, was the emergence of the EU as a force prepared to push this agenda. It had been agreed in the Maastricht Treaty that the states would act together in the economic and social areas in the United Nations: these were areas where the EU had competence which until the early 1990s, and the agreement at Maastricht, it had lacked.

There were three conceivable approaches to the reform of the economic and social arrangements of the UN system. One was to adopt a more supranational or managerial approach, by appointing a central manager such as the Director-General for Development and

International Economic Cooperation (DGDIEC), as had been proposed by A/32/197 in the late 1970s. This was not a promising route.[11] It had proved impossible to give such a manager the authority required to supervise the Agencies, and any efforts to introduce major changes into the Charter, in order to redistribute powers in favour of that officer, or a central organization like the General Assembly or ECOSOC, risked being protracted and bruising. The system's multicentred character had to be one of the givens of the situation.

A second proposal was that the UN system's operations should be considerably scaled down – turned into research institutes with no operational capacity.[12] The money which went to them should then be transferred to the World Bank, which had a reputation for being more efficient, and, happily for those who held this view, had been more generally disposed to favour right-wing economic principles. In the following chapter some alteration in this position is discussed. The problem with this approach was that it was not likely to appeal to the developing states themselves, which generally suspected the Bretton Woods institutions, regarding them as being in the pockets of the developed states. Too often the IMF policies of austerity and low government spending had led directly to serious political unrest. And the World Bank, until the late 1990s, had been firmly linked to the neoliberal policy agenda.

It was highly unlikely that agreement about such radical changes would be found among the various constituencies of states. Another cost was that it involved scaling down the presence of the UN actors in the developing states, which could reduce the attention given by outsiders to their internal problems. Indeed such a system would make it easier for funds to be syphoned off by beneficiary governments for illegitimate purposes.

The third way was that identified and supported in this essay: *entrenched multilateralism*. This would involve the strengthening of system norms within the existing structures, so that they were more likely to impose upon the participating actors. The relationship between the existing actors was to be altered within the present system so that the weight of the injunctions on their behaviour to conform with system rules was strengthened. This essay is largely about identifying how the changes proposed in the 1990s could lead to this quiet revolution.

The meaning of 'entrenched multilateralism' is given in the interlinked ideas of *regime theory*, and of *global governance*. The first of these postulates that there is a hierarchy of 'injunctions on behaviour, of greater or lesser specificity',[13] ranging from 'principles' and 'norms', which are less specific, through to 'formal institutions', which embody precisely defined decision-making procedures. 'Rules' come somewhere in between, but they are of particular importance because they are the point in the hierarchy at which general impulses are translated into explicit constraints on behaviour. They are the specific instruments for realizing common purposes in a society of legal individuals – persons or institutions – and can be applied without further interpretation or enactment. Principles and norms lack this specificity. Global governance involves 'sets of rules that guide the behaviour of participants engaged in identifiable social practices',[14] and can be distinguished from 'government' which requires formal institutions capable of authoritative allocation of values. 'Governance', then, as a form of rule-dominated, ordered society is appropriate to a multicentric system, such as the UN system of states and organizations in which 'government' is of necessity excluded. Rules, however, may be generated through multilateral diplomacy even in the absence of government. They require adhesion by governments to a set of specific injunctions on behaviour which require no further interpretation, which need no further enactment by courts or by other authorities. So 'entrenched multilateralism' arises when multilateral diplomacy is effective in generating rules.

Rules may be developed as a result of particular contingencies which arise in the process of multilateral diplomacy, including fixing the agenda, building supportive interests and empowering them, establishing epistemic communities,[15] or, generally, the creation of circumstances during negotiation in which participants perceive that to opt out is more costly than to opt in. They generate a powerful, self-fulfilling prophecy, such as that which frightened Eurosceptics in the British government with regard to monetary union in the EU in the mid to late 1990s. When multilateral diplomacy takes place in circumstances like these it becomes 'entrenched' in the sense used in this chapter. Negotiation has its own dynamic and tends to create commitments which give rise to a sort of self-fulfilling prophecy, especially when there is a rule of consensus, as applied in the EU and in decisions on UN reform issues.

The argument is illustrated in the history of the British response to the proposal for monetary union. Even though the official position was that Britain retained the right to choose not to join, the British government insisted on participating in the negotiations about the arrangements for the proposed new single currency, and therefore (wittingly, or not) loaded the dice in favour of joining and of accepting the rules of monetary union. British diplomats sought to shape the arrangements to suit British interests, and financial institutions in the country inevitably made changes which they thought would be appropriate to membership, if that were to happen. Adjustments were made in matching technical arrangements within the member states, including Britain, in anticipation of a cooperative outcome. During negotiations there was a tendency for the advantages of participation to be upgraded at each further negotiating step, rather than downgraded: regardless of the objective calculation of costs and benefits, the latter all the time tended to become more evident. So though it was predicated upon the assumption of the right to opt out, multilateral diplomacy in fact shaped circumstances so that all were pushed towards opting in! The form of multilateralism became entrenched because the actors, though retaining the option of non-compliance, became subject to injunctions on behaviour that amounted to rules of the system.

The question which is examined in this chapter, discussed directly in the final section, is that of how far the diplomacy which has been going on over the reform of the economic and social arrangements of the UN system resembled this two-stage process: a first stage of decisions to be in the negotiations because of the pattern of interests concerned (as when the British government decided that the national interest dictated that it had to be involved in negotiations over European Monetary Union, even though it was uncommitted to the goal), and a second of progressively entrenching multilateralism as a consequence of the negotiation process itself so that the specific goal was accepted.

The reform process in the economic and social arrangements of the United Nations

In the 1990s the attempt to reform the UN's economic and social arrangements concentrated at two levels: first, those at the general or headquarters level, especially as regards the role of the Economic and Social Council (ECOSOC); and, second, those concerned with operations in the field within the developing countries. In both cases the reforms were included in a series of key resolutions approved by the General Assembly between 1992 and 1996, namely A/47/199, A/48/162, A/50/120 and A/50/227. The origins of the new phase of reform may be traced further back to the Secretary-General's report on economic and social matters in 1990 (A/45/714), which followed the failure of the Special Commission in 1987 and 1988.[16]

Country level

A key feature of the reforms at the field level was the adoption of Country Strategy Notes.[17] These were statements about the development process tailored to the specific needs of individual countries, which were evolved on the basis of discussions between the Agencies, Funds and Programmes, donors and the host country. They were described in 1996 as a *tour de table* of the plans of the various involved institutions and governments,[18] but had the potential for development into something closer to indicative planning. The UNDP played a key role in instigating the process of formulating such a Note. They were identified as being the property of the host country, and had the obvious merit of setting out targets, roles and priorities.

The role of the UNDP Resident Coordinator as the responsible officer at the country level was also to be reinforced, with greater care to be taken about the selection of officers, and providing any necessary training for them. This was another feature of the reform process: increased concern with professionalizing the way in which services were provided in this area, as in the area of humanitarian crisis responses, and the management of peacekeeping. The pace of change with regard to such reforms had accelerated remarkably quickly since the end of the Cold War in 1989. In the 1990s major steps away from the earnest amateurism of the earlier generation had been taken. There was an increasing professionalization of international organizational service providers which involved the agreeing and monitoring of standards of performance. In this the continuing complaints of NGOs about poor IGO performance in the field had often been a powerful stimulus for reform.[19]

It was recognized that UNDP officers in the past had often not been good performers: they did not have a very favourable press either within or outside the system. The conclusion was that at field level it was necessary for there to be a central coordinating figure and the route of putting right deficiencies in the existing system was chosen (A/47/199 paras 36–8). But the actors were now subject to a wider range of pressures to conform with system norms than earlier: the UNDP Resident would not now be faced with horses which were freely running in all directions, but rather a posse which was more disposed to hunt as one. For instance field-level Agency and Fund Officers were to be given enhanced authority, so that decisions could be taken at that level about the redeployment of Funds within a programme without reference to headquarters (A/47/199, especially para 25); a further attempt to introduce common information-sharing and communication facilities was to be made; the activities of the various involved UN organizations were to be located in single premises, which would bring officers from different UN organizations together on a daily basis and facilitate improvements in inter-Agency communication: the development of inter-Agency collegiality was to be encouraged (see below). The money saved by this would be redirected to the development process. It was also stipulated that the approach was to be an integrated Programmes approach, rather than an approach through distinct projects organized by the various agencies often in blissful ignorance of each other's presence in the same country. Technical improvements, such as changes in information technology, made it more likely that 'stand alone' projects would in the future not be the norm (see below).

There was also a decision to measure achievement through impact and sustainability rather than through the level of inputs of resources, technology or personnel. The Advisory Committee on Coordination (ACC) also cooperated with the Secretariat in setting up a number of Task Forces to promote more effective inter-Agency coordination at the country level. Task force members were chosen from the Agencies concerned with the programme selected, of which four had been identified by 1996. The ACC was pushed away from its traditional reluctance to get close to ECOSOC, the Secretariat or to the major coordination committees of the Assembly such as the CPC. Furthermore the states were to allocate funds to these Task Forces in response to approved plans and Programmes, which was itself an incentive to accept the need to fit into the system at the country level.

Because of these changes it looked as though by the mid-1990s the task of the UNDP Resident Coordinator of promoting enhanced coordination between participating actors in countries had been made much easier than it had been earlier. This was combined with better selection procedures and training for the officers themselves. Certainly their reputation was higher than in the past. There were numerous illustrations of the results of this: the UNDP Resident in Palestine had become a major channel for funding into the area, and the UNDP Capital Development Fund had been used by the World Bank as the pilot for larger-scale investment; in Ghana a UNDP-administered $50,000 project in local development had led to a well-reported large-scale tourism development programme. It was agreed, however, that UNDP needed to be involved operationally only to the extent necessary to get larger programmes off the ground. Some thought this should be the model for the rest of the UN system!

Headquarters level

Nevertheless this was only a part of the story. Supporting changes were also required at the general or headquarters level if the role at the country level was to be effective. At the global level attempts were focused upon the reorganization and rationalization of the work of the Economic and Social Council (A/50/227, section IV). The Council was to hold a single substantive session each year alternately in New York and Geneva. It was to be divided into four primary segments, or parts of the overall meeting – called General, High-level, Coordination and Operational which were to meet over a period of 4–5 weeks (A/45/264). A Humanitarian segment was added later. The High-level segment of four days was to discuss general questions of policy and it was expected that the shorter sessions would facilitate attendance by more senior government representatives, and Agency heads, who would have authority to commit their governments and institutions to action in the chosen areas. The conclusions were in the form of 'Agreed conclusions' and resulted from discussions at the ministerial level. There remained, however, a suspicion that the way topics were chosen for High-level Segment discussion needed further consideration: there was scope for states and agencies to indulge in political manipulation in the preparatory meetings to choose topics which they found less awkward. It was reported that the 1996 segment on Narcotics had been a success. It was also pointed out that the increasing public awareness of global problems, which had been stimulated by the global conferences, made it more difficult for governments to ignore such meetings. The climate of opinion had changed with the climate (see below).

The meetings of the Coordination Segment were to look at cross-sectoral and common themes in the work of so-called functional commissions. These were themes which cut across, or were common in, the sectors of work of global conferences. Each of the global conferences, which had become a routine feature of international society since the 1970s (though with an increasing number in the 1980s and 1990s) – Population in Cairo, Women's interests in Beijing, Human Rights in Vienna, Environment and Development in Rio de Janeiro, etc. – had led to the setting up of a new, or the upgrading of an existing, functional Commission.[20] In July 1996 there were nine such Commissions, the members of which were chosen by the plenary meeting of ECOSOC to represent the various self-identified groupings of states. There were usually 53 members of the Commissions.

The Coordination Segment based its efforts on the *multi-annual programmes of work* of the functional commissions which in turn derived from the agreed conclusions of the global conferences: themes were identified and related to specific proposals for action. The work of the Commissions also helped to identify issues to be considered at the review conferences which were to be held in relation to each of the major global conferences, usually five years after the first meeting. A series of Working Groups was also set up to pursue more coordinated strategies in specific areas of work, such as the Aids Programme. In 1996 attention was focused upon the further rationalization of the relationship between the General Assembly, the functional commissions and ECOSOC. It was agreed that the functional commissions should concentrate upon their particular specialized sectors of activity, but that attention should be given to eliminating any overlap or duplication in their areas of concern. The General Assembly was 'to consider and establish the broad policy framework, the Council was to integrate the work of its functional commissions, to provide guidance to the UN system on coordination issues, and to support the General Assembly in its policy role'.[21] How was the Council to realize this laudable, if vague, ambition?

The question of whether the Commissions had adopted agreed Programmes of work was important in promoting the rationalization of ECOSOC's role. It was realized that the Council could carry out its functions with regard to the Commissions much more effectively if it was able to relate their agreed programmes to each other in advance and identify cross-cutting or common themes. A document produced in July 1996 identified such items and suggested programmes on that basis for the ECOSOC coordination segment meetings over the next five years.[22] The Council's role was most definitely not to duplicate the work of the Commissions, though it had a duty to oversee their operations, and eliminate duplication and waste.

Rather its role was to identify issues which arose in the relationships between their areas of work. Thus Commissions should adopt programmes of work for the next four or five years to follow up the conclusions of UN Conferences, though Human Rights, which hitherto had its own agenda, was an exception: this was the basis on which the ECOSOC could generate proposals which reflected cross-sector concerns, as it allowed proper preparation of studies and documents in advance, as well as ensuring the relevance of the work of ECOSOC to the work of the Commissions. It was reported that the work of this segment in 1996 has been marred by inadequate document preparation. In July 1996 four of the Commissions had a programme of work agreed through until the year 2000.[23] These were the Commission on Sustainable Development, the Commission on the Status of Women, the Commission on Population and Development and the Commission for Social Development. The Commissions on Human Rights, Statistics, Crime Prevention and Criminal Justice, and Narcotic Drugs had not produced such an agreed Programme of work (E/1996/CRP.4), and it was proposed that they should now do so.

Various decisions were taken about the relationship between the segments and other institutions linked with the ECOSOC. The role of the substantive meeting was enhanced at the expense of the subordinate committees, which were subsumed in the plenary as of 1994 (Clause 17 48/162) and the relationship between ECOSOC and the General Assembly was made more specific. There were strict injunctions about not repeating discussions in the various forums, about the need for the plenary meetings to reach firm conclusions, and about avoiding overlapping mandates. In Clause 2.12 2 (A/48/162) 'agreed conclusions containing specific recommendations to various parts of the UN system for their implementation ... were to be agreed' in the High-level segment which had quasi-legal status. The Secretary-General was to inform the Council of steps taken to implement recommendations: the language here was much closer to an assertion of the authority of ECOSOC than had been usual hitherto, which was itself a remarkable development.

This picture was reinforced by the requirement 2.15 (A/48/162) that the operational segment was to ensure that General Assembly policies 'were appropriately implemented on a system-wide basis' and the outcomes of this segment were to be 'reflected in the adoption of *decisions and resolutions* [author's italics]'. This was further reinforced with the injunction in A/50/227, para 37, that 'The Council should fully implement its authority to take final decisions on the activities of its subsidiary bodies and on other matters relating to its system-wide coordination and overall guidance functions in the economic, social and related fields, as appropriate'; and by para 44, which asserted that 'Resolutions, *decisions and agreed conclusions* [my italics] should be implemented and followed up fully by all relevant parts of the United Nations System.' This may be compared with the very modest powers attributed to the General Assembly and ECOSOC in the Charter – they were only asked to issue recommendations and receive reports, which in practice were usually uninformative and banal. Inter-Agency working groups were set up in the Operational Segment to pursue more coordinated programmes in their allotted sectors. The Operational Segment was also to monitor the division of labour between the Funds and Programmes and make recommendations on this as required to the General Assembly.

The theme of ECOSOC's greater assertiveness was also reflected in a new way of agreeing the respective agendas of ECOSOC and the General Assembly, which was so devised that the Assembly would not repeat work done by ECOSOC, and the executive responsibility of ECOSOC in a framework of overall General Assembly policy supervision would be respected. Annexe 2 of 48/162 established a procedure for agreeing a draft programme of work of the General Assembly's Second Committee with the assistance of the bureau of the Council and, once agreed, this '*should be changed only in extreme circumstances* [my italics]'. This effort to rationalize the agendas of the General Assembly's Committees in relation to the ECOSOC was taken further when it was agreed in paras 21–4 and Annex 11 of A/50/227 that the agendas of the Second and Third Committees of the General Assembly should have 'greater coherence and complementarity', a goal supported by the agreement that issues of a procedural nature should be taken by *decision* rather than resolution. This was evidence of an attempt to achieve a more rational and effective relationship between ECOSOC, the Assembly and its committees. ECOSOC had significantly increased it power over the agendas of the Second and indirectly of the Third Committees of the Assembly. The language used in 48/162 and 50/127 was altogether more positive and authoritative than that in earlier resolutions, and, indeed, in the Charter. ECOSOC's leading role in the coordination of the system was asserted and it was correspondingly more assertive. There was evidence by the autumn of 1996 of a rapid increase in the number of conclusions in the form of *decisions* taken by ECOSOC which were more often linked with more concrete proposals. An official reported that the change in this direction had begun in 1994.

The European Union and the United States also pressed for adjustments in the divisions of the Secretariat concerned with economic and social work. These were proposed by the G7 meeting at the Lyons summit in June 1996. They proposed the merger of the three existing divisions, Sustainable Development, Economic and Social Information and Analysis, and Development Support and Management Services. They also argued for placing this work in the charge of a new Under-Secretary-General who would act as Executive Secretary of ECOSOC, and thus strengthen the Council's policy formulation and coordination role. The new officer would also pursue the reform process in collaboration with the heads of Agencies, reducing overlap in mandates, abolishing redundant organizations and generally enhancing effectiveness and efficiency. The outcome was the appointment of a new Deputy-Secretary in 1998 (see below). The appointment would also 'advance the rationalization of UN economic analysis and reporting and maintain a clear oversight in respect of UN funds, Programmes and Agencies while respecting autonomies and competencies' (EU Presidency letter, *op. cit.*, p. 5). The European Union also backed the proposal made in 50/227 of 1 July 1996 to review the 'mandates, composition, functions and working methods of the Functional Commissions and expert groups and bodies with a view to ensuring more effective and coordinated discussions and outcomes of their work'.

The Boards of the Funds and Programmes were also reformed so that their effectiveness with regard to day-to-day management was enhanced. According to 3.21 A/48/162 they were to be transformed into Executive Boards, under the authority of the Council. They were to meet more often for shorter periods, to be more professionally staffed with individuals selected for their managerial and technical skills rather than politicians, and were to be smaller. They were turned into boards of management in a practical sense, rather than being remote committees of semidetached figures, and were required to 'take into account the need for the effective conduct of the work of each Board'. At the same time it was made easier for ECOSOC to evaluate the relationship between them and to approve specific country's programmes under their aegis. They were made more directly subject to the ECOSOC, to which they were accountable, and by which they could be instructed.

Taking the reforms forward in the Funds and Programmes: the Track II process from the late 1990s

In 1997 these reforms were taken forward when the big four Funds and Programmes, UNICEF, UNDP, UNFPA and WFP were joined together to set up a joint UN Development Group (UNDG), made up of the representatives of the four and a small number of other officers, 15 in all, to produce the so-called United Nations Development Assistance Frameworks (UNDAFs). These developments followed from the new Secretary-General's *Report* of July 1997, in which he promised to seek further savings by a further thinning of the UN's administration – by losing up to a thousand jobs – and to use the money saved for development purposes. The General Assembly approved implementing legislation in September 1997 in A/52/12 a and b. The package became known as the Track II process, though the exact meaning of this term – what in specific terms it included and excluded – was hard to determine. Future reforms and increased system-wide coordination were to be considered by the office of a new Deputy-Secretary-General, Louise Frechette, and a new Strategic Planning section was to advise Frechette and the Secretary-General on specific proposals to improve institutions and programmes. The reforms were in essence a parallel route to the ways of working located above in ECOSOC and could replace or supplement them in the future.

They were to be followed by an ambitious programme of further reform in the organization proposed by the Secretary-General for the approval of member governments in future Assembly resolutions. This package included proposals for a Millennium Assembly to consider other aspects of development: a people's assembly for NGOs; a ministerial commission to consider the constitutions of the Specialized Agencies with a view to making them more system sensitive; and the Secretary-General proposed to convert the Trusteeship Council into a Global Commons Council. He also envisaged a revolving credit fund to cover the UN's short-term debts. The dominant sentiment in the UN in the late 1990s was that this ambitious range of proposals was unlikely to attract enough support from UN members.

The one exception was the development process work of the Funds and Programmes about which the judgement was generally favourable, and where extensive changes could be made by the Secretary-General under his own authority as these were formally extensions of the Secretariat. The new process was driven by the energetic head of UNDP, Gus Speth, who had been imaginative enough to allow the other organizations on to the turf previously commanded exclusively by UNDP. For instance, the Resident Coordinators in developing countries, previously exclusively from UNDP, could now be from one of the other partner organizations – in 1998 UNICEF officers had become Resident Coordinators in five countries. And the offices of the Funds and Programmes were now to be brought together in the target countries in what became known as UN Houses. Sixty or so had been set up by March 1998. This was an old idea, which, as already argued, had important implications for promoting savings and better, more coordinated management.

Under Speth the UNDP remained in charge of the grand strategy and determined the allocation of posts in the joint arrangements – it retained what was called a godfather role – and UNDP chaired the UNDG, and the Executive Committee. But the concessions made to the other Funds and Programmes to achieve greater efficiency obviously ran the risk of a declining UNDP role in the future.

The principal members of the new partnership were all within the jurisdiction of the United Nations central system and the new arrangements were a carrying forward of the proposals made in A/48/162 to reform the executive boards of this group of organizations. The idea was that the work of the Funds and Programmes would be more tightly integrated through the UNDG and that indeed their executive committees would hold frequent joint meetings; this happened for the first time in January 1998. The changes stopped short of fusing them into a single entity, a course favoured by the members of the European Union and the Nordic countries. A joint secretariat was, however, set up with secondees from the participating organizations, a remarkable development in view of the earlier resistance to even modest integration. It was reckoned that working together on joint plans in this secretariat, and in the UN Houses in the beneficiary countries, would help to develop agreement between the partner organizations. They could command the development strategy of the United Nations through the UNDG, and create a common evaluation of what the system could provide in relation to the target countries.

One view was that the resulting Country Plans, the UNDAFS, amounted to a supply-side view of development, whereas the Country Strategy Notes represented the demand side. In March 1998 such frameworks had been agreed for eleven countries and the goal was to produce plans for all developing countries. The target states were then invited to accept the plans, not on a take it or leave it basis, but obviously in a context of pressure. The new plans were more specific with regard to policies and finance than the country strategy notes: they were a further step towards more specific planning within the overarching framework of the Country Strategy Notes.

As with the ECOSOC coordination/operational segments the new plans also drew on the work of the Global Conferences through the functional commissions, and aimed at agreeing cross-sector programmes in consultation with field-level officials who worked in such mechanisms as the Agency task forces. The analysis applied above to the ECOSOC arrangements was also relevant to the UNDG/UNDAF system. The latter was also likely to be considered by the operational and coordination segments of ECOSOC and through this to help shape future Country Strategy Notes. Channels were likely to open up in this way which would reinforce the influence of the UNDG/UNDAF process on the Agencies and the member states. But very few Agencies had agreed to join by the time of writing, March 1998. At that date the cohort of the latter was limited to UNIDO, though there was pressure on the other agencies from the Secretary-General and others to join. In late March 1998 a meeting of the Agencies' main coordination committee, the ACC, was to discuss their involvement and it was hoped that there would be a move in that direction. The hope was that this would contribute to the development of a collective sense of best development practice, drawing upon the Global Conference agendas and the related cross-sector programmes, which would become system-wide to include Funds and Programmes, Agencies, donors and beneficiaries. One official argued that the way in which a collective view about population policy had emerged was the model: 'tremendous things are happening'.

The new development frameworks also reflected the new policy of linking development with a wider agenda of creating an enabling environment within which private investment in the developing countries would be encouraged. Like an increasing range of international organizational arrangements in the late 1990s, especially in the UN system and the EU, the new development plans included proposals for creating supporting infrastructures in the economic, social and political contexts. The range of these was wide and startlingly frank in its commitment to liberal pluralist arrangements: it encompassed the elements of a well-founded civil society and democratization as well as such changes as improved credit and insurance arrangements. The significance of this should not be underestimated: for the first time in the history of the United Nations the organization was directly addressing core structures in the state and some argued that even in the difficult continent – Africa – illiberal practices were increasingly delegitimized. The head of UNDP stated that 40 per cent of the resources of his organization now went on governance-improving activities, which was a remarkable alteration in stress. UNICEF's strategy had also been reconsecrated: the new approach was to be 'rights based', meaning that it was to be derived from the Rights of the Child Convention. In the late 1990s another wind of change seemed to be blowing in the UN system: there was increasing perception of the need to give priority to a *strategy* of change in many areas – including human rights and development – rather than a policy of dealing with immediate pressing problems in ways which put the chances of long-term improvement at risk.

For two years or so the donor countries had indicated their preparedness to work within the new framework in the OECD's Development Assistance Committee (DAC). The World Bank, a primary channel of influence for the donor countries, was also willing to link its own development planning process with that of the DAFs. The World Bank and the UNDG had worked together in developing the assistance strategy for Mali and Vietnam and the practice was likely to be repeated elsewhere. But predictably there was some uncertainty in the attitudes of both the target countries and of multilateral companies. The former went along with the new approach reluctantly, seeing it as the only realistic option in the post-Cold War period. The latter were reluctant to see multiple conditionality get in the way of their untrammelled freedom to invest, which was implied in such texts as the recently agreed multilateral investment agreement, but were usually reluctant to come out publicly in favour of protecting social and political underdevelopment. The companies also found the shift in the ideology of development congenial: that one of the purposes of multilateral action was to facilitate enhanced private investment.

The UNDAFs were really enabling instruments, pushing democratization and an improved economic infrastructure, but hoping through this to encourage private business to fill the gaps left by the retreat in the 1990s of official overseas development assistance, even of the more well-disposed countries, such as the Scandinavians. In the longer term improvements in the target states could make it more politically acceptable in the richer states to return to higher levels of official bilateral aid, and to achieve the targets indicated in the UN Development Decade agreements. It would also make it more likely that the developing states would be able to help themselves.

In the debate to approve the new course in the General Assembly in December 1997 the G77 had shown much unease. But the new instruments rested on a powerful coalition – the Funds and Programmes acting together with donor country support were hard to resist – and this was enough to convince a number of actors, including the main beneficiaries, that they needed to concur despite considerable initial opposition. The emerging arrangements reflected an increasing preparedness on the part of the developed world to put pressure on those in the developing world to put their house in order. But this fracture led to a much clearer identification of another: it had become evident by the late 1990s that the developing world, often referred to collectively as the G77, was itself divided between the more developed and the least developed. When the former insisted upon the unity of the whole they got in the way of special efforts to help the latter: there could be a beneficial fracturing of the G77 to make it easier for the richer to help the poorest states.

The logic of the changes: relating global intentions to country programmes

By the late 1990s the three overlapping groups of actors in the system were under increasing pressure to increase their internal coordination: the Agencies, Funds and Programmes and states formed the macro-group, which was involved with the Country Strategy Notes; the Funds and Programmes were a subgroup, now more tightly organized and involved with the Development Assistance Frameworks; and in another subgroup the states were now under increased pressure to fit their bilateral efforts into the emerging multilateral plans. Multinational companies faced the same pressures. This section considers the pressures to coordinate in the macro-group, which was the larger concern of ECOSOC, though similar pressures could be identified within the two subgroups.

The structure of the segments of ECOSOC was of the greatest importance with regard to entrenching the informal pressures to increase the level of programme coordination. Within them the heads of Agencies were brought into close consultation with the main donors and beneficiaries about the programmes for action, which were now increasingly derived from agendas agreed by the Global Conferences, and carried forward by the respective Global Commissions. This was the process of agenda globalization.

In the coordination segments the donors, the heads of the Agencies and the ACC, as well as the Secretary-General, the members of the Committee and Programme and Coordination (CPC) and the beneficiaries were present. This meant that decisions about money were now to be taken in the context of decisions about policy. Agencies were made more aware of a need for good performance with regard to collectively approved programmes. And they were also made more clearly subject to inspection and monitoring by the bodies that took the initial decisions about money and policy. Though difficulties remained in the form of the Agencies' inclination to remain as aloof as possible – as was shown in the Secretary-General's Report of 1997 (June 1997) – they were now under much greater pressure to fit into the system if only to maintain budgetary provision. The new arrangements had the effect of making it politically in the interest of the Agencies to become system-orientated. In this way the multilateral system was adapted to enhance actor compliance.

- The essence of the problem was to relate global *intentions*, which made up global agendas defined in global conferences with regard to a particular sector of problems, to *programmes* which were trans- or cross-sectoral, and which were the functional application of the global intentions in the field. Three developments were necessary to achieve this transfer of intentions to programmes.
- First was a reasonably unobstructed transmission belt transferring one to the other through linked organizations.
- Second was a mechanism by which the sectoral intentions could be translated into cross- or trans-sectoral plans.
- Third was a place where the operational agencies could be subjected to pressures which bound them to the intentions, and which also committed them to pursuing the cross- or trans-sectoral plans. The logic of the process judged in these terms, as it had evolved by the late 1990s, was as follows:

1. Since the late 1980s the number of Global Conferences had been greatly increased, and they had been accepted as one of the routine events of international society. The conferences involved massive amounts of preparation, were a focus of heroic effort by non-governmental organizations throughout the world and promoted intense interaction between the members of participating governments. The mandate they produced reflected compromises that were not always satisfactory, but they did add something new to multilateral diplomacy: the identification of a core of agreed values and purposes, which formed the basis of special actions and programmes over a very wide range of human interests and needs. They were a remarkable contribution to the strengthening among diverse groups of human beings of a sense of common destiny, and of a global agenda.
2. The Conferences spawned two further institutions, the functional Commissions, and follow-up conferences, normally taking place five years after the first event. The Commissions were intended to work out the implications of the Conference conclusions and produce specific plans and costs. One of the features of the Conferences in the 1990s compared with those of earlier periods was that their documentation and concluding statements more frequently included specific targets, timings and policy proposals. A major feature of the Population Conferences of 1974 and 1984 was the determination of the developing states to water down and render less precise the initial World Population Plan of Action. This was a less common inclination in the 1990s with conclusions more often pinned to specifics.
3. ECOSOC was now to oversee the work of the Commissions, to inspect and alter their mandates so that efficiency and effectiveness was enhanced, and to identify cross-cutting and overlapping themes. *In this process the Council undertook a key task: to translate plans evolved in particular sectors of activity, which was the nature of the work of the Commissions, into proposals that were relevant to cross-sectoral programmes.* The creation of such programmes was now recognized as an essential feature of effective development, and that there was now an organizational mechanism for establishing them was one of the two key innovations of the reforms.
4. The next major link between intentions and programmes was established in the second key innovation. The ECOSOC clearly had to find better ways of dealing with the Agencies, Funds and

Programmes, if there was to be a more effective translation of intentions into field-level programmes. The innovation (contained in 48/162 and 50/227), was to bring the Heads of the Agencies and relevant officers into work centred in ECOSOC. They were now under greater pressure to commit themselves to the specifics of programme activities, and fit their own plans into a common framework. Mandates were shaped with them in the presence of the representatives of those countries which might be expected to foot the bill. Officers from the countries were also to be brought into the centre where they could observe the behaviour of their executive masters more closely. This was another element in a cluster of pressures upon Agencies to be much more system-orientated than used to be the case. But it was also in their political and financial interest to do so.

5. There was a further set of interactions generating practical responses to broad intentions in the evolving relationship between the central mechanisms and field activities. Task Forces, which were inter-Agency, received a mandate informed by the cross-sector decisions of the Coordination Segment of ECOSOC. At the same time the Country Strategy Notes, and the greatly enhanced position of the UNDP Resident Coordinator on the ground, provided a machinery through which the programme-related cross-sector and common themes could be specified and operationalized. A number of developments reinforced this tendency: the introduction of unified United Nations premises, which, though by no means universal, were now intended to be common, and the parallel reforms in the arrangements of the Funds and Programmes, encouraged the development of more coordinated cross-sector activities. In consequence, as already noted, in 1996 the number of 'stand-alone' projects had been halved compared with 1991 (these were projects undertaken by Agencies acting alone).

In sum, overall reorganization meant that the two poles of the system – the end where *intentions*, as defined in global agendas, were formulated, and that where *programmes* were implemented, had been, in as sense, stretched further apart, while also being more rationally related. Operations at the programme end, the field level, had been integrated to a greater extent than in the past, and field officers had been given enhanced discretion. *At the other pole, the greater number of Global Conferences encouraged a greater degree of agreement about what should be done;*

and the reform of ECOSOC sharpened its capacity to shape these globally defined intentions, or broad aims, into cross-sectoral programmes with well-defined objectives. At the same time ECOSOC had acquired greater capacity to act as a conduit through which the results of field-level monitoring could be conveyed upwards to the permanent representations of the Global Conferences, namely the Commissions, which then became more capable of formulating well-informed proposals for the consideration of the five yearly Review meetings, and the successor conferences.

6. Procedures had been introduced which strengthened mutual obligations and respect for common rules with regard to the work of the Agencies. At the same time it had become more difficult for both agencies and states to opt out, because the system worked in such a way that the benefits of compliance and the costs of non-compliance were continuously upgraded and there was no supranational challenge or rival pole of action to react against. This is what is meant by entrenching multilateralism. The system had become a forum of obligation.

One source of pressure upon states to conform with plans for multilateral action could be the new plans for development action which included the Country Strategy Notes, which by 1998 subsumed the UNDAFs. If such plans acquired substance, in that they included specific targets and programmes, it would become increasingly difficult for states contemplating bilateral measures to act in opposition. They were formally required to respect them. But the plans would become part of the intellectual environment which had to be taken into account when states determined their own plans; the alternative would be a greater exposure to accusations of deliberately undermining the agreed approach to the development problems of particular states. The plans were multilateral and backed by a consensus of operators, donors and the host country government.

States which flouted the rules of the regime ran the risk of being identified as cheats, and incurring the associated costs. The General Assembly reflected this in 50/227 when it concluded that 'Developing countries are responsible for their development processes and operational activities for development are a joint responsibility of all countries. *Partnership between developed and developing countries should be based on agreed mandates, principles and priorities of the United Nations system in the development field.* All countries should demonstrate their commitment to the Funds and Programmes'

(A/50/227: Annex 1, Clause 7). It was further reinforced in para 63 A/50/227 with the invitation to 'national officials directly involved in the implementation of national development strategies in recipient countries, as well as field-level representatives of the United Nations', to participate in the work of the operational segment.

The new process had the effect of strengthening the norms of a multilateral system. It accepted the obvious: that reform by setting up some kind of supranational manager, or by destroying multilateralism with regard to intentions by transferring money to the Bretton Woods institutions, was impossible. The changes introduced into the budgetary process in the UN and agencies in 1986, in a futile attempt to persuade Congress to return to full funding, was an illustration of the method. Major responsibility for agreeing the budget was given to the Committee for Programme and Coordination, which had a limited membership, usually including the main donors and the representatives of the Group of 77. The agreement that the budget should be approved by consensus in this committee, taken in December 1986, was the key step in creating a system in which the budget was unlikely to be radically altered in favour of the recipient countries by the General Assembly's Fifth Committee.[24] This was easier in the smaller forum because being coopted into it and involved in the details of creating the budget enhanced the sense of being in the inner circle for the representatives of the G77 and the requirement of agreeing by consensus to a detailed budget in this setting reinforced their commitment to it.

Conclusions

With regard to interests, the agencies and the developing countries concurred that strengthening the coordination mechanisms – the route of cooperation – was the preferable course. It could lead to an increase in the level of funding, and at worst could help slow down the reduction in development resources. They expected to be worse off if such mechanisms were not introduced, or if they stayed outside the new system – hence the wan acceptance by the G77 of the proposed changes. The donors for their part had an interest in the mechanisms because they promised greater efficiency in the use of development resources, and could weaken the case for a significant increase in development provision. For them opting out was likely to be the more costly option in terms of development, but also because of the other important agendas, especially democratization.

With regard to the consequences of being in the negotiations: the new mechanisms created two new kinds of rules. First were the progressively defined rules embodied in the new working arrangements; and second, the working decisions produced with regard to policy, programmes and finance in the new system. Entrenching multilateralism meant that sub-system's – actor's – behaviour was more likely to be subject to system-level rules, i.e. rules in the two senses outlined, as determined in the UN's reformed economic and social arrangements, because:

- Finance was a reward for compliance with the new rules for Agencies, developing countries and Funds and Programmes.
- A number of actors had been set up or empowered by the reforms which were system supporters, such as the Task forces, the functional Commissions, the Coordination segment of ECOSOC, the UNDG, and the Agency and Fund and Programme officials who were engaged at the country level in UN premises, who were linked with new communication systems. The weight of system-focused activity generated by this increased range of actors was more difficult to resist. The purpose of the system was shaped by agendas concerning global problems agreed in the global conferences.
- Actors within the developing states were likely to become system supporters, working for the global agendas, like the national courts in the EU, because they were empowered in the new arrangements through finance and function. Taking more decisions about the content and financing of programmes within local mechanisms, including national governmental and inter- and non-governmental organizations, created a system clientele. Democratization reinforced system orientation, but also enhanced loyalty to extra-state system actors.
- Bilateral providers were also now more likely to be system-responsive, as they were required to take note of the Country Strategy Notes. They were also together in the key ECOSOC committees and exposed to socialization into system norms. The global agendas impinged more frequently on them. Officials in provider ministries, like the DfID in Britain, were likely to be pushed to support system orientations, as there had been open commitment to support for the concept of the reforms; the alternative would imply a flat contradiction of the concept.

Behaving badly remained an option but would be a more public transgression.
- The juxtaposition of three functions in a single unit – ECOSOC – created what was potentially a powerful instrument. The three functions were the translation of sector proposals into integrated programmes which were more easily related to country plans; the allocation of resources for programme implementation within countries; and the monitoring of operational performance under the scrutiny of the main providers and programme formulators. Doing these three things in the same forum had a multiplier effect on pressure towards system-orientated behaviour for policy formulators, resource contributors and programme implementors alike. Contributors, implementors and formulators were locked into a way of working which supported system rules.

In sum once a pattern of interrelated interests existed, ensuing negotiations could lead to developments which trapped cautious and willing actors alike. They were pushed to compliance with system rules by: a fear of losing benefits by exclusion; an unwillingness to weaken a related existing regime which was regarded as beneficial; the creating and empowerment of new or existing actors which favoured cooperation; specifying sets of rules about cooperation, like the Country Strategy Notes, which could be evaded only by appearing to abandon the agreed concept, i.e. abandoning cooperation; and being involved in a forum where the only alternative to system compliance was marginalization. In this sense the reform of ECOSOC, so that the three functions were juxtaposed – and membership was correspondingly fixed – turned it, from the point of view of cautious actors, into something like the Intergovernmental Conferences of the EU in the 1990s from the point of view of the British. They had to stay in because leaving would lead to even greater costs.

The future agenda

The points of importance for a future-orientated agenda are now identified. Given the changes proposed and their implications for new ways of working in the economic and social spheres of UN activity, what specific developments needed to be stressed and further pursued?

1. It was necessary to develop schedules of topics for the discussions of the High-level segments for each succeeding five-year

period. The possibility existed of playing politics to minimize attention on areas which did not suit the winning players, be they agencies or governments. In general in the new system the working assumption should not be that everything depended on the good will of the participating actors. What needed to be identified were a set of specific advantages of being system-orientated, and the disadvantages of going against the grain.

This was one of the ways in which the new multilateral arrangements in this area could be entrenched: that is embedded in the system so that they became irresistible to the individual actors in the system, even in the absence of central direction. The trick was always to involve the elements in the multicentric system in processes which led to their entrapment.

2. The work on improving the technology of communication between the different participating actors in the field, including NGOs, should be pursued energetically. Vigorously pursuing a policy of setting up single UN premises would help this process. Similarly the single premises would assist with the development of programme-officer collegiality.

The idea of improving the financing of the programmes should be pursued. The proposal to have multi-annual pledging commitments for voluntary contributions was a sensible halfway stage between regular budget assessment and traditional voluntary contributions. It was an adaptation of the Consolidated Appeal Funding approach developed with regard to financing crisis intervention by the DHA. The implication of this was that funding would be tied more to specific programmes, and operational activities would have necessarily an inter-organizational element. The focus of the provision of funds would be inter-organizational.

3. The specification of Country Strategy Notes and UNDAFs should be further refined. They should become more specific and more comprehensive. Along with this, care should be taken to inform all contributors and participating organizations about the Notes.

4. Attention should be given to the further enhancement of the capacity of the Coordination segment to translate sector-specific proposals, deriving from the Global Conferences, the global agendas and the functional commissions, into relevant and effective guidelines for country-specific programmes within the

overall context of the Country Strategy Notes. One possible way was to make greater use of Task forces, such as those set up by the ACC and the Secretariat, with representatives from all participating organizations at the country level, which would link up with the coordination committee and the inter-organizational mechanisms at the country level. The country-level operations would be under the supervision of the UNDP Resident Coordinator. Four such Inter-Agency Task forces existed in 1996, which received guidance from Agencies after participation in the coordination segment.

5. In the new arrangements the Agencies already had a greater incentive than they had previously to be good system performers. One reason for this was that financial stringency led them to calculate that they were likely to get more money by accepting enhanced coordination. But attention could be given, and the opportunity seized in the present context, to increase the range of penalties which could be imposed on any participating institutions, possibly including NGOs, which proved to be non-cooperative. The reasons for this would increase if money returned possibly through the new budgetary arrangements mentioned at 2. above. This could mean that operational activity money was directed away from the Agencies towards the field, and was likely to be managed at that level. Unless penalties were introduced, Agencies in particular might begin to play a different game: of circumventing the new arrangements in order to acquire greater control over operational spending.

6. The main donor states should formalize their own overseeing mechanisms in New York on the economic and social side. Their involvement in the segments naturally provided a method of enhancing their overview, in a collective context, of the translation of sector goals into programmes. They should be aware of this and this should be recognized in programme-orientated discussions. The goal to be achieved would be a greater degree of solidarity of position on the part of their members in the Agencies. There would be enhanced donor collegiality about the details of programmes, alongside enhanced Agency solidarity. Discussion in the various segments, but especially that concerned with coordination, would facilitate this, as it would involve contributors, players and monitors in a context where decisions about money were related to decisions about policy.

7. Above all, however, it was necessary to ensure that ECSOC

attracted staff of the highest quality and indeed, without this, it would be impossible to realize the full potential of the changes discussed here. There remained a good case for arguing that an international body such as ECOSOC could not be redeemed once discredited, and some member states looked to alternative frameworks. It would be ironic indeed if such disillusionment were to lead to the abandonment of the UN system just at a point when such promising rearrangements had been agreed.[25]

8. These arrangements needed to take account of the advantages of working for development, and other linked social and economic goals, within groups of contiguous states. Throughout the above discussion the assumption was that global agendas reflected an increasing level of agreement about the general interest – there were global intentions – which could be developed into programmes in territories where they could be most effectively realized. Indeed effectiveness was the top priority, whether in development or the linked agendas of sustainability or human rights. There was in this context nothing magical about regions, but regionalization could be the consequence of simply asking the question of which territory was most appropriate for the realization of an integrated programme.

This was really the same principle which had been introduced into the EU in the Maastricht Treaty, the principle of subsidiarity.[26] Things could be done at the level of the Union, the regional level, if that seemed necessary for 'reasons of scale or effect'. In the Maastricht Treaty the goal attached to this by Eurosceptics was that of stopping the transfer to the region of functions that could not be performed by the separate states. But the argument also worked when turned upside-down: things that could not be done effectively by the state should be done by the region. There was a simple functional logic about this at the global level which followed directly from the acceptance of the overwhelming importance of the global agendas. The UNAFS and Country Strategy Notes did not have to be just concerned with separate individual states, but could be related together in regional groupings of states for the sake of effectiveness.

International organizations, especially those of the UN system, were uniquely qualified to act as the partners of developing states in developing their own perspective on the plans. In this capacity they could promote regionalization as a way of helping to develop a stronger voice for the developing countries. Here again, regionalization was a positive strategy in a period in which global agendas were evolving. Indeed in this context too the conclusion was unavoidable that globalization required regionalization. If the global agenda was so important why should it not be sought in the areas where it could be most effectively applied? This simple, but powerful argument is revisited in the next chapter.

The way in which reform had been approached was consistent with the principles of the multicentric system: it was evolutionary rather than revolutionary, which was usually the more difficult course to comprehend but at the same time the most practical. The changes involved something quite simple, making it less likely that the actors involved, which were both states and international institutions, would evade or wish to evade system rules. This effect was achieved by a combination of tangible incentives, and of less specific injunctions on behaviour. Most important, however, was modifying the perception of the self-interest of the actors. The negotiation process itself could generate a powerful self-fulfilling prophecy, in circumstances such as those which applied here, in which cooperation came to be seen as the right choice.

CHAPTER 5

Development and Labour Welfare in the Age of Globalization: Aspects of the US International Economic Stance and International Organization

> Globalization is a fact of life. But I believe we have underestimated its fragility. The problem is this. The spread of markets outpaces the ability of societies and their political systems to adjust to them, let alone to guide the course they take. History teaches us that such an imbalance between the economic, social and political realms can never be sustained for very long.
>
> Kofi Annan[1]

> Where one group is strong enough to push another around and stands to gain by it, it will do so. Even if the state would abstain from aggression, companies and individuals will not wait for permission.
>
> David Landes, *The Wealth and Poverty of Nations*, New York, Norton, 1998, p. 63

In this chapter the clash between the proponents and opponents of the major approaches to globalization is explored with regard to its implications for two major issues: development and the conditions of employment and wealth distribution. These are taken as particularly expressive of the differences between neoliberals and their critics about the management of the international economic system in the early twenty-first century, with the dominant coalition in the US taken as the main representatives of the former. These are not questions which an observer of the effects of globalization can ignore, since they relate to the achievement of the minimum tolerable standards for life. There is an obligation to see what can be said which this author cannot avoid.

Several economic and political developments of the late twentieth and early twenty-first centuries amounted to a pathology of globalized capitalism and attracted critical responses in an increasing literature, and in public protests such as those in Seattle, Genoa, Paris and London.[2] Regardless of the dangers to civil order of such protests, the balanced judgement of them has to be that 'the movement will remain an important counterbalance within the international system, and will continue to prod decision-makers towards addressing issues of exclusion, inequality and injustice'.[3] The disagreements about neoliberal globalization, and the responses to it, were an excellent illustration of the fallacy of the end of ideology.[4] The struggle to produce a socially responsible capitalism for the global economy was highly ideological, and carried a charged emotional baggage for both opponents and proponents. This chapter is concerned with locating the elements of that pathology and considers the strategies for dealing with it. Inevitably it identifies the parties to the dispute, their strategies and their motivations – what might be called the clashing visions. On the one side were a group of politicians and companies in the first world, among which right-wing Republicans in the US, and neoliberal economists and their allies, played a leading role. On the other was a more diverse group of academics, activists and politicians. The discussion in effect becomes an account of US economic macromanagement,[5] and its critics, in the early twenty-first century.

Neoliberal globalization could be seen as part of a long wave in the development of the international economy. The state had earlier moved from a period of *laisser faire* economic arrangements, which included such socially costly devices as the gold standard, to a Keynesian concern with full employment and demand management. Similarly in the early twenty-first century the social problems resulting from neoliberal globalization, which was also a form of *laisser faire* capitalism, demanded a new theory of employment that took account of globalization. The point will also emerge that the processes and principles of neoliberal globalization were dependent upon a particular kind of global structure of states and international organizations, and that effectively countering its less desirable aspects depended on recognizing the ways in which that structure was changing. In particular a global system of states was being overridden by groupings of states which, to a lesser or greater extent, were more closely connected with each other than with outsiders. Behind the arguments in this essay lurks the assumption, evident throughout this book, that regionalization and globalization were positively related, and that, far from challenging globalization, regionalization was its natural corollary. It was also a positive factor in dealing with the more pernicious aspects of globalization.

Neoliberal globalization was a collection of theories and ideas about global economic arrangements. But it was also a political ideology in the sense that the theories had been taken over by politicians such as those in charge of the so-called Anglo-American economies. They were pushed more or less vigorously and interpreted more or less perversely to suit their political agenda. Because of this it was misleading to talk of the practice of neoliberalism as if it were entirely a matter of the thoughts of economists translated into practice. Rather neoliberal practice was a reflection of a wider range of influences which included political culture, the distribution of power within and between states, and the views of political elites. In this chapter there is less concern with the analysis of what might be called academic neoliberalism and more with the consequences of its adoption by political elites. It is an essay about a set of related practices on the part of the dominant power in the early twenty-first century, and possible responses to them, rather than an examination of the theories of neoliberals.

The practice of development in neoliberal perspective

These propositions are explored in the context of two major areas of political economic activity, namely development and welfare. First, development:

There were two opposing views about how to practise development in the early twenty-first century. First was the view that there could be no distinctive policies on development, as the only acceptable approach was that of liberal deregulation, with development following from the success of this. The other was that development did indeed need special policies and that they demanded a compromise with hard-line globalizing deregulation. After the financial crises of the mid to late 1990s it was the latter approach that seemed to prevail, and this meant that, far from there being a globalization-induced convergence in economic arrangements on a neoliberal model, there was in fact a new divergence.[6]

It naturally led to a preference for distinctive responses in the world's major political-economic regions in which development paths were chosen which suited their particular circumstances. In the 1990s, and later, the disagreement was expressed particularly clearly between those in the US who supported neoliberalism, who were often associated with right-wing Republicanism, and those who argued that it came at too high a political and social price. The neoliberals in the US were particularly vehement in opposing any attempt to enshrine development in international law as a right. In this they continued an American tradition, often supported by other developed state governments, especially when they moved to the right.

The Right to Development, as a legal construct embodied formally in treaties, was a contentious issue that had to be qualified before it was acceptable to the main G7 countries. It had been implicit in the demand for a New International Economic Order in the early 1970s. And in 1986 it was incorporated in a General Assembly Declaration, when the USA voted against it and the other leading developed OECD states abstained.[7] In 1992 the Declaration of the Rio Conference on Environment and Development included it in Principle 3, though the US, Canada and the European Community had opposed it. The US government entered an interpretative statement as follows, which was revealing about the overt and covert agendas of the US. It asserted that 'the United States does not, by joining consensus on the Rio Declaration, change its long-standing opposition to the so-called right to development. Development is not a right. On the contrary, development is a goal we all hold, which depends for its realization in large part on the promotion and protection of the human rights set out in the Universal Declaration of Human Rights.'[8]

The US insisted that individual political and civil rights had precedence over economic rights in the form of development. Such a view can be defended on the grounds that individual rights exist but state rights do not. But it also represented a particular, and, for them, convenient take on an ancient dilemma, namely what to do about standards for individuals when there were failures of human rights. The danger was that the view would lead to limiting development support, because of the failures of developing country governments, rather than adopting the more positive approach of accepting a right to development as well as the need for democracy and respect for human rights. The US position, as represented in this form of words, contains a reason for doing nothing directly about development, a position which is inherent in neoliberal globalization. Unfortunately, as will be seen, this tended to be the position of the Republican tendency which supported President George W. Bush.

The position of the US right and its alternatives

Elements in US policy

The elements in the position of the US right, which came through from the Clinton regime, but were likely to be more vigorously expressed in the Bush Administration, can be set out succinctly as follows. The reader should note that in what follows the reference is to the US position, which should be understood as the position of the US right, which came to power in 2001.

- The US wanted the market to have pride of place.
- The US view was that the right to development was equivalent to the right to welfare, and was reluctant to make any concessions to the alternative view that the market was often a flawed instrument for providing both welfare and development and that there was a need for adjustment to other factors, like culture, or the phase of economic development, or to correct the imperfections in the market. Therefore the US was against the right to development.
- The US neoliberals wanted civil society promotion, such as building working democracies, better administrations and getting rid of corruption, but not including the development of labour organizations, or any device which could be described as government regulation. There was emphasis on the need for strong and effective financial-sector regulation, but by independent agencies. Hence the record of the US on the ILO was generally one of hostility and, as with the negotiations about the proposed Multilateral Agreement on Investment (MAI), anything that approached negotiations with labour was to be eschewed if at all possible. Labour considered itself grossly underrepresented in those negotiations.
- The US neoliberals wanted to give capital the ability to evade the costs of welfare, and development, by maximizing, as within the context of the MAI, its freedom to exit a country where government taxation was judged, in their eyes, to be inconsistent with neoliberal norms. Governments could tax but

companies could leave! The dominant view was, however, that there was no such thing as development costs in the sense that development could involve any special kind of costly economic activity in addition to that found normally in an unregulated market.
- The US actively lobbied to oppose direct government provision of key services such as health even in developing states and sought to project its national preference for private provision as the universal standard. The US strongly opposed any attempt to permit the WHO, from its early days to the present, to be directly involved in providing health services in the field. This would have got in the way of the US preference for private health provision and reflected a deep-seated ideological aversion to a broad range of alternatives placed under the general heading of 'socialized medicine,' even when these were organized by national governments rather than international institutions.
- The US wanted no specific mechanism for the redistribution of wealth from North to South, and was uncomfortable with the setting of targets for government aid provision.
- The US was opposed to any inequality of obligation to pay economic dues – i.e. there was disquiet about the idea of debt relief, or interest subsidies, and these were accepted only partially and with reluctance. The US position was one of the reasons for the slow progress of the debt-relief programme. In early 2001 the progress of the heavily indebted poor country initiative (HIPC) was slow, and its limited nature was apparent.

The effects of US political culture

In discussing the US position on development it was well to remember that the agendas of economic management, welfare provision and development were close together and shaped by a common ideology. It was therefore likely that views on one would have immediate and direct implications for the other. Similarly it was to be expected that attitudes on social provision and economic management within the US would be reflected in US positions on North–South economic and political relationships. Far too little attention was paid to the role of domestic political culture in these international policies. It was highly unlikely that there would be tolerance for a measure of redistribution from North to South when this was increasingly unacceptable from rich to poor within much of the US.

In 2001 the US was transferring less and less to developing states. It had fallen well below the 0.7 per cent of GDP stipulated in the UN Development Decade agreements. The development agenda of right-wing Republicans, who moved into power in 2001, was unlikely to reverse this trend. This was a country where it was unwise in public life to advocate policies which could be called Liberal – the term had become one of abuse. For liberal Democrats, as for right-wing Republicans, the least developed states could not be distinguished in this agenda from the poor in the US. But the conclusions drawn were diametrically opposed. The former argued that they should be helped with better welfare provision, but for the latter they were equally undeserving and equally part of the dependency culture. One appointment to the new Bush Administration, Myron Magnet, distinguished between the deserving and undeserving poor, while another, Marvin olasky, had made his reputation by urging the replacement of government welfare provision with that of charities, including right-wing religious organizations.[9] The US right-wing policy positions on linked questions such as environmental policy also reflected this ideology, and were hardening under the government of George W. Bush.

After the tragedy of the attacks of 11 September 2001 the question arose of whether the Bush regime would now adopt a more liberal multilateralism. It should be remembered that before that date the new regime had announced its withdrawal from the Kyoto agreements on pollution control, as well as showing a general inclination to unilateralism in a range of other environmental, and security issues. The President had emerged, after an uncertain start, as a capable leader in a time of crisis. But there was no evidence whatsoever of any change of position on the issues discussed in this chapter. Why should there be?

The position on environmental questions of the 'economic rationalists' and the 'Prometheans', as John Drysek characterized them,[10] was likely to be strengthened with the appointment of Gale Norton as Interior Minister, who had a reputation for pushing for the rights of logging and mining companies to open up US National Parks to exploitation. North–South policy was likely to follow similar lines, with attempts, in collusion with venal governments, to head off the efforts of environmental lobbies to restrict the exploitation of natural resources in developing countries. In March 2001 it was reported that the US had gone back on its promise made in the Kyoto Treaty[11] to scale back the emission of damaging greenhouse gasses. Those who denied that there was an environmental problem, and argued that the earth had an infinite capacity for regeneration, or who held that the one necessary step was to attach property rights and a price to chunks of the environment, had come into their own.[12] It was to be expected that this political group in the US would be strongly opposed to any strengthening of the role of the institutions which might adopt more liberal approaches.

The emerging debate

The debate about development had to be related to a long-term process of changing thinking about the process of globalization, and of the associated development of more liberal arrangements. By the 1980s the agenda of neoliberalism was in the ascendant and academics such as Biersteker reported its widespread adoption in the developing world in the 1980s and 1990s.[13] The reasons for this, according to Biersteker, were mainly a coincidence of the development of ideas, the appearance of favouring interests in the states, the obvious failures of the previous policies, and the crisis of the early 1980s. First reactions to the crisis in Mexico in 1994, and the financial crises in the Far East, were that this was an indication of the folly of any alternative to the approach.

But by the late 1990s doubts were being expressed by influential people, such as Joseph Stiglitz, Chief Economist at the World Bank,[14] and were reflected in the increasing problems in negotiating the Multilateral Agreement on Investment (MAI) in the OECD framework, eventually abandoned in 1998. In the late 1990s there were a number of shifts in the pattern of alliances on neoliberalism, which were reflected in thinking about the way to develop successfully.

The alliances were, first, the developing countries which, despite their abandonment of the principles of the New Economic Order in favour of liberalism, nevertheless wanted a greater degree of development support, in terms of finance, and in terms of policies. Attached to this lobby was a large number of sympathetic citizens and groups based in the North. This group preferred to work through the parts of the UN system which it judged most favoured its interests, and where it had a majority, such as the General Assembly, and UNCTAD. A number of development NGOs were attached to this group. Second was an alliance of multilateral companies, right-wingers in the US Administration and Congress, and some EU governments, which preferred to work through the institutions where they had a majority. This group supported a neoliberal agenda and tended to be cautious about the continuing extension of aid to the developing world. The institutions which they favoured included the International Monetary Fund (IMF), the World Bank and, to a lesser extent, the World Trade Organization (WTO). The US, as shown in a statement by the US ambassador to the UN, Betty King, was anxious to protect the role of the IMF and World Bank where the US could lead, and opposed any move of responsibility to the UN's central system.

In response to this the UN Secretariat, and leading UN officials, began in the late 1990s placing greater stress on working with business to promote development and responsible social policies in the development process. The Secretary-General stated in December 1999: 'Today, I am pleased to acknowledge that, in the past two years, our relationship has taken great strides. We have shown through cooperative ventures – both at the policy level and on the ground – that the goals of the United Nations and those of business can, indeed, be mutually supportive.'[15] Some of the business organizations themselves saw advantage in this and entered into agreements, and working arrangements, with parts of the UN system including UNDP.[16] At the same time the more cautious institutions, such as the World Bank, were brought to face the need to adopt a social agenda alongside the economic one. The argument that social change would be a natural result of liberalization, and therefore need not be addressed directly, was modified.

The British New Labour government also supported this change. A part of this development was a degree of fracturing of the so-called Washington Consensus, which was an informal agreement among leading figures in the US capital to push the neoliberal vision of the globalization process. Some influential academics in the US, such as Rodrik, came out openly on the side of the need for a more active social agenda to offset damage within the US to those who were not benefiting from the liberalization process, an argument which had obvious implications for globalization and development policy.[17] He argued that, though the benefits of the liberal approach to international trade and capital movements were large, they were not being distributed even to sections of the US population. The fears about globalization were increasingly seen to be not only about North–South issues, but also about rich–poor issues in the developed world. Given the ability of the US system to tolerate very large differentials of living standards the questions remained, however, of how disadvantaged people would have to be in the US before there was any policy response, and whether any response would have implications for thinking on North–South differentials.

But this development now produced a further counter-movement. A rival group within the neoliberal coalition was visible, made up especially of right-wing Republicans in the US and a New Right intellectual community, involving such organizations as the CATO institute, which was determined to continue with the purer version of the neoliberal agenda. They found arguments and institutions to counter any dilution of the hard version of neoliberalism, a view that was associated with more xenophobic and isolationist attitudes in the US.

Major cleavages in the new confrontation included disagreements about the rights of countries, even in the developed world, to insist upon their own right to restrict imports of goods that they judged to be damaging to the environment or to health. The disagreement about the export of hormone-laced beef from the US to Europe, and of an allegedly toxic additive to petrol made by the Ethyl Corporation and exported to Canada, were examples of this. There was concern that in both cases the WTO would judge that these were simply ruses to keep out goods, in other words, disguised protectionism. The Canadian government agreed to give compensation to Ethyl, thereby further fuelling suspicions that the agenda of the business community would now prevail over social considerations, such as maintaining good health.[18]

This problem was also illustrated by the WTO's decision that the European Union's ban on the sale of hormone-fed beef was an unfair trade barrier and illegal under GATT, even though the ban applied equally to both imported and domestic beef. The WTO based its decision on its conclusion that there was insufficient scientific evidence that hormone-fed beef was dangerous to human health.[19] Critics of globalization argued that creating the WTO, and investing it with the power to make such decisions, would infringe the sovereignty of national governments, and lead to the subordination of more important considerations concerning the welfare of individuals. They viewed the hormone-fed beef decision as a perfect example of how precautionary regulations could be overridden by international economic agreements. Opponents believed that the MAI, with its investor–state dispute-resolution mechanism, would create a vehicle more powerful than the WTO for challenging national laws. The view was often found among the governments of developing countries that the WTO was really a first world institution.[20]

Another fracture was about the appropriate institutional location of the agenda. Generally speaking the neoliberals strongly opposed the involvement of the United Nations directly in financial and trade issues. There was also the problem of which agendas and which rules should have priority, the rules of the WTO or those of agreements on environmental issues. A typical neoliberal response was to insist on institutional specialization, while the new liberal alliance, made up of the Social Democratic states of the EU, NGOS, the United Nations Secretariat, and the Secretary-General, and its linked machinery, as well as the GA and ECOSOC, and most of the Specialized Agencies, Funds and Programmes, pushed for a new holism. That is they accepted that related issues should be considered in relation to each other in a particular forum. In contrast the new right in the US tended, as was predictable, to argue for the total exclusion of international multilateral agencies from this work, and this meant reasserting US hegemony.

Those who were now questioning neoliberal positions, and by implication were opposing US government policy, took a different view. There was now a requirement, they argued, to look for consistency among the various parts of the matrix of interrelated policy issues. This meant finding ways of linking more effectively the activities of diverse agencies, which had responsibilities in various parts of the agenda. Such was the progress of the ongoing debate about the relationship between the argument for a rational division of labour on the one hand, and the need for effective coordination on the other!

There was some evidence of the linking of agendas and institutions in the light of the apparent need for a new, more holistic approach. One illustration was the attendance of the G8 finance ministers at the high-level meetings of the Economic and Social Committee in April 1999, and security issues in the broader sense, which impinged on issues of sustainable development and social stability, were discussed at the Security Council. The UN also entered into new agreements with the IMF and World Bank.[21] And, before it was abandoned in 1998, diplomacy about the Multilateral Agreement on Investment became embroiled in problems concerning the extent to which it should take account of a binding code of responsible corporate practice about short-term and long-term social considerations. After this breakdown the OECD sought to bring up to date and invest with new force its lengthy list of guidelines to multilateral companies about responsible behaviour. But for all its efforts the OECD codes remained voluntary: pressures had to be moral or intelligent self-interest.[22] In the late 1990s a range of other frameworks were set in place to improve the regulation of banking and financial institutions and activities in developing countries by subjecting them to international rules.[23]

The UN could be seen as increasingly attempting to build a new agreement with business. The UN had been anxious to demonstrate its preparedness to work with the private sector, as was reflected in Kofi Annan's speech to businessmen at the World Economic Forum conference at Davos in January 1999. He repeated this form of words in later such conferences. He also stressed the need for business to accept a code of social practice. 'Without your active commitment and support, there is a danger that universal values will remain little more than fine words,' he said, 'and unless those values are really seen to be taking hold, I fear we may find it increasingly difficult to make a persuasive case for the open global market.' British Chancellor of the Exchequer, Gordon Brown, also argued for such a code. This would be a 'code of global best practice in social policy which will apply for every country, will set minimum standards and will ensure that when IMF and World Bank help a country in trouble the agreed programme of reform will preserve investments in the social, education, and employment programmes which are essential for growth'. Moreover this code 'should not be seen in narrow terms as merely the creation of social safety nets. We should see it as creating opportunities for all by investing more not less in education, employment and vital public services.'[24] It was suggested by him that this code should be agreed at the next meeting of the World Bank in spring 1999. It fell to Robert Holzmann as Director of the newly created Social Protection division of the Human Resources Network of the Bank to formulate this. Some initial thinking was provided by the Social Development Section of the UK New Labour government's Department for International Development. It was suggested that best practice in social policy involved a) equitable access to basic social services, health, education, water and sanitation, shelter; b) social protection enabling individuals to reduce their vulnerability to shocks; and c) core labour standards.[25] There was therefore some evidence that the major international financial institutions, particularly the World Bank, had decided to humanize their approach to development questions, and had moved to be more involved with 'issues of social capital, good governance, safety nets and so on'.[26] In February 2000 Holzmann, and his colleague Jørgensen, produced a report on Social Risk Management for the World Bank.[27] In this the need for a holistic approach involving cooperation between all the relevant actors, including the UN system, was stressed. By the spring of 2001 the Bank appeared to have moved to the point at which old hands, who were 'more attuned with the cold calculus of structural adjustment packages', were unhappy with the new approach which was concerned with 'the complexities of sustainable development, human capital and cultural economics'.[28]

Even organizations such as the United Nations Development Programme (UNDP)[29] had moved by early 1999 to cooperate in a rather controversial arrangement with sixteen international companies which had contributed a seed fund of around $50,000 each to what was described as a 'privatized shell institution' called the Global Sustainable Development Facility. At the end of 1999 UN Secretary-General Kofi Annan's targeting of international financial instability as a central concern in his end-of-the-year review, and his promise of new initiatives to link the United Nations with business, were among indications that the world body was responding to globalization and its adverse consequences by stepping up participation in international economic dialogue. What seemed to be happening was that the UN had moved to stressing the role of regulating international business in development precisely when the US administration was likely to move to a harder right-wing position. The UN was now trying to capture business, having recognized it as a primary target, while the US government was increasingly disposed to leave it to respond to the call of the wild. Some UN people were nevertheless at pains to point out that it was not only money that was needed, but also expertise.[30]

But perhaps the most important change in institutional relationships, from the point of view of development policy in the late 1990s and early twenty-first century, was the moving together into an overlapping policy space of the main financial institutions, the IMF and World Bank, and the United Nations agencies. Previously they had been frequently at loggerheads, with the former pursuing the Western-style neoliberal agenda, and the latter retaining an aura of radicalism left by the New International Economic Order (NIEO). Both had changed in the direction of the other by 2001, which made it possible for there now to be cooperation. The biggest changes were of course the abandonment of the triumphalism of the Bretton Woods agencies, and the compromise with business of the UN.

Ironically the emergence of this alliance was taking place when the weight of opinion in the US political elite inclined differently.

The US and abroad: terra nullius *or international cooperation?*

The power abroad of a rather small but powerful neoliberal US elite was left unchallenged by an American public which was largely uninterested in the idea of abroad, despite the appearance of widespread passive support for the United Nations.[31] The US was the only state in the world with an extensively developed body of doctrine and practice favouring the extraterritorial application of its laws.[32] Hence at the beginning of the twenty-first century the US was often somewhat cavalier in its attitude, and response, to international law, and an opponent of any system that claimed priority, even in greater justice and right, over the US. This point, often made, was illustrated by the reluctance of the US authorities to apply the Geneva codes on the treatment of prisoners of war to those captured in Afghanistan and imprisoned in a US camp set up in Cuba. The US also strongly opposed the setting up of an International Criminal Court, and had always refused to accept the binding jurisdiction of the International Court of Justice. The same view was evident in the US stance on international economic arrangements.

The US was split on the necessary response to the new development crisis in the early 2000s. The outcome of the split was critical. On the one hand there had been a recognition of the need to deal directly with social problems among a number of prominent Americans, but the political power remained unreformed in its attitude to international welfare, as it was to national redistribution. But the judgement would have to be that the overall movement of the US official line was away from support for any increased or more organized effort on development policy. This was in line with the strategic stance of right-wing elements in the US towards *abroad*, which had a long tradition. This characterized the lands beyond America as a *terra nullius*, rather like that on the far side of the Western Frontier, or beyond the frontiers of ancient Rome, which was open for exploitation, but which was an area of potential US dominance with regard to law and culture. Abroad was an area of inferior, less principled, practice which could be subordinated at the discretion of the

US authorities, federal and state, to that of the true civilized realm within. It was because of this that the habit in the US was to seek to apply US law outside its own territory – the only country in the world to do so. The Bush regime's unilateral abandonment of attempts to reduce emissions of greenhouse gases, mentioned above, reflected this attitude. So was the membership of the US Vice-President and the Secretary of Defense in a well-funded lobby which was to discuss and pursue by all available means the reshaping of international society to suit US interests.

Gus Speth, an American who had held senior positions in the UN, most recently as head of UNDP, was reported to be deeply frustrated with the US position on the UN. 'He deplored what he called American "ignorance" of the "extraordinary" role played by the United Nations in preventing and containing conflict, sustaining development and reducing poverty. He criticized not only the Republican-led Congress, which had been holding $1.6 billion in past dues hostage to anti-abortion and other domestic concerns, but also the Democratic Administration that had nominated him.'[33] The point might be added that even when a compromise about the paying of the UN dues was reached in late 2000, which included the reduction of US contributions on the regular budget to 22 per cent and on the peacekeeping budget to 27 per cent, the Republican-dominated Congress did not have the decency to make up the remaining shortfall from its trillion-dollar budget. To reveal the scale of the offence, the shortfall was made up in one payment from the personal account of a single enlightened US citizen, namely, Ted Turner.

While 'a lot more supportive' than Congress, the Clinton Administration had also in Speth's view given the United Nations too little priority. The US, he said, too often indulged in 'going it alone' as a superpower and failed to press for the implementation of its pledge to reward the reforms it advocated. A troubling indication that Washington had given up its leadership here, many United Nations officials said, was the Administration's decision to permit a non-American to replace Mr Speth, who was the sixth American to hold the post of head of UNDP. Several diplomats and American officials said that Washington had given up the post in hopes of further reducing its contribution to United Nations development aid. The new head of UNDP was Mark Malloch Brown, the British-born World Bank Vice-President, who had been nominated by the Secretary-General, and was regarded as a good thing despite the negative symbolism of his appointment. It was, of course, possible that his appointment had been helped by the conversion of the World Bank to a more social agenda, like the one which UNDP under Speth had vigorously espoused.

There had been a twenty-year cycle, from the general acceptance of the neoliberal agenda in the 1980s, to a measure of loss of confidence in that agenda in the first years of the twenty-first century. There was an increasing sense of running into a trap formed, on the one side by US governmental weakness and lack of leadership, and on the other by the increasing danger of serious turbulence resulting from the very nature of globalization. The primary agenda in a range of international institutions such as UNDFP and the World Bank, and in the G7 governments, had become a push for better domestic governance, though this was unlikely to appear without the parallel development of more effective global governance.

The clash of visions in greater detail

By the late 1990s and the early years of the twenty-first century the neoliberal/US vision and its alternatives could be discussed usefully in greater detail in the context of three agendas. These were all defined in the context of globalization, with its linked neoliberal agenda of removing regulations on trade and the movement of capital.

Agenda I

First there was the agenda of the 1980s which was the range of changes which developing countries generally thought they needed to introduce after the apparent failure of the planning approach of the New International Economic Order. Biersteker pointed out that 'virtually everywhere, developing countries began restructuring the nature of their intervention in the domestic economy, liberalizing their domestic trade and investment regime, privatizing state-owned enterprises, and pursuing a variety of economic reforms more generally'.[34] This involved a reduction and redirection of state economic intervention in the economy, in combination with an increased reliance on the market for the allocation of scarce resources and commodities.

A number of specific activities was linked with this in the new policies of developing countries. There was an effort to institutionalize nominal devaluation of the currency in order to generate and sustain real exchange-rate adjustment. Fiscal policy reform meant reducing or constraining the rate of growth in government spending, reforming the tax structure, rationalizing expenditure, phasing out or reducing government subsidies, and improving the efficiency of public investment, namely scaling down and shifting the focus from manufacturing to infrastructure and social sectors. It also involved trade liberalization, in particular the replacement of quantitative restrictions on trade by tariffs and the general lowering of tariff levels. Financial reform was also often carried out in the form of controlling the rate of growth of the money supply, liberalizing foreign exchange controls, and eliminating the subsidizing of credit.

By the time of the first wave of the Asian crisis in late 1997 liberalization 'was deemed to have triumphed over rival Asian developmental statism and Latin American heterodoxy'.[35]

Agenda 2

There were those who favoured building on the changes introduced in the 1980s, and furthering the globalization/liberalization process, but there were also those who opposed such an extension and wished to re-examine the model of the Development State. The two sides of this argument were conveniently and succinctly captured in the positions of proponents and opponents of the Multinational Agreement on Investment (MAI).[36] They are now discussed under Agendas 2 and 3 respectively.

The changes that were wanted in the MAI were the most noteworthy in this discussion as they remained the goals of the right-wing lobby, and essentially captured in 2001 the right-wing position on development. It argued that most existing regulatory practices, for example, restrictions on foreign investment, which the MAI would prohibit, actually caused 'distortions'. By 'distortions' they meant economic outcomes that were less efficient than those that would occur in the absence of regulation. In their view, an investment agreement like the MAI could establish clear rules that would eliminate a host of distortions and inefficiencies that had been written into law through the efforts of special interests – yielding benefits for the general public.

For proponents of the MAI, a set of global rules governing investment was needed to lock in the liberalization that had already taken place over the previous two decades. This was needed to protect the rights of investors to free, equal and safe access to markets, and to resolve the conflicts that were inevitable between governments and transnational corporations (TNCs). The primary purpose of such rules would be to reduce the distorting effects of such policies. Examples of the latter were requiring foreign investors to form partnerships with local firms, and performance requirements, like maintaining certain employment levels, which required TNCs to act in ways other than those indicated, in their view, by market forces in making their production decisions. Business and industry groups argued that the MAI was a necessary step toward minimizing the substantial risks of investing overseas.

Accordingly obstacles to the increasing integration, i.e. the globalization, of the world economy should be removed. In order to accomplish this a set of rules was needed to limit the ability of governments to restrict foreign investment. These rules would in effect also curtail, to a certain extent, a nation's regulatory authority over both foreign and domestic corporations with respect to performance requirements. The basic principle was that of non-discrimination. From the perspective of proponents these rules would do no more than ensure a level playing field for international investors and protect the security of investments in countries that were party to the agreement. Furthermore, the final treaty would include many country-specific reservations and exceptions to the rules, which proponents maintained would address the concerns of critics.

Specific rules would included:

1. A rule which required countries to treat foreign investors and investments no less favourably than domestic ones. Under this rule countries could not, for example, place special restrictions on what foreign investors could own, maintain economic assistance programmes that solely benefited domestic companies or require that a corporation hired a certain percentage of managers locally. Under one version of the text, which might be termed the hard neoliberal one, laws that had a discriminatory effect on foreign investors would be prohibited whether or not such discrimination was intentional. While governments would be prohibited from discriminating against foreign investors, there would be nothing to stop governments from treating foreign corporations more favourably than domestic ones (for example, by offering special incentives to attract foreign investment).

2. Most Favoured Nation (MFN) treatment was to be applied to capital, as it had been applied under GATT to trade. This would require governments to treat all foreign countries and all foreign investors the same. Laws prohibited by MFN would include economic sanctions that punished a country for human rights violations by preventing corporations from doing business there. This would make illegal any action by a government against a company which it judged was behaving irresponsibly, by for instance, destroying valuable habitats, in other parts of the world.

3. Performance requirements imposed on business by host governments were to be excluded. These were rules which, for instance, required investors to meet certain conditions if they wanted to establish an enterprise in a particular locale or if they wanted to be eligible for tax incentives or other government aid (for example, low-interest development loans). A requirement that corporations used some percentage of *domestic* inputs was an example of a performance requirement that would be prohibited by the MAI. Performance requirements would be banned even where they applied equally to domestic and foreign firms. The extent to which the MAI would limit performance requirements had not been agreed when negotiations ceased, but the preferred outcome of this lobby was clear.

4. There was to be a ban on the uncompensated expropriation of assets. The MAI would require signatory governments, when they deprived foreign investors of any portion of their property, to compensate the investors immediately and in full. Expropriation would be defined not just as the outright seizure of a property but would also include governmental actions 'tantamount to expropriation'. The aim here was to have in place rules which would compensate firms for any kind of loss resulting from host government action, and to take jurisdiction in these cases away from the host government in favour of an international mechanism. Private investors and corporations were to be empowered to sue national governments, and seek monetary compensation, in the event that a law, practice or policy violated investor rights as established in the agreement.

International investors would have the option to sue a country before an international tribunal rather than in the country's domestic courts. This investor–state dispute resolution mechanism was an illustration of the continued move away from the

practice of earlier economic agreements like GATT, which allowed only governments to bring complaints against other governments. NAFTA employed investor–state dispute resolution in limited cases, as did most of the 1600 plus bilateral investment treaties.
5. There would be a ban on restrictions on the repatriation of profits or the movement of capital. Countries would not be able to prevent an investor from moving profits from the operation or sale of a local enterprise to that investor's home country. Nor could countries delay or prohibit investors from moving any portion of their assets, including financial instruments like stocks or currency. Negotiators were debating the question of whether an exception would be made in the case of national financial crises, like the Mexican peso collapse, when countries might choose to put brakes on disinvestment in an effort to avert a financial meltdown.
6. Also on this agenda were a range of 'roll-back' and 'standstill' provisions, which were designed further to liberalize the rules for international investment and to ensure that transnational investors had access to new markets as they emerged. These provisions required nations to eliminate laws that violated MAI rules (either immediately or over a set period of time) and to refrain from passing any such laws in the future. Country-specific exemptions could be made for some existing laws as part of the negotiating process, but these would be for future negotiation.
7. The agenda *did not* include any binding code on the responsibilities of investors regarding fair competition, treatment of employees, environmental protection or other issues. Proponents evaded this issue by arguing it should be tackled in the framework of other institutions. There was discussion of including existing OECD codes of corporate responsibility in the MAI, but these provisions would be non-binding. How these various proposals would affect businesses, workers, consumers, the environment and the general public was an area of intense disagreement among opponents and supporters of the agreement.

Agenda 3

In response to this set of proposed neoliberal add-ons to the post-NIEO changes a number of points were made by development economists and the governments of the developing states. The crises in the Far East in the 1990s in particular led to a re-examination of the neoliberal agenda and a reassertion of arguments favouring an intelligent adaptation of the theory of the development state. The intellectual roots of this response were also traceable in the arguments of those who opposed the MAI. These responses constituted the third agenda on development of the early twenty-first century. The roots of the argument were concerned with the issue of welfare, which is discussed more fully below. There had been a sharp increase in inequality which had coincided with the acceleration of the process of globalization, and which needed specific counter-measures. The positions on this agenda were:

1. The Agreement promoted investor rights without investor responsibilities. The view was that countries could have legitimate reasons for treating foreign investors differently from domestic firms or for imposing performance requirements on investors, and that by limiting such policies the MAI would sharply restrict the ability of governments to shape investment policy to promote social, economic and environmental goals.
2. Opponents viewed the MAI as an attempt to create rights for multinational companies and other investors, and to defend these rights even when they were in conflict with the rights, needs or interests of individual nations and their citizens. The MAI clearly provided binding legal protections for the rights of investors, but there was no confidence in its commitments to respect labour rights, environmental standards or anti-competitive business practices. To opponents, this imbalance reflected a conscious effort by the MAI's drafters to place investors' rights in a privileged position relative to environmental, labour and other concerns. This was hardly surprising: the negotiations had been in private and almost exclusively between the representatives of business and governments. Labour and other interests had been limited to just one out of thirty odd committees, and this was one of the reasons for moving the talks to the OECD framework and locating the talks in Paris. They would be less visible there.
3. Opponents further argued that by increasing the ability of investors to shift production around the world, the MAI would hasten the 'race to the bottom', in which countries were pressured to lower living standards and weaken regulatory regimes in an effort to attract needed investment capital. In this view, even regulatory laws that were not in direct conflict with the MAI

could be threatened by an increasingly intense competition for capital. Opponents did not accept the idea that increasing the flow of capital around the globe would necessarily benefit the people, even in the USA. They pointed to the fact that the US trade deficit had grown substantially with increasing trade in goods and services. Exports had grown, as defenders of globalization predicted, but imports had grown faster.
4. Opponents were particularly concerned that corporations would abuse the power, granted them under the MAI, to sue governments for damages. They feared that investors would take an expansive view of the MAI's definition of investors' rights and bring legal challenges that the MAI's drafters might not anticipate. Opponents also worried that investors could use the threat of potentially costly lawsuits to intimidate governments that were considering the passage of new regulatory laws.

The range of laws that could violate the MAI was wide. They included a wide range of laws that protected the environment, public health and the welfare of individuals, as they were vulnerable to the charge that they discriminated against foreign investors, constituted expropriation of investor assets, or were illegal performance requirements.

Examples included:

- laws designed to conserve valuable natural resources or land
- requirements that recycled content be used, when possible, in the production process
- public contract preferences for environmentally responsible firms
- laws encouraging local economic development which could put foreign investors at a competitive disadvantage. These included programmes earmarking economic development funds for local businesses, community reinvestment laws requiring banks to invest in economically deprived areas, set-asides for minority- and women-owned businesses, state and municipal programmes earmarking loans and subsidies to home-grown businesses, rules promoting the investment of public pension funds in local businesses and/or in socially responsible businesses; and set-asides, targeted loan and grant programmes, and special regulatory relief for small businesses.
- laws designed to enhance financial and economic security could also be illegal under the MAI, opponents asserted. Laws that

could be challenged included 'speed bumps' or other restrictions on short-term stock, bond and currency transactions which countries might wish to use to avoid financial crises, and laws designed to protect jobs by requiring corporations that moved jobs out of a country to pay tax penalties.

The above list of objections to MAI constituted a comprehensive account of the kinds of arrangements that might fall under a positive development agenda. Though stated in the negative, and framed as objections, they implied a list of positive policy objectives. It would be redundant to restate those. But they were illustrated dramatically by one particular example, that of Malaysia. In response to the currency crisis in the late 1990s Malaysia introduced a ban on the repatriation of capital, a ban on the trading of the ringgit overseas, a freeze of the dollar–ringgit exchange rate and limitations on the amount of national currency Malaysians could take overseas.[37] The first response of Washington was one of horror. But by late 1999 the Malaysian policies were being hailed as a success, in that they dealt with the crisis and made it possible to return fairly quickly to more open policies, to attract inward FDI, without undue cost.

The new practice and theories of employment in neoliberal perspective

The discussion now moves to focus more directly on welfare policies, particularly concerning the interests of workers. It will be noticed that the arguments extend the discussion of development issues above, and that again there were in the early twenty-first century two primary visions, a neoliberal one, captured and interpreted by the US right-wing political and business elite, and a reaction to that on the part of those who were more prepared to accept deliberate intervention in the market to correct its anti-welfare tendencies.

A number of charges were frequently levelled against what was seen by critics as a syndrome of dangerous and costly practices with regard to employment in the neoliberal globalized economy. They were:

- The wealth was not distributed in a way that could be seen as equitable. Income differentials had increased greatly after the early 1990s between the poorest and the richest in the developing world, between median incomes in the poorest and richest countries, but also within the developed world. In the developed world the appearance of full employment was misleading, especially in those states where neoliberal management procedures had taken the strongest hold. More of labour was part-time and more was subject to exploitative practices such as firing and then rehiring on less advantageous terms. Long-term employees in some of the rich countries, including the USA and the UK, found themselves facing redundancy with no alternative but to accept, on rehiring – even in the same job – a worsening of the conditions of employment, including lower pensions and, in the USA, health insurance.

One example was Microsoft in the 1990s, a company which had once prided itself on its long-term commitment to its employees and the loyalty of its employees. After being found guilty of illegal hiring practices, it eventually succeeded in getting its people to do the same job for less after firing and rehiring through subsidiary connected companies. Such were the implications of US macro-management. The appearance of full employment in the UK and the US concealed the undermining of employment standards: more jobs were part-time and less secure, compared say with Germany or France, and the package of social protection had been diluted. Indeed in the so-called Anglo-American economies – those most adapted to neoliberal practices – gross figures on levels of employment concealed as much as they revealed about the condition of the economy. More people were worse off than they had been, though some were richer.

- The proportion of global wealth in the developing world, compared with the developed one, had declined further during the 1990s from an already low level. Production of a range of goods, but particularly clothing, shoes and electronics, was often carried out by underpaid and exploited labour in tax-free economic production zones (EPZs), a principle originally approved by the Economic and Social Council of the UN as a way of promoting development, but since appropriated by some multinational companies, and governments, as a way of maximizing their own profits and minimizing labour costs. Around 27 million people worked in such zones. These people could not increase wages or improve working conditions as they were unable to exert any collective pressure. Owners could relocate at very short notice to other countries offering even lower costs: the so-called 'race to the bottom'. The EPZs were an extreme example of a general driving down of wages in the developing world.

By the late 1990s some companies, including major high-street brands, did not make anything themselves but bought in from producers who ran production in the third world. The owners of the production enterprises, often from newly industrialized countries such as South Korea, sought the cheapest locations of production in Indonesia, the Philippines, Mexico and the like.

- This arrangement reflected the interest, newly discovered by companies, in separating their market from their labour, and illustrated a post-Fordist view of production.[38] The mass-production philosophy of Henry Ford had the advantage of balancing increasing production with an expanding market based on an increasing capacity to consume by workers spending their wages. This was a view which derived from the thinking of the British political economist John Hobson at the London School of Economics in the early twentieth century. He argued that there was a natural balance between the need to produce and the need to consume. In the age of neoliberal globalization, in contrast, it was argued that the global market was limited to a middle-class population of about 2.1 billion people, whose money was earned increasingly not from the real economy but from rent and financial instruments of various kinds. And for the time being the wages of workers producing the goods were irrelevant to the scale of consumption.
- Companies had taken on a number of organizational characteristics, each of which carried a social cost. They were *downsizing*, and *outsourcing*, according to modern management practice, so that they did not bear direct responsibility for production or its costs. In some sectors they existed solely in the form of an administrative headquarters and local branches, and outlets, and a brand or logo, which identified the goods they sold. For many companies, particularly in clothing, the brand name was the main repository of the value of the core company; its primary economic purpose was the protection and promotion of its reputation, as symbolized by its brand image. Another change, however, was that, as they outsourced and downsized the operations inherent in their original purpose, companies were becoming increasingly concerned with stock and currency market activities to increase profits, rather than production and market expansion. Even companies which were nominally

involved in the world of making and selling goods were in fact becoming more remote from the real economy, and more involved in 'casino capitalism'.[39] Hence in the 1980s and 1990s profits continued to increase much faster than growth.[40]

This development was a logical consequence of their multinational character, and the structure of international society, as much as of changing fashions with regard to management methods and the organization of production. A large number of small, and weak states, with relatively weak international governance, provided the opportunities for companies which could be light on their feet. And the multinational character of the companies was a necessary underpinning of their capacity to exploit opportunities for cheap production in different states. They now found advantage in having a range of currencies generated in the market available *in house* so that purchasing goods could be switched rapidly as production relocated at short notice between states in response to changing costs. In this vicious circle the lack of responsibility of producers for their workers was matched by the lack of obligation of the branded companies to their producers. In consequence there was a general tendency for companies to get involved in banking. Hence in the UK a good number of high-street stores had set up as banks, and companies that had once specialized in a particular sector of the capital market, like building societies in Britain, re-invented themselves as general-purpose banks.

- Their banking activity had paradoxical implications. To the extent that they invested in developing countries they had an interest in their stability and growth. But to the extent that their currency and stock-market portfolios increased they had acquired a capacity for speculation and increased their ease of exit. In this they were more likely to behave without regard to economic stability, social justice, environmental protection and political stability in any particular country. Indeed by playing a kind of musical chairs with the poorer countries they increased instability and uncertainty for them. They were interested in cutting costs, with all the social and economic risks this entailed, but if things went wrong they could exit. In turn that increased the determination of the companies to protect their ability to leave. The exit had to be kept open.

The economic problems in some countries in East Asia in the 1990s, such as Indonesia, were of benefit to multinational companies in some sectors in the short term since they led to the paying of even lower wages to workers in dollar terms and the consequent further reduction of production costs. This related to a key problem in the way of development from the perspective of neoliberal globalization. To the extent to which they were post-Fordist, multinationals had an active interest in reducing production costs by preserving underdevelopment, and indeed increasing rather than narrowing the North–South divide. Neoliberal globalization was certainly ambiguous with regard to development, and there was something in it which prized development failure for many companies.

- In contrast some of the very big banks, which had invested more directly in building capital infrastructure in the developing world, were less ambivalent about the need for stability. But their anxiety about fast profits often tempted them to take big risks, which, it appeared, were likely to be insured out of taxation in rich countries, as with the massive loans, totalling more than $50 billion, by the US to help Mexico deal with the crisis of 1994. This habit was supported by the close relations often found between top politicians and the major investment banks in the first world. US Treasury Secretary Robert Rubin had been vice-chairman of Goldman Sachs which had invested massively in Mexico and stood to lose massively if Mexico became insolvent. Goldman Sachs had also contributed massively to Bill Clinton's presidential campaign. The massive support for Mexico can be seen, therefore, as a consequence of both the fear of structural crisis, and the fear of massive private loss. The bill for all of this was of course ultimately paid by the taxpayers of the developed world. Hence the judgement was made by critics that in this situation the profits were privatized and the risks socialized.[41]
- In 2001 this way of organizing capital had its strongest and most ideologically motivated backers among right-wing Americans, such as a number of those Republicans who supported and worked for the new Bush Administration. These were people who were ideologically committed to the removal of any regulation on economic activity, which amounted to a determined and well-financed effort to abolish any attempt to restrict the maximizing of private profit, and to avoid any kind of social cost. Hence in 2001 any attempt to challenge the problems of globalized capitalism also amounted to an attack on the policies of the Bush Administration. It followed that the machinery for protecting

private profit had to be protected: hence opposition to any regulation of tax havens and the demonizing of the OECD attempt to regulate them in 2001. The argument proposed by the Bush officials, like Treasury Secretary Paul O'Neill, was that regulating such havens would get in the way of driving down tax levels in general. After the loss of the Republican majority in the Senate, it was reported that the US might sign up to regulation on condition that a requirement to equalize tax rates between foreign and domestic companies was dropped.[42] What this meant of course was that tax havens were seen as a way of forcing down social welfare costs. Suddenly what had been regarded as a vice, tax havens for the hiding of profit and tax evasion, came to be seen as a virtue.

The most visible manifestations of the pathology of globalized capitalism with regard to labour welfare in 2001 were therefore:

- The greater uncertainties imposed on labour in the developing and developed world, but particularly the former. This was the primary social sin of the practice of neoliberal globalization.
- In some cases companies had been brought to realize that it was necessary to achieve higher standards in some areas, particularly on the environment and the content of goods, as consumers could refuse to buy those which fell short. But companies struggled to conceal low labour standards, and would get away with what they could in other areas.
- The separation of profits from real value, in that increasingly money was made from monetary and financial speculation rather than producing and selling 'stuff'. There was less concern with growth in productive capacity, as with the Fordist approach, and more with increasing profit without growth by such activities as playing the stock, securities and currency markets.
- There was an increasingly conspicuous strategy of deliberately destroying the regulatory capacity of governments. This was promoted by a pernicious coalition of heads of multinational companies, right-wing supply-side economists, rightist political elites in the developed world and, until the late 1990s, the global financial institutions. The political agenda of this group was dominated by the goal of privatizing profits and socializing costs, weakly justified as being in the long-term interest of the poor – bitter medicine for their own good – with discredited

mantras from the 1980s such as the trickle-down effect, or freeing energies by getting governments off backs.
- There was indeed a return to a political economy dominated by ideological conflict of a kind reminiscent of the quarrels between left and right of the Cold War. Right-wing politicians and economists demonized any opposing entity and any attempt to construct an opposing coalition, while those who pushed what they thought was an agenda of social responsibility were inclined to castigate the neoliberals. In this strategy the neoliberals were, however, able to command vast resources, and enlisted the support of a range of professionals in banking, politics and the media. The organizations containing these professionals were themselves often US-based multinationals and obviously had an interest in the neoliberal agenda. These multinationals often also financed the research to justify their behaviour.

Responses to the problem

Agents of the pathology

Before any realistic proposals could be made to regulate globalized capitalism – as captured in this account of the syndrome – it was necessary to be clear about the targets to which they had to be addressed. These were the entities which bore some responsibility for triggering the pathology and which had to be persuaded, or made, to act as agents for its mitigation.

The targets, as the responsible agents, were:

- the rich in the first world when they demanded ever-lower prices and the driving down of levels of taxation. In the USA there was likely to be resistance to any proposal for a tax on consumption in favour of the worse off, both in the US itself, but especially overseas. By the last quarter of the twentieth century advocating the redistribution of wealth, however modestly, from rich to poor, was a sure road to defeat in US elections. Indeed even the word liberal had come to acquire dangerous connotations in US public discourse
- the political and economic elites of developing countries, who often colluded with the exploitation of citizens of their own country, and of the state itself.[43] Sometimes this was because of

personal greed and opportunism, combined with a tendency to view the state as a 'pork-barrel'. It was rarely because of an explicit socio-economic strategy
- right-wing political elites and their associates in business, such as Exxon, in the US. (Exxon contributed substantially to the Bush election fund and in return expected to obtain US withdrawal from the Kyoto agreement on the environment and the relaxation of environmental standards in the US to permit exploration for oil in hitherto protected areas.) Commercial interests were particularly pressing because of the scrabble to have access to scarce resources such as oil, and to exploit break-through technologies in areas such as information technology and genetic engineering
- the boards of multinational companies. Although some had been brought to act more responsibly, the assumption had to be that the managers often allowed short-term economic rationality to prevail over social responsibility, even though in the long term the social costs would produce indeterminate economic costs

Agents of a counter-strategy

There were agents which were capable of exercising power against the target actors identified above. Each agent could exploit a particular kind of power, with the resources available to it; the power varied with the agent. Both of these are now identified.

- Consumers in first-world countries constituted the first agent, which could be empowered by the provision of reliable market and production information. Consumers were more likely to pursue enlightened self-interest than were producers and, given access to information, they were likely to act. This was because every additional purchasing decision was likely to be of minor consequence for their overall economic standing. Paying a little more for a 'good' product, or refusing to buy a 'bad' one was unlikely to involve anything more than small inconvenience or monetary cost. The power of the consumer was, however, also dependent on a range of supporting changes. For instance companies could refuse to provide information, as Nike had done concerning the sources of its production. The power of the consumer required that companies should be required to reveal their product sources. This information should be about the conditions of employment, and about the record of compliance with labour legislation. Often such legislation existed but was ignored. Indonesian workers were fired in Malaysia in 2001 in open defiance of existing Malaysian rules for workers on such matters as notice and compensation.[44] Compliance should be monitored by global organizations such as the UN, with the aim of providing reliable information, on a regular basis and in a transparent fashion, for consumers in the first world.

- A second agent was the epistemic communities and NGOs which acted as the verifiers of evidence and argument, and the shapers of agendas, and of informed and expert opinion. They were also frequently the primary agents of transparency with regard to what was going on in the developing world. Their power had a number of dimensions. It included the capacity to challenge what neoliberals often claimed were the givens of the globalized world. Some aspects of the arguments of neoliberals were more contentious than they claimed and they often – intentionally or not – concealed the facts. For instance in the argument about the advantages of giving priority to exports over import substitution the discussion was prematurely closed, as many economists had come to recognize by 2001. These agents could be actively concerned with challenging such givens and in consequence promoting a positive agenda which was supported by a sufficient coalition of political elites.

Neoliberal doctrine held that the pursuit of export-led growth was necessarily superior to the traditional strategy of developing countries' import substitution.[45] This was because of the theory of free trade which it was thought would bring general benefit. But even a cursory glance at the logic of this gave some cause for doubt. Export priority required import priority as giving exports the lead in a closed system for all states also required them all to give imports the lead. But the developed states were usually very reluctant to permit this especially in areas where developing states could have a competitive advantage, such as textiles. They recognized that there were social, economic and political costs in accepting imports unconditionally, and because of their power were able to insist on countervailing measures, and in effect to make developing states pay the social costs of the policy.

But this was merely an expression of a general situation: that free trade could involve social and political costs for all states.

The rational course of action was therefore to measure the costs against the benefits of free trade and to calculate a strategy for balancing the costs against the benefits over time. Of course it was necessary to measure how far to defend local production against any gains that might arise from freeing trade. But the error was in seeing export-led growth as the only trade policy when a sensible strategy was to seek the right mix of exports and import substitution. To insist on the superiority of export-led growth was to promote a dogma that could ignore social and political realities. It reflected a determination to put trade before people.

A similar argument concerned the belief that development was linked with increasing income differentials, and that these in general were good. This argument, which was always an ideological one, was challenged increasingly by economists in the 1990s. Indeed Persson and Tabellini argued that inequality was actually harmful for growth.[46] The argument that maintaining higher levels of welfare spending was necessarily against the interests of companies was another neoliberal given that was open to attack. All these arguments could be considered by relevant organizations and epistemic communities and forced on to the political agenda. There were also those who denied the increase in income differentials within states and across them.[47] The argument usually depended on the use of gross statistics and the ignoring of significant exceptions. It stressed the mean rather than the difference between the best and the worst.

- A third agent was transnational labour organizations acting together. In the US labour had always been seen as the enemy of big business – Kapstein in effect said that this had always been the case – but individual trade union members could still escape culpability as they were also citizens and in this role had to be judged more favourably. The prejudice was that labour did not need any special protection, even against predatory management, as inevitable growth and expansion of production – a natural endowment of the American way – meant that another job would always come along. Workers in the USA were persuaded to accept this because they subscribed to the national myth of upward mobility – which was not borne out by the facts of US socio-economic life in the last quarter of the twentieth century. Indeed upward mobility in the US, in the face of this myth, was no different from that in Western Europe.

It was likely, therefore, that any initiative to organize labour transnationally would need to come from those able to act from outside the US, which would probably be the unions of social democratic Europe. Its goal would be to strengthen the capacity of labour to act transnationally, in particular, to impose costs on multinationals over the range of their operations in different countries if they transgressed labour codes. Tight transnational organization of unions was necessary to ensure collective action, and this probably meant moving towards the transnational federalization of such civil society organizations. This was a development which was a natural corollary of the globalization of production and was likely to be strongly resisted by multinationals.

It had been argued, especially by hopeful Americans, that the globalization of the economy had led as much to a levelling up of standards as to a levelling down. Companies, they claimed, had to accept environmental standards or standards on the specification of goods, in order that they could be sold in the first world. This could be acknowledged. But it was small beer compared with what was perceived as the general degradation of the conditions of employment, and it was hard to avoid the judgement that lowering welfare costs was one of the main purposes of neoliberal globalization as interpreted by political/ economic elites. The neoliberals also argued that the wider distribution of productive enterprise was bound to bring benefits for labour because of so-called 'trickle-down' effects. There would be technology transfer and job creation. Unfortunately this proved to be simply untrue. More and more exploited workers were, until quite late in the process of degradation, perfectly capable of upholding better and better standards in production processes, and the quality of goods. They were also capable of working with increasingly sophisticated technology without any commensurate benefit for themselves.

These arguments were taken up in the late 1990s in negotiations about what came to be called the social clause in the WTO, which was generally opposed by first-world governments as well as leaders in developing countries such as Malaysia.[48] The latter argued that a social clause which obliged employers, under penalty of legal sanction, to uphold responsible labour standards, would carry costs which could even lead to protection measures to offset the additional costs such standards would produce in the internal market. They would make it more difficult to uphold the Most Favoured Nation clause of GATT. So, instead, the strategy of choice was to agree core labour standards which would be incorporated into codes to be agreed and supervised by the ILO. The main point about these – the reason for preferring them – was that they were not linked closely to the WTO – though the WTO would cooperate to some degree with the ILO to supervise them – and that they were not subject to clear sanctions. They were to be upheld on the basis of informal arrangement, self-regulation and moral persuasion. In other words they could be avoided.

In the face of this failure to obtain a social clause at the global level, the way forward favoured by interested organizations, like the International Confederation of Free Trade Unions (ICFTU) was to turn attention away from the global level to the regional one.[49] At the global level the strategy of those opposed to stronger social action was often to insist on an institutional specialization. So, the WTO could not adopt the social clause, because this area of activity was the responsibity of the ILO, and insisting on this had the advantage of lessening the chances of a stronger, more coordinated social policy, increased the chances of dilution by multiplying the contexts of negotiation and capitalized on the weaknesses of the traditional forms of action in the ILO. The latter had built up a process of persuasion in drafting its codes and applying them, which was the result of a long experience of labour–employer hostility, and of disagreement between East and West during the period of the Cold War. It had certainly made a positive contribution, but more in a period of political than economic risk. It was, by temperament and experience, unlikely to see binding codes, backed by legal sanction as the way forward. All this suited the interest of those who preferred a minimalist strategy.

But there was strong evidence that labour codes with stronger backing from the law were being agreed and pursued through regional arrangements in the EU, but also in APEC and MERCOSUR. In the regions the pressures to have stronger social policies were more strongly felt because of a measure of cultural identity, and because the decision-making centres seemed closer and more controllable. But this was also linked with the trend for an increasing proportion of world trade to be at the regional level. At higher levels of trade interdependence the need to bring social costs into line was more pressing, as the effects of low standards of labour support and protection in some areas were more apparent, and their consequences for trade, if there were significant differences in cost, were manifest. In this case, as in so many others, the regional level was the preferred level of regulation. States which hesitated to accept stronger mechanisms in global organizations could accept them if they were operated in a context where standards were more likely to be related to local practice, and decisions made by a smaller more closely related group.

- A fourth agent was the guardians and rule-makers of big markets, especially the EU. The three or four big economic blocks acting together could win, but it was a problem that there was a powerful and, in 2002, dominant coalition in the US which was on the side of the big multilateral companies. Therefore it would need to be the EU plus regional groups such as ASEAN-APEC, and MERCOSUR in alliance against NAFTA. The EU had to recognize that it needed to take the lead on this. This was a position that the UK government of New Labour had yet to recognize at the time of writing. Getting better global standards demanded stronger leading regions. It was therefore also necessary to consider the ways in which the ability and willingness of Europeans to act could be strengthened. This would inevitably involve an increased risk of collision with right-wing USA.

The broad goal in this context – discussed further below – was to find ways of identifying social costs when multinationals relocated between countries within regions and between regions, and of finding a principle according to which these could be allocated between the company, the countries and the regions affected. It was entirely logical to enter social costs into this calculation, as economic costs did not have any natural independent existence. This could involve negotiating relocation codes among regions. In the first world too it was necessary to have an agreed response in the face of the irresponsible behaviour of companies. For instance the steel-making company, Corus, closed a works in South Wales in the UK at the cost of 6000 jobs, and defiantly refused any discussion with unions or government; and the UK retailer Marks and Spencer simply abandoned its stores in France. This would not be a simple matter, but it was clear that it could be tackled more effectively at the regional level and through trans-regional agreements. Rules were also needed which would not get in the way of new investment into less developed regions.

- A fifth agent was those able to build responsible coalitions, e.g. the United Nations. The global organization had the kind of initiative opportunity to be proactive in this context which did not often occur. It was the natural forum for encouraging the continuing consolidation of trade and investment regions and of a denser range of labour legislation. It could also promote greater transparency about labour practices, and work on codes to govern inter- and intra-regional investment. It could build on its extensive experience hitherto in the area of development by concentrating through its agencies as well as the Central Secretariat on working to strengthen the structures through which the developing world dealt with multinational companies. In other words the UN could be the primary agent of developing world regionalism in a cluster of economic activities, including production and labour standards.

Most importantly the UN could exploit the new structure of multinational companies to the advantage of the developing world. Their reliance on developing world production made them vulnerable to a collective strategy of cost enhancement. This would have to be carefully managed within and across regions, so that there was a maximum inflow of new investment to all regions, and a minimum relocation of old investment across regions. The agencies of the United Nations system, especially UNDP, and the economic departments in the central Secretariat, as well as agencies such the ILO, were uniquely placed to manage this process. The important thing was to realize what could be done, and define the codes, and set up the supporting machinery.

Strategies of the counter-strategy

It is possible to identify a range of possible strategies, that might be taken, and adapted, from a number of sources, such as successful past practice, or from *a priori* argument about existing circumstances and the possibilities they suggest. They amount to a set of reasoned statements about what could be done.

- *Explore the model of OPEC with regard to production processes?* The power of the branded companies comes from their ability to exploit competing producers. But what would be the prospects for getting elites in EPZs and developing countries to accept multi-country production agreements for manufacturing on the OPEC model? The problem hitherto had been that producers could exit in response to any relative increases in labour and social costs. But agreements among large groups of states to protect standards could make this more difficult. There was a need for a smaller number of larger groupings of producer states, between which capital movement would be subject to the kinds of codes alluded to above. Examples of these could be the UNDP country strategy notes, and the United Nations Development Assistance Frameworks developed through the United Nations Development Group. In principle there was a difference between new investment and the relocation of old investment. The former should be easy within the production area chosen by the investor, the latter would be more complex, subject to calculation and sharing of social costs.
- *Retain controls on capital movements?* This was an area where neoliberal apologists exaggerated the difficulty. In fact the number of channels through which international capital moved was limited to four major ones, Reuters, Minex, EBS/Quotron and Bloomberg; controlling capital movements again, or subjecting them to forms of toll payment, would not be difficult. In this instance too the neoliberals preferred to exaggerate the number of channels and the difficulty of effective control. Hence the idea of a tax on international currency speculation, the so-called Tobin tax or its equivalent, re-entered the agenda in the late 1990s. But other possibilities included a requirement to place a proportion of inward moving funds, or any value proportionate to that inflow (in liquid form), in a joint holding with host governments, or with an international agency such as UNDP to insure them against the social costs of leaving, subject to a code under the jurisdiction of an international authority. The reasoning behind this proposal is discussed more fully below. Neoliberals deliberately exaggerated the difficulty of control of capital movement and the multiplicity of channels, though their concern with the Multilateral Agreement on Investment in the 1990s rather gave the lie to this!

- *Explore and advertise the systemic risks of capitalism in the early twenty-first century?* One source of the risk of collapse was the separation of nominal value from real value, which led to too many financial instruments which were tradable in themselves and increasingly remote from the market in 'stuff'. Profits were being derived from a virtual market rather than a real one. The complexity of these markets, and its vulnerability to unforeseen developments, made it dependent on the decisions of fewer and fewer people who were more and more likely to make mistakes, and more and more capable of abusing the system for their own ends. Finding ways of reinforcing the need for an increased mass market would increase the likelihood of a return to a more Fordist practice in which producers would have an interest in higher rather than lower levels of wages. There was a danger in abandoning Fordism arising from uncertainty about the point at which the numbers of engaged consumers declined beyond a critical point. Restrictions on the growth of leveraged instruments like hedge funds, futures markets, etc., were needed.
- *Develop strategies for deciding the allocation of social costs of relocation?* In this section a set of arguments is developed to illustrate the way in which the key actors could be targeted in one of their sites of vulnerability, that of access and exit to valued territories, especially economic regions. The assumption is made, a fair one, that all regions have something which the companies capable of moving capital want. Even in Africa there is a market of value, and there are production resources. All regions therefore have bargaining counters which can be used in negotiations with capital about location or relocation. This is intended to identify points for consideration and for refining or rejecting.

The arguments can be set out as follows:

The underlying assumption was that capital should be required to contribute directly to the social costs arising from its relocation or liquidation. The problem is to work out the principles and limits of such a scheme, how it would operate, and how it would be upheld. In order to reduce the risks of free-riding and evasion it would be necessary to have a limited number of investment regions, which would be large areas made up of clusters of states or large single states. The regions would also be big enough to have something which the companies would want, a market, even a small one, and resources. (There are some areas of course where the market is very big indeed, as with the market for anti-Aids drugs.) Thinking through the principles is made easier by:

1. assuming the existence of investment regions in the form of two or more groupings of developing states, A and B, and of developed states, C and D, and an international agency such as UNDP;
2. assuming capital investment in production facilities in region A;
3. assuming either increase in social charges in region A or C or decrease in social charges in region B or D;
4. assuming access to the same market from A or B or C and D, e.g. global or A + B or C + D or A + B + C + D, i.e. the market of the investment regions or the global market.

The question is then: how is relocation from A to B, or liquidation in A, to be compensated? The compensation is the mechanism for discouraging the irresponsible movement of capital.

The proposal is that the social charges would be calculated, and stated as an amount payable – a liability – to an investment agency such as UNDP, when capital moved into investment region A. The sum would be actually payable in full at the time of movement from A to B, or liquidation in A, and companies would be obliged to maintain their fluid assets at a level at which it could be paid. The sum would be applied by UNDP to financing improvements in A, e.g. to infrastructure, or social adjustment programmes, so that its competitive position would be improved. Monies held by UNDP could be invested and proceeds added to total available capital. Sums which were credits, to be realized if the company moved, could also be used by UNDP as collateral to raise funding in the market, or as a basis for a futures market.

The formula to be used in calculating the liability would be weighted as follows:

1. Inversely related to per capita GDP of the receiving region when that was classed as developing.
2. Positively related to the per capital GDP of the receiving region when that was classed as developed. Whether groups were developed or developing countries would be determined on the basis of per capita GDP.
3. Positively related to the scale of the inward investment.

The social charge would be actually payable when capital moved from one region to another and a new liability would be calculated on entry into the region. A sum equal to the sum paid would be available for social support expenditures in region A. Social charges would also apply, in the same way, to movements between groups of developed countries. No liability would be applied to new investment i.e. when there was no relocation, but investment was financed by the raising of new capital. No actual charges would exceed the taxation payable on the profits of the company and all its associated branches in all countries where it was located.

The means of change

Finally, in this account of the possibilities for action to counter the undesirable effects of neoliberal globalization, it is appropriate to discuss the kinds of mechanisms that could be used.

Moral persuasion

Instruments for achieving this include:

- ensuring open access to information: ensuring the right to presence for monitoring purpose of organizations such as NGOs, relevant IGHOs, and the media;
- setting up mechanisms for determining the saleability of goods through consumer associations, and effective national watchdogs;
- founding competent research organizations to explore the medium-term and long-term consequences of various modes of production and exploitation, and thereby exploiting anxiety about the future of the environment and of succeeding generations. Protecting the inheritance for posterity!

Imposition of charges and conditions

Instruments include:

- manipulating charges on exit and access. Establishing conditionality on access to factors of production and markets: seeking appropriate structures such as regional groupings of states (as above);
- generating conditions and tolls on system use: currency movements, stock movements, digital value transfers. Acting to maintain the manageability of transfer systems – Reuters (currency

transactions), Minex, EBS/Quotron and Bloomberg (stock trading).[50]

Social and legal regulation

Instruments include:

- drawing up codes and adherence incentives. Seeking to ensure compliance through informal sanctions through the international civil society of governments, formal procedures, through international courts, tribunals, etc., the internalizing international conventions, and linking national legal and policing jurisdictions together;
- agreeing a code, and linking it with penalties, for the economic performance of individual leaders. (There could be an audit of outgoing leaders.) The leaders of all states needed to subscribe to a code of good practice which was internationally and effectively monitored. There should be a requirement to justify and explain high levels of personal wealth in political leaders (it was often noticed that the richest leaders came from the poorest countries).

Using international institutional agency such as the UN machinery

In developing the means of power and facilitating its exercise the world of international organizations has an important role to play. Its role would be:

- to promote the necessary structural conditions – i.e. the existence of the regions, as indicated at various points of this chapter;
- to determine the structure of the investing companies, taking into account their global components and all locations;
- to calculate the scale of the liabilities, taking into account a number of guiding principles – transparency of economic benefits and social costs of relocation, disincentives to relocating from developing to developed regions, incentives to relocate from developed to developing regions;
- to negotiate agreement to the system across A, B, C and D;
- to set up a machinery to ensure the paying of the charges when due;
- to ensure they were applied to 'useful' investment.

Conclusions: clashing visions

This chapter has been about the clash of two visions of global economic macro-management. Each has been explored in comparison with the other. But in the first years of the twenty-first century this was not a contest of equals. On the one side was a coalition of the powers-that-be that broadly favoured neoliberal globalization, sometimes making timely concessions in the light of a likely challenge, but usually having their way. This involved risks. The primary risk was that the costs imposed upon labour, in developed as well as developing countries – mitigated only by the uncertain promise that everything would be better in the longer term, and that the medicine was necessary – would prove unbearable and generate massive political turbulence. The further risk was of a failure to manage the globalized system, because of a complete mismatch between the capacity of global governance and the weight and complexity of the global economy.

On the other hand was a coalition of academics, some enlightened governments, and business managers, which favoured a more people-friendly vision of globalization, which could be called a global theory of employment. In the international society of the early twenty-first century such a theory needed to relate to the linked problems of development and wealth distribution. These were not the powers that be, and the task facing them was to identify strategies for enhancing that power to the point at which it could be effective. But this was not an argument against globalization. Rather it was an argument in favour of a more liberal form.

Several changes in the 1990s and early twenty-first century had given the United Nations opportunities to enhance its impact on the practice and ideology of development. There had been a convergence among international agencies on the need for domestic reform within developing states across a wide agenda, in each part of which there was a requirement for positive action. In this work it was bound to find itself in the process of shaping alliances in opposition to those which were promoting versions of neoliberal globalization.

The changes needed included the discrediting of the intellectual community of the pure neoliberals and their agents in the main institutions of the first world. Their view that the development of states was merely an incidental, though desirable, consequence of more liberal policies, had to be discredited. The crises in the Far East and in Latin America in the 1990s were, eventually, capable of contributing to this. There was now a more widespread belief that a new approach to development was needed, which nevertheless built on the liberalization in the developing world of the 1980s and early 1990s. There were several different ways in which development could be helped in different regions, and it was no longer appropriate to talk of a single model of economic management, development and welfare provision, all under the umbrella heading of globalization. There was also a need for a new holism, meaning a realization that all these agendas, though separate, were linked, and that they demanded cooperation between the wider range of institutions.

There was also an increasing realization of the need for an active social agenda, rather than expecting better governance and welfare to follow naturally from the unregulated market. The appearance that the World Bank and IMF had become more actively involved in this could underline the need for cooperation between them and the members of the UN system. But there was a need for joined-up policy-making, in that the link between employment and wealth distribution policies, as promoted by multinational companies, and the development process, had to be clearly recognized. The UN system could make a useful contribution to this. Indeed the UN was now more likely to move back into a key position among these institutions, building on its contribution to development as recognized by Gus Speth. It was the natural primary forum for the emerging holism of this approach.

But what also emerged was that these arguments converged in support of the view that regionalization was a concomitant of globalization. It was not that the latter was a unified force, but rather that it needed unpacking into a number of separate but related dimensions. Within the three or four primary political-economic regions the various dimensions had different regional responses. There was a response which was primarily economic, which called for distinctive development policies within the regions, but also one which had political and social elements that asserted that there had to be local and varied responses to the pressures towards improved governance. There was of course a general pressure from globalization to raise standards, but this left a lot of scope for regional divergences. These issues are dealt with in greater depth at various points in this volume.

CHAPTER 6

The Principle of Consonance in Global Organization: The Case of the United Nations

Introduction

This chapter concentrates upon the consequences for global organization, taking the United Nations as the example, of the changing structure of international society. It sees the need to act collectively in the light of the globalization of problems and concerns. Difficulties and shortfalls have to be acknowledged in this context. But it also notes that there had emerged a new potential for regionalism in the light of globalization. The argument is that the global organization needs to reflect that changing structure. Too often it has been ignored in the discussions about changing the mechanisms of the UN, despite the obvious fact that the organization has contained regional groupings from the beginning. The broad assumption here is, however, that regions are continuing to solidify, that this is a positive development, and that UN structures should not get in its way. Changing international society should run in parallel with changes in global organization.

Sometimes UN problems had produced surprising results. For instance the shortage of finance – the squeeze – was certainly a major source of difficulty, but it also had positive aspects.[1] In late 1998, the USA had been close to losing its vote in the General Assembly, following Article 19 of the Charter, because of its failure to pay what it owed the organization. But a positive effect of the financial stringency was that the Agencies, and other organizations, were generally persuaded to be more system-orientated – to accept more coordination – so that they could get a larger piece of the smaller pie. The collapse of the Soviet Union, which in a united stable form in the late Gorbachev period had been a positive factor for the United Nations, also helped the agenda of democratization in developing countries. They could no longer avoid the pressures to build better civil societies, and promote human rights, by playing one superpower against the other. But the weakening of the Soviet Union's successor state, Russia, made it more difficult for the Security Council to act effectively.

In the phase of development of the international economic system which followed the fall of the Iron Curtain, which combined the triumph of liberal capitalism with budgetary constraint, it became apparent that developing states needed to attract private money, which was more likely to be available if societies were more open and more stable. This was of course often a dangerous game: openness was too often at the expense of mass unemployment which in turn could create civil unrest. Even the development of the new global systems had positive, as well as negative implications, from the point of view of entrenching multilateralism – i.e. strengthening the system of informal rules that governed relationships between states. The revolution in information technology was a part of the destabilizing process, with such developments as the computerization of currency speculation weakening governments' ability to maintain a stable system.

But at the same time the evolution of the global village meant that peace was now indivisible, and gross violations of human rights were likely to be brought to the attention of a wide public. This was part of the process of softening the old distinction between national interest and moral action. It was more likely that the national interest would be served by acting morally, as not do so would lead to a loss of status and the appearance of weakness.

Approaching the problems

There were a number of scholarly conferences on the Treaties of Westphalia in the years around the millennium – and with good reason: there was a useful comparison to be made between the situation which the emerging states faced in the early seventeenth century and that which faced states in the early years of the twenty-first century. In the first case states were faced with the problem of how to deal with fading transnational systems, in particular the secular empire of the Catholic church, as their power increased and as they gathered the appurtenances of sovereignty. In the latter case states were faced with the problem of relating their statehood and continuing sovereignty to emerging transnational forces. As Langhorne put it:

> In the first case, those developments had to do with secularisation following the Reformation in Europe, the successful establishment of independently acting states and the retreat of non-state jurisdictions and universalist ideas. The result was the gradual construction of an international system based on the principle that states alone had the right to be actors. What followed was a long period in which that principle was unchallenged and allowed the international system to exert pressure to conform on the actors: a reversal of what had happened during the emergence of the system. In the present case, *raison de système* has ceased to operate, or at least to operate reliably, and once again it is factors external to the system which have the whip hand: an international system consisting only of states or organizations which are the creatures of states cannot cope with developments and pressures which, because of the effects of the global communications revolution, extend horizontally across state boundaries and evade the controlling policies of their governments. Only when the process of change has produced a *really new world order* [my italics] reflecting the realities of the distribution of power among both the old and the new possessors of it, will a new system develop able to extrude similar pressures to conform.[2]

Changes in the mechanisms of the United Nations had to be considered in the context of the need for such a 'really new' world order. The preceding chapters indicate that the organization could be seen as a part of the transformation, helping with the entrenchment of multilateral rules, procedures and decision-making centres, so that global mechanisms for managing the global systems were developed. But its relationship with the environment of the society of states was also important. It could be assisted by the constellation of power or it could be enfeebled by changing structures and circumstances. The UN could help with the development of an international structure – of symbiotically related regions and global arrangements – in which governments would find it easier to cope with the new horizontal pressures. But alongside this was concern with the optimum organization of the UN itself – how might it be best governed? – so that it emerged as an effective actor in the new order? The latter is closely related to the former, and therefore care – often missing – needs to be taken to relate plans for the reform of the institution to the preferred pattern of evolution of international society.

The relationship could be a negative or a positive one. Plans for internal reorganization in the UN could be negated by an adverse international society, as is shown below; but, if properly conceived, they might also help a more supportive international society to develop. In sum: internal reforms needed to be related to the emerging world order. This chapter concentrates on the institutional mechanisms and the operational principles, but it attempts to relate arguments about internal change in the UN to the context in the international system. What is not discussed are the details of operational impact within particular states, or the shortfalls of resources in specific contexts.

Two approaches to the problem of controlling the transnational forces are conceivable. First the international mechanisms could be strengthened to maximize the potential for common control by states – which would inevitably be limited to the extent that their interests differed. Second the ability of the states to withstand disturbances generated by the transnational forces could be augmented: to the extent that the universal mechanisms fell short the local mechanisms needed to be strengthened. The best strategy for achieving the latter in the early twenty-first century remained the further development of the dominant structural trend of the second half of the twentieth century, namely progress towards denser organization at the regional level.[3]

Until countervailing global systems emerged, only further consolidation of regional organization could create circumstances in which the social, local interests of citizens could prevail over the global, profit-maximizing interests of multinational companies and other systems which could be tempted to pursue asocial strategies. Paradoxically, however, enhancing the strength of the regions was also a way of strengthening the global mechanisms. Stronger regions could more effectively resist multinationals but also make better, more densely constructed building blocks of a stronger set of international institutions, including the United Nations. The general requirement was that a *consonance* was required between the institution, how it was arranged, what it did, and its setting in society. The characteristics of society had to fit its instrument of governance, and international society was no exception.

Consonance is seen as having two levels. Internal consonance is when the sub-institutions are consonant with each other – the structure, processes and roles in one sub-institution complement and reinforce the structure, processes and roles in other sub-institutions. External consonance is when the overall set of institutions is consonant with its environment in international society – its internal consonance, as defined above, is promoted by the structure of international society, which is its primary environment, and the sub-institutions together promote a favourable structure of international society. Therefore it is necessary to avoid changes in one sub-institution which create contradictions in other sub-institutions in that their structure, processes and roles are in consequence reduced in efficiency and effect: and nothing should be done which gets in the way of the development of a more supportive international society or which inhibits the implications of the positive aspects of international society for internal consonance.

Obviously to carry out a full examination of the UN with these principles in mind would be a massive enterprise; in this chapter they are outlined and illustrated. This is at least a first step towards understanding how it could be made a more effective player in the current international system, able to contribute positively to the *really new world order*. Three elements of the institutions within the United Nations were selected for closer examination. First was the structure of the membership, defined in terms of members' orientation towards the institution in comparison with their status in international society; second was the form of collective activity undertaken in the various sub-institutions; and third was the structure of the institution in terms of its sub-institutions (Security Council, General Assembly, etc.). The points argued here are that: each of the elements has features which might be consonant or dissonant in relation to those of the other elements; a lack of consonance between the features in each of the three elements would lead to tensions and inefficiencies in the institution – i.e. the ideal was overall consonance, both among the sub-institutions of the UN system and between them and the environment of the society of states.

There were, then, two interrelated questions to be discussed: what were the general guidelines on how to construct the best kind of United Nations and how should it be related to the society of states? The next two sections focus on the first two elements which are relevant to consonance; the third is discussed *passim*. In the third section examples of consonance and dissonance are addressed more directly.

The pattern of UN membership

The following typology of state memberships in the United Nations is based on two criteria: the orientation of their governments towards the organization and their status in the hierarchy of states at the global and regional level. Groups of states can be identified which constitute the structure of membership. In the later discussion frequent reference is made to this typology.

1. *Status quo powers, having a position in the organization which matched their status* in global international society (e.g. US, China, and late USSR). These were states where governments were largely supportive of the system and prepared to work through it. They saw the UN as an instrument of their foreign policy, and their role and status in the organization matched their perceived position in the international hierarchy. They had major vetoing or promotional capacity in the context of the institution.

2. *Status quo powers, having a position in the organization which exceeded their status* in global international society, but which could claim to be representative of a region (e.g. UK, France). These were states which occupied a position in the international hierarchy which was lower than that which they occupied in the structure of the United Nations. But they saw that mismatch as suiting their interests in that their position in the organization added to their status outside it. It was said that the British position in the UN allowed that state to 'punch above its weight', which was also true of France. But there was a coincidence between their regional position and their global institutional one in that the convergence of regional interests was sufficient for their role in the UN to be seen as compatible with a representative element. This convergence, together with their overall contribution, justified their UN status.

3. *Reformist states* (e.g. Germany, Japan). These were states which were significant contributors to the organization – they had high informal status – but which saw a mismatch between their emergent global status and their formal status in the organization. They therefore wished to enhance their position in the latter to reflect the former. This interest was not seen as posing any problems for their regional partners, for reasons discussed below, even though the latter might not always positively support it, as with the case of Italy's policy on Germany's claim to membership of the Security Council. (This group is discussed in comparison with others more fully below.)

4. *System-reinforcing problem-solvers* (e.g. Sweden, Netherlands, Norway, Finland, Canada). These were countries which made no claims for enhancement in the formal structure of the

organization, even though they were significant contributors and had high informal status. They were relatively unconcerned about obtaining a match between their status in the international hierarchy and their formal status in the UN. They had no claims based on regional representation. They were positive about their membership – seeing it as bringing proportionate benefits, and being prepared to contribute positively to its work and the solving of problems within it – without attaching these to formal promotion in the institutions – e.g. they refrained from demanding special Security Council membership for themselves to reflect their status as good citizens in the UN and in the global international hierarchy. They were significant net contributors to the resources of the institution, in terms of money, and/or supportive involvement and policy development.

5. *Reformist states.* These were states which made claims for formal enhancement in the organization which exceeded their general status in the international hierarchy, and which presented a contested claim to represent regions (e.g. Brazil, India, Nigeria). They saw the promotion of their position in the global organization as an instrument for promoting their status among the states of the region to which they belonged, as well as in global international society. For instance, for Brazil, becoming a member of the Security Council would multiply its power but also increase its status in comparison with other Latin American states, in particular the Argentine. (This is discussed further below.) Moving up the institutional hierarchy was likely to increase divergence at the regional level. Similar arguments applied to India and to Nigeria.

6. *System-loading claimants* (e.g. failing and non-developed: G77 and most of Africa). These were states which looked to the organization for the solution of their economic, social political problems, were low in the global international hierarchy, and did not claim to represent a region. They made little contribution to the development of the institution's resources, and were generally short of the skills and resources required for efficient administration and the maintenance of a modern civil society – i.e. they were generally claimants, and beneficiaries, rather than contributors. But they were prepared to work in the existing structures. In the late 1990s this group could be subdivided into two groups: the least developed, which were close to collapse as states, and included states in Africa south of the Sahara; and

those which were somewhat more advanced in economic and political terms and which could be fairly described as developing. The latter's claims in some ways got in the way of attempts to solve the problems of the worse off.
7. *The new dissatisfied powers.* These were states which saw the institution as being in need of drastic reform in order to meet their interests, but at the same time were claimants on the system (e.g. Yemen, Cuba, Sudan, Malaysia, sometimes Algeria). They were constantly working for system revolution, and had no expectation of position enhancement within it in its existing form. In particular they sought to acquire structural power by actively promoting collective action in the plenary meetings, and thereby enhancing their position in a more populist UN, but they had little regional base.
8. *The Al Capone-syndrome states* (Libya, Iran, Iraq, Burma). These were states which remained members in order to do what they could to prevent further moves against themselves, and in the late 1990s could be regarded as semi-detached from the UN. As with the decision to be with or against the Chicago gangster in the 1930s: 'If they weren't there it would be worse for them.' Their strategy was the negative one of remaining in the organization, even though they saw no particular 'positive' benefit in this, simply because leaving would risk even greater costs. They had little or no regional status or representative claims.

A further comparison of the orientation of states in groups 2, 3 and 5 is illuminating. The UK is taken as illustrative of Group 2, Brazil of Group 5 and Germany of Group 3. By the late 1990s the attitude of the UK towards the reform of the UN, particularly the Security Council, was strongly affected by its membership of the European Union. Unlike 1945, arguments about the role of the British and the Brazilians were crucially affected by their relationship with regional institutions in Europe and Latin America. The situation in the late 1990s was that the UK and France still reserved their right to decide for themselves on issues which were on the agenda of the UN. They agreed to inform the other members of the EU through the machinery in New York but would not be bound by instructions from their partners. This was protected by agreements in the Single European Act and the Maastricht Treaty. Because of the EU's gradual development of stronger mechanisms for a Common Foreign and Security Policy (CFSP) this position was becoming more difficult to maintain.[4] To the extent that the CFSP became stronger, interests and policies of which the UK approved and which it had helped to shape, would be collectively pursued.

A regional identity in foreign policy would paradoxically make the question of whether the British and French should lose their membership of the Security Council a less sensitive one. If they stayed they could represent the EU; if they went the EU representative could take over – the difference was not critical. But in the late 1990s, although the British remained unwilling to renounce their ability to act independently on the Council, and to promote its unilateral position in that context, the matter was by no means as sensitive as it would have been if the EU had not existed. Indeed the whole question of German accession to the Security Council as a veto-bearing permanent member was less important to the extent that the regional partnership made the precise nature of the Union's representation in the Council less sensitive.

In contrast some countries sought seats in the Security Council for more traditional reasons. Brazil, for instance, saw membership of the Council as one of the steps in its emergence as a ranking power, a confirmation of status and acceptance by the states that mattered. It saw that membership as confirming its leadership of the regional group of which it was a member, MERCOSUR, which aspired in the late 1990s to emulate the EU. Unlike the case with Britain, membership was seen as an aspect of the defining of Brazilian identity, and its role in the world, and could not be mediated through the notion of an emerging regionalism in Latin America. While British attitudes towards protecting its Security Council position were mixed, it was conceivable by the late 1990s that there could be a regional successor or – more likely – a stronger form of mandating of members by the partners. In contrast Brazil's position was an indication of the weakness of MERCOSUR in that it would help to assert its separate foreign policy identity especially in relation to Argentina. If anything Brazilian membership would challenge rather than enhance regional integration, in that it would increase the status of the biggest regional state at a point in the evolution of MERCOSUR when countervailing regionally located institutions and policy-making arrangements were weak.

From the point of view of the reform of the United Nations it was unlikely that the Security Council membership of states such as Brazil, India and Nigeria would be helpful. Such reforms would be unlikely to increase the effectiveness or efficiency of the Security

Council. Brazil could not claim to represent a set of regionally agreed interests, in the sense that they emerged by consultation in a set of legitimate institutions embodying common interests, as potentially with the CFSP of the EU: membership looked like a form of triumphalism in relations with the Argentine. In the arguments for membership the question of the capabilities of Brazil in performing UN tasks got little attention, though there was some reference to the modest involvement of Brazilian forces in peacekeeping: it was more a question of entitlements and claims, entitlements because of emerging national economic strength and claims to be promoting international democracy by representing Latin America more effectively in the UN. Both arguments rested on uncertain foundations: would economic recovery continue? In what sense could Brazil represent other Latin American countries which expressed doubts about its right to do so?

By the late 1990s Britain appeared to have accepted without enthusiasm the case for enlargement of the Council to include Germany, Japan and an undetermined number of non-permanent members. Japan had taken the United Kingdom's 'second place' in the International Monetary Fund (IMF), and both Japan and Germany had provided high-ranking international civil servants in WHO and NATO respectively. But the United Kingdom was seen as a reliable member of the Council, with a wealth of experience in multilateral diplomacy – more than the US – and first-rate diplomats in New York. It was acknowledged by other members that the United Kingdom (and France) were different from countries such as Germany and Japan. The United Kingdom was a nuclear power and had a global military reach surpassed only by the United States. Moreover, again like France, the United Kingdom had an inclination to act, which seemed likely to be stronger under New Labour. The British were unique in having both a large number of technical skills, in drafting, committee work and so on, and great ability in the processes of multilateral diplomacy, and in the possession of a world-view.

The question of the resources, tangible and intangible, which candidate and member states could bring to the Security Council was highly significant. In contrast with the members of the first 4 groups, Group 5 members were more likely to be net consumers than contributors of resources! They were, taken as a group, of uncertain internal stability, with challenges from other states in their regions, and without global experience or interests. In the late 1990s they also had to be taken as lacking a reserve of tangible resources which could be significant additions to the UN's peacekeeping or development capacity; both tasks had greatly expanded so that the resources of the big players were inevitably critical. Placed in the context of the hierarchy of states, it was therefore easy to see that there would be serious dissonance between the formal status of such states in the UN and their actual status in international society, such that they would be more likely to detract from than add to the overall capacity of the institution.

The principles of collective actions

Three types of collective actions are referred to here:

First form

A first form included action to initiate major operations for norm maintenance, such as peacekeeping, humanitarian intervention or enforcement under Chapter VII, but could include executive action in other member organizations to initiate forceful – not necessarily violent – action. The main forum of this form of collective action was the Security Council, which could take decisions in the event of threats to international peace and security, decisions involving significant expenditure in such areas as peacekeeping and enforcement; and approve major expenditures on humanitarian intervention operations.

In the late 1990s the United Nations seemed to be very much improved as regards its mechanisms, but nevertheless the strong impression was that it was not succeeding. There had been relative failures in Rwanda–Burundi and the Congo, and it looked as though the Western states would back away from their commitment to remove chemical, nuclear and bacteriological weapons from Iraq through the UN inspection teams.[5] Only a few months earlier military action had been threatened in the face of Iraqi obduracy. The question was constantly put: who or what was to blame? There was talk of a failure of political will and often the accusation was addressed explicitly at the United States. That country had emerged as the triumphant superpower at the end of the Cold War and yet was seen as being primarily responsible for the failure of the UN to act as the world's policeman. There was no doubt that some of the blame could fairly be attached to the United States, but that was only a part of the picture.

A brief discussion of the more obvious rules of collective action develops this point.

1. It is a truism to say that action to protect global standards would be more likely if that action coincided with the perceived interests of the states. But the history of the United Nations showed positive developments in this context, as has been argued in the previous chapters: it was more likely that in the late 1990s moral action – to protect a norm – in fact coincided with national interests. It would add to the status of a state in the community of states, would be seen as a qualification for high office in the institutions of international society and would help a government with its electorate. The role of the mass media in this was crucial. It ensured that for the first time in the development of global society peace was indeed indivisible.
2. The chance that a large number of actors would agree to take decisive action to enforce global standards – meaning to act firmly, accepting costs and not merely expressing support for action – was less than was the case with a smaller number of actors. But there were reasons for supposing that a *single* actor, even the most powerful one, would also be unlikely to wish to go it alone; the costs would be relatively high because unshared, and the perception that others were free-loading would be strong; there would be the risk that the acting state would be blamed for failure, would be too exposed to adverse judgement if things began to go wrong and would get little credit if they went right. Success was rarely clear-cut and in any case was only to be expected if undertaken by a superpower. The risks of going it alone would be high, and others' failure to act would make it look morally acceptable to do nothing, especially as their hesitation would inevitably attract the attention of the media.
3. The chances of action being taken would be greater if the decision depended upon agreement to act among a small number of states. In this case the risks of incurring the costs outlined in paragraph 2 would be less. It would be easier to get agreement among a small group first and then to persuade others to that position, than it would be to get agreement at the outset among the members of the larger group. But even in a small group it would be necessary that a subgroup, possibly of just one – but probably of no more than two – should be prepared to initiate

action and to appear to be prepared to risk going ahead of the others. Action could not depend upon the general and equal commitment of members, even of a small group. The expectation of this would lead to paralysis. Someone had *to appear* to be prepared to go ahead. But the conviction had to be general that a failure to follow would be greeted with opprobrium and create serious costs. If no state was prepared to go ahead the collective will would be undermined, though the conviction that support for the initiator would be forthcoming was essential.

This rather basic piece of reasoning is highly significant from the point of view of understanding the failures of the UN in the late 1990s. The internal problems of the Clinton regime in the United States, which included the difficulties with his private life, as well as the powerful position of anti-internationalist Republicans in Congress, were only one source of the appearance of institutional *lourdeur* in the UN. But equally important was the lack of any other significant actor in the international system which was prepared to support action, to contribute resources which were enough to make a significant difference to the chance of success and to stay in convoy. The position of the European Union had become a difficulty rather than an asset from the point of view of successful action.

A comparison of circumstances in the early and late 1990s is illustrative. The move towards effective action in the Gulf in 1991–2 had been much helped by the emergence of a close coalition, under US, UK and French leadership, which had been institutionalized in the P5 arrangement. An informal amendment to Security Council practice was initiated by the then British ambassador, Sir John Thomson, in the mid-1980s, who, sensing a change in mood in the Iran–Iraq war and in Soviet attitudes towards the United Nations, acted as a catalyst. The idea was that the permanent members would meet before full Council meetings to agree proposals if possible. Thomson talked to his French counterpart with a view to making a joint suggestion for P5 consultation. However, for various reasons of an accidental nature, it was Thomson who made the telephone calls. He did not consult the FCO before issuing the invitations, and his Soviet colleague responded without consulting Moscow. The Chinese dithered but, in fact, were present at the initial meeting in the autumn of 1986. A second meeting took place two days later, and on that occasion the FCO and the Secretary-General were both informed. The Secretary-General, however, was not invited to join the group, a sign that the group was not prepared to commit itself in advance to a general rule of mediation, which would have been the implication of Secretary-General involvement. It could be more activist than that! As the initial coordinator Thomson (and his successor, Sir Crispin Tickell) briefed the Secretary-General and others, such as the non-permanent members and the non-aligned movement, either alone or with representatives of the other permanent members. The meetings were weekly or even more frequent, depending on items on the agenda. The meetings themselves were informal, of a confidential character, and work, in English, was on the basis of consensus.

Coordination rotated on a three-monthly basis: France resisted a 'permanent' coordinating role for the United Kingdom. The ground rules were that no member should insist on discussing an issue that another member did not wish to have considered. However, any question could be raised. The work, which started at the end of 1986, was on the basis of written documents and came into operation when the Five had a definite objective in mind. It therefore met on demand. There were also occasional meetings of the five foreign ministers with the Secretary-General – another British initiative. Moreover, it was under British chairmanship in January 1992 that the heads of government of the members of the Security Council met in session for the first time – a meeting that invited the Secretary-General to prepare his *Agenda for Peace*. Reflecting on his experience with coordinating permanent member cooperation, Sir Crispin Tickell told a University of Georgia audience:

> Two things are necessary for success. First is an identification of common interest and political will to construct joint policies based on it. Second is a good relationship between the Permanent and non-Permanent Members: for while the Five can stop anything, they do not, by themselves, carry a majority in the Security Council. You will note an important point: the negative power of the Five has always been vital; but now we are seeing the development of the positive power of the Five, and that may turn out to be more important still.[6]

The *positive power* of the P5 arrangement was of key importance in the UN's success in the late 1980s and the early 1990s: ending the Iran–Iraq war and winning the enforcement action against Saddam Hussein.[7] By the late 1990s, however, the ties of the successful coalition had been much weakened. The failure of the member states of the EU, including Britain and France, to act decisively in the early days of the Yugoslavia crisis, was of crucial importance from the point of view of the later failure of the UN. It began a noticeable pattern of failure to achieve in the EU an acceptable consensus on foreign policy, illustrated by the root and branch opposition of some states to majority voting on foreign policy questions in the Council of Ministers; and the determination of some states to widen the EU's membership which, intentionally or not, was bound to lead to a weakening of its central institutions and to lessen the chances of agreement to push effective action in the UN. The EU now began to appear in the unhappy position of not being united enough to act together decisively in *high politics* aspects of foreign policy, including in relation to Security Council decisions, and in support of the US; but of being united enough for dissent among members to handicap the ability of any one member to act alone.

This was true of the most willing ally – Britain – whose independent military resources, in any case, were insufficient to act alone, or indeed to make much difference in crises which required the strength of the US. In other words the failure of the UN in the late 1990s was as much to do with the failure of the EU to push a more integrated foreign policy and to emerge as a significant actor, as it was to do with US failures. For the time being at least the CFSP had become a mechanism for the mutual enfeeblement of its members in the UN context, and in particular that of the Security Council. It was strong enough to get in the way of an activist P5 coalition, but not strong enough to provide a reliable partner for the US. And this meant a partner which, in principle, if necessary, was capable of acting effectively alone.

The end of the Cold War was also in the circumstances of the 1990s unhelpful. It provided a context in which the EU would be enfeebled by pressures towards enlargement, and by disagreement over East European policy. At the same time, as events turned out, the new Russia was a broken reed, incapable of effective action but strong enough to put large road blocks in the way of states which wished to do so in the Security Council. By the late 1990s both Russia and the EU had become relatively ineffective in foreign policy. If one was in the business of attaching blame for the failure of the UN in the late 1990s blame should also be attached to those in the EU who failed to appreciate the way in which the regional and global systems fitted together, and the way in which a stronger, necessarily non-enlarged, EU could more effectively act with the US in promoting world order. Russia could conceivably also have done this had it been possible to move more easily from communism to capitalism.

Unfortunately another historical disjunction meant that extreme economic liberalism became the ideological flavour of the 1980s and 1990s and pushed the Russians to destroy their existing systems without putting anything in their place. In consequence it made sense to blame the shallow sentimental nationalisms of some of the member states of the EU, and even the orthodoxies of the right-wing supply-side economists, as much as the US Administration of Bill Clinton, for the failures of the UN in the late 1990s.

Second form

A second form of collective action was appropriate to a second major type of decision-making in the UN system: that on expenditure out of assessed budget in economic/social decision forums. These were where decisions on expenditure were made for economic and social programmes over the wide range of UN concerns, usually involving an attempt to relate policy decisions with budgetary plans on a biennial basis. The UN central system's main forum for this type of collective action was the CPC but by the late 1990s almost all the Agencies had a similar forum. The introduction and implications of this procedure were discussed as follows in the author's 1993 account:[8]

> The budgetary process agreed on 18 December 1986 could be seen as a compromise between the Committee of Eighteen's first and second sets of proposals. It rejected the proposal in the third set that the CPC should determine in advance the resources available, but accepted the CPC's primary role in considering the Secretary-General's outline budget and proffering advice on it to the General Assembly in the 'off-budget' years. In the budget years, however, after the budget had been reconsidered by the Assembly, and turned into firm proposals by the Secretary-General, it would be forwarded to both the CPC and the ACABQ which were to advise the Fifth Committee 'in accordance with their respective mandates'. The Resolution also accepted the various proposals concerning the upgrading of the CPC and it looked as though it would now be a more formidable institution, expected to play a key role in relating the budgetary proposals to the Medium Term Plan, and in shaping the latter. It was to be involved from the beginning in the process of shaping the budget. In other words it was accepted that the CPC would be the principal 'advisory' and 'intergovernmental' committee on these matters.
>
> In view of this, one particular decision in the resolution attracted particular attention, and was regarded as a breakthrough by United States officials. This was the agreement in paragraph 6 that the CPC should continue its existing practice of reaching decisions by consensus. Paragraph 7 took this further with the stipulation that 'all

possible efforts' should be made in the Fifth Committee 'with a view to establishing the broadest possible agreement'. The argument seemed to be that though consensus had been the established way of reaching agreement before the reforms, this was not significant as long as the CPC's role was modest. With the development of that role, however, there was a greater risk that voting would take place, and lines drawn between the larger number of smaller contributors, and the smaller number of larger contributors. Conversely, the requirement of consensus would greatly increase the leverage which could be exercised by the major contributing states over the others. The client states would be more frequently placed in a situation in which they either concurred with the contributing states, or risked losing the latter's funds. The consensus approach, in other words, was viewed as a weapon in the hands of the rich which could be used to get the poor states to accept the discipline of the Medium Term Plan. The rich states would also, however, have been able to play a decisive role in shaping the Medium Term Plan in the CPC: decisions in that process would also be taken on the basis of consensus. There is evidence to suggest that the US Administration, or at least, officials within it, regarded these arrangements as largely satisfying the demands made at the time of the Kassebaum Amendment, and that they were now prepared to make approaches to Congress, with a view to restoring full funding to the UN system.

It is not, of course, that the CPC could be sure that its budgetary proposals would be accepted by the Fifth Committee or the General Assembly. But the richer states could be expected to exercise greater authority in the smaller CPC. The question of whether insisting upon consensus voting was compatible with the Charter – that it was legal – also remained to be examined. The appeal for consensus in the Fifth Committee would only marginally reduce the chances of adverse votes. A more important disincentive, however, would be that it would be more difficult, and, from the point of view of the poorer states, even dangerous, to unravel a carefully structured budget, relating resources to priorities, monetary commitments to programmes and intentions, which had already been agreed in the CPC. It was, therefore, more a question of tipping the balance of probabilities in favour of the richer states, of making it easier for them to lead and more difficult for the poorer states not to follow, rather than one of eliminating opposition. It would be a matter of management, not of control.

It is, however, arguable that the financial weapon, as used by the US, was likely to prove a powerful incentive for the more general reform of the United Nations system. The report of the Committee of Eighteen itself exemplified this. The proposed changes in the budgetary process may be seen as attempts at institutionalizing in the United Nations arrangements the ability of the rich to use the financial weapon to press on a continuing basis for reforms which they preferred. In other words, they were aimed at in effect incorporating the Kassebaum Amendment informally into the United Nations Charter. The discrepancy between voting power and financial power, which had long irritated the US, was to be reduced. That this prospect was in the minds of US officials was revealed by their view that improving the budgetary process in the central system was only the beginning of the reform effort. The agenda, no longer hidden, was for similar reforms to be introduced into all the Specialized Agencies: they were all to be required to accept consensus voting in their key budgetary committees as a condition of full funding. Even the International Labour Organization, which was regarded as having reformed its budgetary arrangements after the 1978 US withdrawal, was nevertheless to be deprived of funds unless and until the consensus procedure had been introduced. This was the position taken by US officials in the summer of 1987. Consensus became the practical alternative in US eyes to weighted voting.[9]

The procedure found an echo in the reformed arrangements of ECOSOC. Decisions about spending were to be considered in the context of decisions about policy in a single forum which included the major donors, the major spending institutions, and the major beneficiaries. Decisions were taken by consensus. The expectation was that the participants' involvement with each other would create pressures on them in favour of supporting the approved package in other forums. In the case of the CPC process this assumption proved to be correct, in that the Fifth Committee of the General Assembly accepted the CPC's budget with little dissent after the new procedure was introduced in December 1986.

Third form

The third major form of collective action in the UN system was found when an institution's main functions were, for example, to agree general policy recommendations, to assert a norm or a broadly defined objective, rather than a precise command. Plenary meetings of international representatives such as the General Assembly, were usually not empowered to take legally binding decisions: their acts had the status of recommendations. This was also characteristic of advocacy institutions such as UNCTAD, which were concerned with mobilizing a large group of states in support of a strategic plan such as the New International Economic Order. Why was a plenary body, such as the General Assembly, *not* likely to be effective in making decisions to pursue specific goals energetically and effectively, as was the ideal in the case of Security Council action? The range of contributions of the Assembly, such as identifying coalitions of states, and promoting quiet diplomacy, were considered in depth: but rarely the question of what it was *unfit* to do.

The difficulty of agreeing about more precisely defined and targeted action was likely to increase as the number of members increased. A plenary body of two hundred was very unlikely to achieve consensus on such action. Indeed, the history of the General Assembly indicated an opposite inclination. The trend in 1990s' resolutions was for an increasing number of decisions to be taken on the basis of consensus or 'approval without vote', but this reflected more a failure of will than a genuine agreement.[9] It was a consequence of formulating resolutions in more general terms, and concealed the level of potential dissent, which would become more explicit as the wording became tighter. This habit had certain advantages from the point of view of getting agreement about general codes or rules. Governments could agree on a general expression, precisely because they believed they could evade its implications for actual behaviour in the short term. And in the long term it represented the beginning of a ratchet process. In time instruments were set up for pressing more practical and direct application of the codes which had been approved.

But there were a number of problems when resolutions became more explicit and directly targeted. One could be called the problem of *false echo*, when different and contradictory versions of the resolution were approved. This could result from the difficulty of establishing an agreed hierarchy of priorities among so many governments. The issue might be regarded as important by everybody but not equally as their first priority. The context was an opportunity for the pursuit of individual agendas which did not precisely overlap, and hence a number of resolutions, each an imperfect echo of the other, would be pressed, even if one or other of them was pushed to approval by majority vote. This would naturally be likely to cause uncertainty of purpose and irresolution in execution. Another problem was that of maintaining consistency over time among a series of linked resolutions, which, as with the Security Council and the Gulf War in the early 1990s, would be required in the various stages of a protracted operation. In large assemblies, like the General Assembly, it was more likely that new majorities would need to be constructed for each new resolution, increasing the risk of inconsistency among the resolutions over time: this was a problem, even in the Security Council, illustrated by *mission creep*, but the risk would be greater in the larger body.

There would also be problems connected with the setting up of an executive committee, which would often be a necessary mechanism: it would be required to take on responsibility for the day-to-day running of an operation. Such a committee was built into the structure of the Security Council, but in the Assembly protracted diplomacy about initial membership was likely, and the qualifications of particular governments to remain members as circumstances changed would be disputed. One reason for a number of these difficulties was the rather more diffuse social cement in the larger bodies compared with the smaller ones. The development of a degree of collegiality, based on personal acquaintance and common experience, often lay at the heart of a sustained consensus in active, and costly, pursuit of specific goals. It would be more difficult for an individual to behave irrationally or inconsistently in a small group as the disapproval would be more personal and direct.

These are the three major forms of collective action which are each necessary in the overall functioning of the United Nations. It was important to note, however, that each required different ways of making decisions, with regard to different purposes, among different memberships. There was an implied consonance between these various elements in the sense that a different matching would lead to inefficiencies: having a different pattern of memberships, purposes and forms of action, would increase the difficulties in the way of effective action. At the same time the relationships of the sub-institutions, thus conceived, to each other fitted a rational overall institutional design. There was an element of executive agency, for instance in the Security Council, and in the implications of the reforms for ECOSOC; there was an element of code making, and consensus building, in the various plenary meetings; there was an appropriate mix of contributor and recipient inputs in the budgetary mechanisms; and, as will be argued below, there was an element of distinctive secretariat provision. These, and other elements, added up to an overall structure the internal elements of which were rationally related to each other by dint of membership, purpose and style of collective action. There were, therefore, good reasons why a particular institution should not behave as if it were another institution, and should not attempt to acquire the colouration of the whole – as one official said about UNCTAD in the 1970s.[10] Decisions about spending had to be taken in institutions which looked like the CPC. Decisions about norms, or general principles needed to be taken by institutions such as the General Assembly, which could not, because of its membership and necessary relationship with the other institutions, take binding decisions which were precisely targeted.

The idea that the Assembly could act as a manager of the Specialized Agencies was therefore misconceived, as was the idea that the ECOSOC and CPC should be made up of all members. The reform of the ECOSOC to strengthen its coordination role, and the ability of CPC to decide the budget, would be obstructed by such a move. But the Security Council was not constructed to define norms and general standards. A lot more could be said about this, but the general principle was clear: the institutions of the UN had to concentrate on doing better what their positions in the system, the nature of their membership and the style of their activity – each related to the other – indicated they could do. Reforms of the various parts of the system needed to start from the assumption that there was a requirement for consonance between the features of the different elements in the system.

Principles of consonance in the United Nations

Any attempt to locate the principles, which should be taken into account when proposing reforms of the United Nations, should respect the need for consonance of the membership structure, the various forms of collective action, and the overall structure of the institution itself. A consonant relationship of this overall structure with its environment in the society of states was also necessary. What follows is a selection of the resulting injunctions.

1. *States which contributed most to funding should have the biggest say in budgets and spending.* An implication of this was that the main contributing states could not be required to pay for operations of which they disapproved. This point is not particularly startling, and after the reform of the budgetary arrangements of the UN and of a number of the agencies in the late 1980s it became an accepted principle. What it pointed to was the need to obtain donor approval for operations, and to have in place consensus-maximizing practices. This moved into the area of judgement of proper and acceptable expenditure which was very much a matter of norms and expectations. It was necessary that the arrangements should promote, rather than get in the way of, the development of these. One sure way of increasing the resistance of donors was to have decisions about the budget controlled by beneficiaries, which appeared to be the case before the mid-1980s in many of the budgets of the UN system. In the terminology of this chapter this was a situation of dissonance between activities and the structure of membership.

   This is not to deny that the UN and the system was in serious financial difficulties in the late 1990s. Some of the reasons for this were not directly related to the budgetary process and the norms and expectations of expenditure among members. But it was important to create a context in which agreement to return to paying contributions by all members, but particularly the US, could be sustained. The principle of consonance was an essential part of this. The implications for the arrangements of the UN system was that decisions which involved spending, and making itemized budgets, should be taken in small joint committees of donors, representatives of the beneficiaries and the spending agencies, on the basis of consensus. The model for this was the CPC, and the emerging pattern of ECOSOC segments.

2. *The specialized character of the various component institutions of the United Nations should be recognized and asserted.* The functional and membership differentiation had been built into the original design but had been maintained precariously over the years in response to various *ad hoc* challenges. In the late 1990s claims to make the UN more democratic, i.e. to make all decisions in plenary meetings on the basis of majoritarian democratic principles, were still being pressed; and, at the other end of the spectrum of opinion, were still those, of decreasing weight and number, who held that their superpower of choice should act unilaterally regardless of the views of the UN membership. These were the clashing visions mediated in this chapter.

A specific example of the confusion of procedural principles – of dissonance between structure, activities and procedure – was when an organization, such as an Agency, or a Fund or Programme like UNCTAD, began to move from its original function as a forum of policy development, into direct operational activities.[11] When this happened hopes were raised for the majoritarians that decisions about expenditure would be made in ways other than those recommended here, i.e. by committees dominated by beneficiaries or by agencies anxious for self-aggrandizement. Such developments would inevitably lead to deadlock. The first two kinds of collective action should always involve maximum non-binding consultation with the other categories of state. But they must be led by category 1 and 2 states, not the states from other categories, and they could only be effective if the diplomatic patterns reflected the principles of collective action outlined above.

3. *The international hierarchy of states should be reflected consistently in relation to the three forms of collective action across the UN's component institutions.* States should not have a higher status with regard to diplomatic/policy decisions than they had with regard to economic/social decisions. In plain English: it would get in the way of effective action if a beneficiary/system reformer state could command decisions on sanctions in the Security Council. Effective leadership by countries which were the major donors and the main contributors to the UN was essential.

   Enlarging the Security Council to include countries in Group 5, such as Brazil, raised the issue of whether this was compatible with other aspects of the reform of the UN system. Would it produce consonance or dissonance? How would this help to solve the problems of the Security Council, which in the late 1990s were judged to include the poor definition of mandates, the production of vague resolutions which were deliberately couched in general terms to facilitate a consensus of members, the problem of mission creep and the difficulty of agreeing to provide enough resources to pay for the agreed policies?

   Enlargement was at best irrelevant to these problems and it could exacerbate them. Was it likely that the states which contributed the overwhelming majority of resources for peacekeeping would accept decisions about military activity shaped by developing countries? But there was also the problem of the relationship between the Security Council and the economic and social areas of the UN. The complex crises of the late 1990s demanded the coordination of peacekeeping activities, political activities, development activities and humanitarian activities. Maintaining consistency between these various sectors was likely to be undermined by placing control in each in the hands of varying coalitions of states, especially when a major beneficiary from activity in one sector was instrumental in generating activity in another. The major donor states would feel unhappy about footing the bills for peacekeeping or humanitarian assistance operations that had been set up by coalitions of minor contributors. Different hierarchies in different institutions with regard to collective action would lead to increased problems of system-wide coordination.

4. *But supranational management principles were to be avoided.* This injunction emerged clearly from the lengthy discussion of ways

to obtain a more effective global policy on population control and how to manage the humanitarian aid process. The structure of the international system, and of the system of international institutions, was polycentric and any central organization claiming authority over the systems would inevitably be resisted. Proposals for reconstituting the agencies to bring them under more effective centralized control flew in the face of the logic of the system.

It would be impossible to get sufficient agreement among member states to achieve fundamental reforms of this kind. And the proposals could not achieve a safe answer to the question of who or what would do the controlling. The different categories of states had their own client institutions, and reform always raised the spectre that some other state category could gain control. Similarly the fact that this was a society of sovereign states meant that compromises between effectiveness and autonomy had to be made continuously. The best that could be hoped for was, therefore, enhanced consonance and in this context more effective coordination. This was precisely what was sought in the reformed ECOSOC and in the humanitarian arrangements under OCHA.[12]

5. *The UN should reflect in its internal reform process the need to encourage the emergence of an international society which was more favourable to its work*. This meant helping with the emergence of stronger multilateral frameworks, but also stronger subunits. For example there was a need for UN organizations to reflect and encourage regional consolidation: for example, any claim to promotion to membership of the Security Council, should be based on the ability of the candidate to enhance or reflect regional solidarity as well as to contribute resources to UN activities. The idea that non-permanent members of the Security Council should satisfy these criteria was already widely accepted in the late 1990s: those states which did were likely to return to membership more frequently. But as Bertrand pointed out, regions in the UN should be more consistently and rationally organized: different principles on groupings in different institutional settings encouraged division. It also got in the way of consolidating regional arrangements among the members of the regions outside the UN. The UN should be positively involved in strengthening the qualifications of states for promotion within the institution, by encouraging real regional

representation, as well as the more obvious enhancements, such as development.
6. *The donor states needed to multilateralize their leadership functions in the system.* For instance the few main contributor governments should develop their *mutual* consultation procedures and also those to coordinate policy towards the UN system *within* themselves. A part of the problem of UN coordination was a lack of donor agreement and of agreement among departments of the same government. It was remarkable that the main donor countries had not initiated more substantial mechanisms for coordinating their plans for spending among themselves, and, at the same time, for linking those with developing a consensus on policy so that multilateral arrangements would be strengthened. The Geneva Group was a long-standing institution, which brought the donor states together to talk about keeping control of the budget. But this had never been linked with a mechanism for building donor-country consensus on a rational overall plan for the programmes of the various spending institutions. There was a very important connection here: such coordination would confront donor states squarely with the problem of coordinating policy within and between the range of organizations in the system, which would in turn imply a stronger commitment to the resulting multilateral frameworks. The effort to coordinate more widely and more deeply between national administrations would strengthen common rules: i.e. it would entrench multilateralism.

The failure to do this was extraordinary: it would not be an exaggeration to say that the donor states could easily have obtained close control of the UN system by creating and bringing together the parts of their various policy-planning departments which were concerned with UN business. If the donors had been better coordinated in their policies towards the Agencies there would have been no coordination problem with them. A meeting of UN correspondents within states, could easily be linked with the Geneva Group, and the fact that the number of major UN donors was so few made this project relatively simple. But behind this failure was another: that too many governments had inadequate mechanisms to coordinate policy towards the UN between the various relevant sections of their own administrations. The British had developed their arrangements relatively recently but others still lacked them.

A brief sketch of the UK arrangement in the late 1990s indicates the kind of problem and the stage of development of UN coordination in the government. Although many home ministries maintained direct relations with the specialized agencies, as did British-based INGOs and NGOs, the organizational hub was the UN Department (UND) in the Foreign and Commonwealth Office (FCO), which fell under the remit of an Assistant Under-Secretary responsible for a range of departments in the FCO. It was a relatively small department in part because the FCO's structure tended to give priority to issues over particular institutions. In the 1950s and the early 1960s, the United Kingdom even had two ambassadors at the United Nations in New York, one of whom was solely concerned with Fourth Committee and Trusteeship Council affairs. There was then a long period during which Her Majesty's Government (HMG) considered that the United Nations' role on the issues that mattered was marginal and consequently the UND was then not a front-rank FCO department.[13]

This changed as governments came to feel that the United Kingdom could use the United Nations positively, especially the Security Council. Indeed as Britain's power in the world declined increasing stress was placed on doing well in the UN to make the most of what was left. *However, the geographical and functional departments generally took the lead*, and the role of the UND was to get them to think of the UN angle, a way of working which indicated that UN policy was a secondary, not a primary, concern of coordination. In the new climate after the end of the Cold War the UND made more policy suggestions, and policy in the United Nations was no longer a damage-limitation exercise. Nevertheless, the African department, for example, would lead on the Great Lakes problems, and the same was true of the Middle East, the problem of drugs and the like. From the outside it did not seem likely that the UND would be strong enough in relations with the geographical or functional departments to ensure overall coordination of relevant UN system policies.

The structure of the FCO's UN administration reflected this in 1998. Before possible changes by the new Blair government there were about 32 people doing UN policy work, ranging from Heads of Department to Assistant Desk Officer level. There were 20 UND policy posts, 6 policy posts in the Human Rights

Policy Department (HRPD), 3.5 in the Environment, Science and Energy Department (ESED) and 2.5 in the Drugs and International Crime Department (DCID). Many officers, particulary in HRPD, ESED and DCID, combined their UN work with other responsibilities. For example the head of HRPD had responsibility for human rights policy across the board, both bilateral and multilateral. Similarly the Geographical Departments had a strong input into UN decision-making when their particular country or region was the focus of UN attention. The UND worked in a 'mutual education' process with geographical and functional departments. But only 8 per cent of FCO personnel were assigned to intergovernmental organizations (IGOs). Subscriptions to international organizations amounted to £79.7 million out of a total financial provision for the FCO in 1988/89 of £725.4 million.[14]

The UND did not, therefore, have a central position in the FCO, but there was a trend towards task expansion and a greater prominence for UN questions. This account illustrates the general proposition that failures of coordination in the UN system are a reflection of the lack of coordination about UN issues within states. There was dissonance between the way in which governments were organized and *expectations* about the organization of the United Nations. It was simply not possible for the latter to be more effectively organized than the former.

7. *There was a need for improved, more consonant administrative arrangements. An international institution has at its core a secretariat.* Indeed there was a sense in which that secretariat *was* the international institution, in that it was its single permanent feature. What did the principle of consonance suggest about the pattern of reform of the secretariat? Were there any general principles which could be added to the frenzy of reform of the 1980s and 1990s, from Boutros-Ghali to the Track I and II of Kofi Annan? Some of those reforms were beneficial, producing the banal judgement that the institution was now leaner but fitter. The lead governments lost no opportunity to get at the UN's civil servants, leading to a series of sackings and a loss of around a thousand staff in the central system over a five-year period, with the prospect in 1997 of another thousand lost (A/51/1950, p. 2). And there were a number of reorganizations of departments and offices in the central system, many of which have been discussed in the preceding chapters.

But the effects of the reforms of the Secretariat was not entirely positive, and some more advisable reforms had not been stressed, such as the need for improved overall management. This implied an executive committee for the institution involving the heads of the various sections in frequent meetings to discuss overall activity and resolve problems. A start on this had been made by Secretary-General Annan with the setting up in January 1997 of four Executive Committees (A/51/950, July 1997, para 28). It remained to be seen how this would work, but the case for a single committee, with real powers, meeting frequently, remained persuasive. What was needed was a secretariat that was the best possible support for the activities and government committees of the United Nations: the most consonant interaction between government representatives and international civil servants. This required a highly qualified personnel, loyal to the organization, and with skills matched to the job specification. This implied a greater degree of staff mobility, and flexibility: the ability to move the right people to the right job. It also meant being more proactive in finding and keeping the best people. As it was, in the late 1990s, the best people had been lost because of the indiscriminate scaling down. Attention had been paid to reducing the numbers and less attention had been paid to retaining and indeed recruiting the most able.

One element of consonance was, therefore, getting as close a fit as possible between personnel, their skills and the requirements of the job, and between the international civil servants and the governmental representatives with whom they were required to deal. Another was getting as wide a range as possible of relevant experience input into the central system. One of the major weaknesses in a number of areas, was that the number of exchanges between field and headquarters personnel was limited. In some areas, such as humanitarian assistance, and economic development, an attempt had been made in the late 1990s to tackle this problem. The point was made that the perspective of headquarters personnel was likely to be different from that of those with field experience. As the UN's range of operations became wider in the 1990s, it became increasingly necessary to find a compromise between the longer planning period, usually five years, of the headquarters people, and the shorter perspective of the field people, who were more concerned with getting an immediate and effective response. Indeed the more active UN of the 1990s required a modified personnel strategy: consonance of staffing with activities required a flexible, mobile staff, with high technical skills, and hands-on field experience.

The kind of adjustments that had taken place were too often unhelpful from that perspective, though a beginning had been made in some areas. What further reforms could have helped? A few rather basic points are made here:

All levels of the Secretariat should be filled through neutral, professional procedures, that is, through procedures which did not involve barter among states, but rather a professional search and evaluation. The recommendations of Urquart and Childers on the Secretary-General's appointment were very much on the right lines.[15] The UN needed stricter controls of appointments and a more flexible approach to the principle of equitable geographical representation if there were no candidates of suitable calibre from a particular state or group. It was important to avoid simply filling posts with West European and other people, but groups could be asked to approve suitable people from out of their area. It was, moreover, very important to have a regular rotation of staff, so that no institution could be identified, as ECOSOC had been, as a poor performer because of the quality and attitudes of its staff.

This argument could be taken further! Scrutiny of the performance of members of government delegations when they were attached to UN institutions could be introduced without compromising their responsibility as the representatives of states. The purpose of this would be to reduce the chance of the repeated return of incompetent, free-loading representatives to scheduled meetings of institutions such as ECOSOC or the various forums of the General Assembly. By extending the idea that good standards of performance were required among national government delegates, and that there should be international ways of monitoring these, the general interest in optimum system performance would be underlined. International procedures for maintaining good technical standards could be extended outwards, from full-time international civil servants, to those on secondment from national governments, and, beyond that, to national delegates. The last would at least be encouraged to achieve good professional standards, even when instructed to be obstructive in a particular diplomatic setting, and at best would be motivated to a more professional reconciliation, wherever possible, of particular and general interests. At the same time the UN could make a contribution to improving national standards of technical competence among national officers, and even political elites.

Conclusions

In this chapter some of the general rules that applied to the reform of the United Nations have been discussed. What could be done, and what should not be done to make it work effectively? They have been placed under the general heading of consonance, meaning the existence of relationships between key parts of the system which were mutually supportive: they were conducive to effectiveness and efficiency. The institutional structure of the UN was taken as a given, that is, no alterations in the constitutive parts of the institution, or their mutual relations, have been suggested, nor were they necessary. The requirement was for what existed to be improved. At the end of the day there was a natural limit to what could be done, because that depended upon the will of governments and the resources and time which they were prepared to commit. The relationship of the institution to its environment in the society of states was also important. But satisfactory arrangements, and well-considered reforms, were more likely to be the focus of national enthusiasm.

The rules can be organized into four clusters concerning the three types of collective action in the UN system and the nature of the relationship between the institutions and international society.

1. The first type of collective action depends upon general agreement among the members of a small group. If action depended upon general agreement among members of a large group it would be much more difficult to obtain and to sustain. If the small group acts for the large group in some sense, it must also represent leadership. It must involve the states which are recognized as those having the resources, and the commitment to act effectively together to defend the system. The members of the group must also be committed to norm maintenance. Leadership is weakened if members of the group put their own reinforcement at the regional or global level ahead of collective action, or if they are perceived as being liable to do this. As argued above, within the small leadership group, it is necessary that a subgroup be prepared to go ahead of the others, and that the others will join the convoy.
2. Decisions on the second type of collective action, such as the budgetary process, must be responsible. They must involve the donors at an early stage, and not involve procedures through which their disagreement with particular spending can be

evaded by groups of beneficiaries. Similarly beneficiaries should not be in a position in one part of an institution to push decisions which oblige donors in other parts of the system to spending which they would otherwise refuse. For example, it would create serious problems, and the reduction of the commitment of donors, if beneficiary states took decisions with regard to the management of humanitarian crises which then required donors to foot the bill. This danger is reminiscent of the situation which arose in the 1960s when decisions to set up peacekeeping operations were linked with a general obligation to pay.

3. The third type of collective action involves the whole membership, or the majority of members, which also has rights and responsibilities. These are mainly the right to be consulted with regard to category one and two collective actions, and not to have supranational plans thrust upon them. In the forums which takes decisions on money and high diplomacy they have to be informed and to advise, through their representatives, but they will inevitably be subject to pressure to conform if the leadership is in agreement. They do have the right to impose limits on what they consider unacceptable action, as in the British system of government: the right to say 'no'. The meetings of the general membership of the institutions are where broad questions of principle and purpose are agreed, but those forums should not take on the colouring of the whole, for instance, in the form of directly controlling specific programmes or issuing specific instructions. This indicates also that their can be no centralized management of programmes in the UN system – the system of international institutions is like the system of states in that it is essentially multicentred, and requires to be persuaded into coordination rather than ordered by a central institution.

4. In the relationship between the institution and international society the important point is not to introduce internal alterations which weaken the sources of support for the institution in that society, and to have in mind the need to relate the institution to the changing system. It is necessary to have a consistent image of the most favourable structure of international society, which, it is proposed here, is a society organized into regional groups of states. Attempts on the part of some states to gain internal promotion in the UN, which is likely to increase division rather than unity in their region of origin, should be resisted. Conversely

regions should be the basis of representation in the UN wherever there is a reasonable regional accord.

One element in consonance was the way in which alterations in one part of the system might be assisted or frustrated by the lack of matching changes in other parts of the system. Conversely they might lead to changes elsewhere which were positive in their impact on the reform. The way in which the whole system was interconnected needed to be borne in mind when considering reform and this was often forgotten by designers of change. One link, mentioned in the opening paragraphs of this chapter, was that between the arrangements in the United Nations, and other international institutions, and the structure of international society. That link had to be placed in the context of overall system change, the primary element of which was the declining capacity of individual states to control their environment. The United Nations could become an element in an arrangement which achieved that control, though in the course of that evolution it could also respond to and create favourable changes in international society.

This is not a trivial point, although it has not been discussed at length in this chapter. The United Nations should be organized so that it promotes rather than gets in the way of the development of the most favourable structure of international society. Such a favourable structure was likely to be one in which there were stronger regions, made up of state members which inclined to policy consensus. The United Nations should be seen, therefore, both as a framework within which multilateral rules would be progressively strengthened, and superordinate interests in the *really new* world order defined; but also as a framework for the consolidation of a system of regional groupings of states which could pursue welfare for individuals more effectively, especially the classical Keynesian purpose of full employment, in the face of increasingly antisocial global forces.

The relationship of the United Nations with the regions was a vital consideration: it should not get in the way of their consolidation; it should promote their emergence; it should reflect them rationally and effectively, and consistently, in its internal arrangements.

CHAPTER 7

Conclusions: Globalization, International Organization and Regionalization

Introduction

According to John Ruggie three developments between the fourteenth and the fifteenth centuries began the process which led to the emergence of modern international society. Though they interacted, they could be *differentiated* from each other, spatially and temporarily. Their modern equivalents are discussed below. By the seventeenth century these developments had led to the emergence of sovereign states, the main characteristic of which was that they occupied different territories, but carried out similar functions within their own territories. Ruggie preferred this kind of explanation because it did not assume the outcome, the emergence of the state, from the outset. In other words it allowed for change.

The three sets of developments were, first, changes in material circumstances, second, changes in strategic behaviour on the part of key actors; and, third, the development of what were called 'supportive social epistemes'. The last were sets of interrelated ideas believed by significant groups of people which favoured a form of polity like the state. A fourth development, namely appropriate *social empowerment*,[1] was the mechanism by which the potential of the three others for creating states was realized: the people with the ideas acquired the power to get what they thought they wanted. In other words they were persuaded to prefer certain things, in this case a state, and came to have the power to get them.

As pointed out in the Introduction, the problem with a number of theories about international society, particularly those in the realist tradition, was that they found it hard to say anything useful about the way the system changed. Theorists made assumptions about the underlying structure which were external to the theory and could not be tested by it. So if the assumption was that it was dominated by power-seeking states that was the way it had to be. Ruggie concluded that

> providing an account of things in contemporary international relations research typically means specifying their causes. That in turn requires that we have a theory – in this case, a theory of international transformation. But we have no such theory ... we can barely even describe transformation in the international polity.... The modern theory of states is socially constructed.... I find that developments in three dimensions of European collective experience were particularly salient, and that the three dimensions are irreducible to one another: namely material environment, strategic behaviour, and social epistemology[2]

The present writer agrees that the alternative categories are those which need to be tested.

Even the developments listed did not *explain* the appearance of the society of states, since the way they developed and interacted was often a matter of unintended consequences. But together they created a context in which it became, we can say in hindsight, progressively more likely that a set of states, each territorially defined, would appear, each of which had to accept the idea of the other's sovereignty. But what was happening was a set of interacting material developments and at the same time a movement in ideas about what was possible and necessary. Hence the relevance of the ideas which were a reaction to, but not caused by, the material changes: the state was constructed out of perceptions and imaginings though these were linked with actual needs and arrangements.

In attempting to understand the changes that were going on at the start of the twenty-first century the same question could be put: what were the actual material developments and what were the perceptions and imaginings about them which could lead to change? Ruggie implicitly set us the task of trying to decide whether there were any equivalents to the differentiated developments he found at the beginning of modernity.

Material changes in the international system

He found one example of current change in the European Union which, he argued, may have constituted the 'first multi-perspectival polity to emerge since the advent of the modern era'.[3] The main reason for this was that in this polity, 'a collectivity of members as a singularity, in addition to the central institutional apparatus of the EU, [had] become party to the interstate strategic interaction game'. In other words the polity of the European Union had two discrete levels, that of the states and that of the collectivity, and elements in each of these interacted directly with each other across national frontiers, and, in turn, views about what constituted the state and their society were altered.

The current writer has argued that this had not altered the location of sovereignty, but there was surely a multilevel allocation of competences – which Ruggie calls multiperspectival – and an unbundling of the various attributes of the state.[4] But it was also important to stress that there was no indication that this was likely to lead to a federal state, since this would merely replicate on a larger scale the traditional political form. If there was a federal outcome it would not be a changed unit or society. This was one reason why neorealism could not deal with the EU! It could not grasp the idea of the multiperspectival or of unbundling. Neorealism was about the relations between states in a society of states and any mixture of the two, an in-between situation, was incomprehensible in neorealist terms.

The same question can be put about international society beyond the European Union: were there in the early twenty-first century any comparable developments at the global level which could lead to an unbundling of territoriality so that there was a multilevel allocation of competences? It would contain entities which could still be called states – that is an assumption about the underlying reality – but they would represent a 'multiperspectival polity' in that aspects of them would have been fundamentally altered or 'unbundled'. It depended on what was meant by unbundling. The answers to this question would also form an answer to the question of whether further change was likely or unlikely in international organization.

What could be meant by 'unbundling' in the international system in the early twenty-first century? The material circumstances, which deserved to be noted, included the appearance of a world which was a single capitalist entity, working within a unified system for production and marketing, crossing the boundaries of states. This capitalist system would have had a tendency towards an increasing industrialization and mechanization of production, involving an increasingly rapid and sophisticated degree of information generation and exchange. It would also be characterized by a single financial system, and rapid, computer-generated capital flows. A key feature was, however, that there were also serious inequalities in this global system, with industrial production being concentrated in some areas, and rewards generated being unevenly spread. There were serious shortfalls of supply in some parts of the world, the main divisions being between North and South, but also with some divergence within the North. In sum, there was inequality and inequity, which coexisted with unity and a high degree of integration in some areas, such as the financial market and the information system.

These developments in the material situation contained impulses towards greater cooperation among governments from three sources. One was the impulse to exercise control to prevent the overexploitation of the world resources, material and human, by non-governmental organizations such as multinational companies, or by irresponsible governments. The social episteme was such that it was generally believed that the costs of allowing such exploitation exceeded the benefits. It was, therefore, necessary to act together to persuade the companies to fulfil a social purpose which, as capitalists, concerned primarily with short-term profit maximization, they would otherwise not wish to do.

Second it was important to obtain an acceptable distribution of the values produced in the system, so that crises did not arise simply from maldistribution. The global entity could not rely on spontaneously arranged effective and equitable distribution any more than that could be relied upon within states, or within the EU, despite the common advantage for states of membership.

Third it was necessary for governments to cooperate together to make it easier to deal with crises in the system. The system had a constant tendency to disequilibrium – to move towards crisis – which those who were working within it could not understand, recognize, or respond to, possibly because of the inherent difficulties in theorizing alluded to above! Governments needed to develop and maintain an effective apparatus for minimizing shocks within the system and their external effects.

The material circumstances were the context of a number of different behavioural responses. Ruggie pointed to the importance of the appearance of trade fairs in the late Middle Ages, which, as concentrations of economic activity, facilitated the appearance of forms of political control to manage this more complex socio-economic entity, but were also accessible to control and exploitation by higher political authorities. They became a conduit through which the power of the latter was consolidated. They emerged as a consequence of a functional need to enhance productive and distributional capacity but also became important as generators of centralized political power.

An equivalent strategic behavioural response in the early twenty-first century was the recurrent efforts to gain control of the unified but differentiated production and supply universe. Key in this was the international financial system. In a number of ways states had made a start on attempting to regulate the global financial system which was increasingly a threat to the pattern of production locally. Even though there were disagreements about how to do it there was the idea – the imagining – of a problem and a need to tackle it. Each territorial entity was threatened by the dislocations of universality and therefore each was impelled to seek to regain control by consultation with others regionally or globally. The various international institutions discussed in this volume also represented an attempt to achieve control so that acceptable standards could be achieved, both with regard to avoiding crises in material circumstances, and crises in human values, which it was increasingly believed, were often linked together. But it should be stressed that there were both regional and global, as well as interventionist and deregulatory responses.

The achievements of governments in strengthening control in the range of economic and social contexts was striking, even though serious limitations remained. The general achievement can be illustrated by reference to the particular cases referred to in this volume, which may be taken as typical of the behavioural response of governments to changing material circumstances. The conclusion was unavoidable that in these areas the mechanisms were significantly improved. The conclusions presented in Chapter 1 are applicable: that intentions that had been defined in a global context now had an increased possibility of being translated into action at the local level, or in a specific context. Other general achievements or ambitions included improving the process of gathering and interpreting relevant information, professionalizing the work of the central institutions, greatly improving the coordination process between the various actors involved and facilitating more rapid reaction.

An international society of individuals

Underlying all of these changes was the apparent strengthening of the norms of collective action in general forums of the specialized actors involved, namely those providing resources, those in receipt of them and those charged with carrying out the job – the technical and operational actors. (A point discussed in the context of social epistemes below.) The point is also highly significant that the scope of international cooperative activity had been greatly expanded. Despite the difficulties, never before in the history of humanity had such strategic behaviour applied to such a broad spectrum of activities. The appropriate analogy was that of the development of a motor car with the intention of making a journey: the car had been much improved, indeed there was now a fleet of cars, but there was still a shortfall in the availability of petrol to fuel them, and the drivers could not always agree precisely about the route.

To apply the concept of social epistemes, what was striking was the increasing number of individuals in international institutions, but also in member governments, their missions in New York and the like, and generally in societies within states, who were committed to the idea of international cooperation. There was no way of measuring the precise numbers, but the changes in views about the merits of stronger international organization, acting in areas which were appropriate, could be safely regarded as enormous compared, say, with the 1930s. The real change in the weight of changes in international trade, compared, say, with 1913, may be disputed, but there was no denying the changes in the numbers of personnel involved in managing one or other section of related international organization. This was not to deny there was frequently anxiety about the implication of this for the sovereign state, and uncertainty about how stronger international cooperation could be reconciled with the felt need to protect degrees of local control. And in some states, such as the US, the anti-modern minority had acquired power in the early 2000s as a result of accidents of the political process. But the set of beliefs about the meaning of sovereignty was surely in the process of transmutation, both in terms of the changing values about international cooperation, and in terms of the global distribution of those changes in values among states.

In the early twenty-first century this could surely be described as an epochal shift in values, a new social episteme. These changes, of course, were likely to be promoted further by the increasing range of movements of individuals around the world, the strengthening of diasporas, increasing numbers of refugees, of international civil servants, of steadily increasing links between national officers, and deracinated individuals. For the first time in the modern world a social episteme which was becoming global, and which carried an image of an interdependent and cooperative global society, had appeared. The great problem, of course, was whether this social espisteme could grow to a point at which it could hold sway. Was the process of social change running ahead of or behind the functional need for crisis-management? Were the material circumstances changing faster than the social ones?

By the early twenty-first century, in addition to the formal structures of states and regional and global organizations, there had been a widening of the range of the international society of individuals. This had come to include:

- *An a-national deracinated society of individuals and groups.* These were individuals and groups which had become separated from their roots, and which owed no loyalty to any community, but only to some a-national goal, even such as making money. In the late twentieth century an increasing number of multinational companies included such individuals, such as Rupert Murdoch, the media emperor, but there might also be an increasing number of such individuals in groups of refugees, stateless persons and diasporas.
- *A transnational society of groups.* This society was made up of individuals and groups which acknowledged a national base, but which had also developed a significant capacity for building transnational alliances, or communities and working through them. They might share technical or specialized expertise, or wish to act together to promote an interest, or be involved in advising governments or international organizations. The movement in forms of national governments, including the collapse of state-capitalist or communist systems, only added to these.
- *An international civil society of members of governments.* This was the number of individuals involved in the increasingly dense network of transnational relations between governments, working through a variety of international frameworks, including international institutions, consultation committees, lobbies and so on. In this case individuals from different national backgrounds related to each other as if they were members of a single civil society, seeking individual rewards, promotions and status defined in that context. What should be stressed is that such individuals were not just members of international organizations, but also increasingly were national representatives. Those

who behaved in this way also included an increasing number of those who were formally members of national governments.

Individuals in the last group had two roles. First they defined and projected the ideals of the state, in which capacity they had symbolic and representative roles, just as individuals might possess formal roles, defined as such by the society of which they were a part, such as the role of father or priest. Another role which coexisted with the first was that of an individual member of a civil society, in which there were self-defined ambitions and responsibilities, reflecting individual character and abilities. An illustration of this distinction was the different self-image an individual might have in a formal role, such as a father, when compared with the non-formal role as an individual. Hence someone might say when asked for advice: 'as a lawyer I would say this, but as a friend I would say this other'.

This was related to the role of the state in the modern world in that in some parts of the world the view of the state had been attenuated in that individuals had a weaker perception of their symbolic roles when acting for the states. It was important to realize that the state could not act except through individuals, when they were leaders, heads of state, or diplomats, or other kinds of representative. What happened was that these individuals took on such symbolic roles when acting for the state, and in this case might become completely dominated, even to the extent of the complete infusion of their personality, by the impact of these roles. Hence an Emperor in pre-modern China might become pretty much completely a representative of a traditional formal role at the cost of an individual one. In modern states the combination of these two roles was normally such that the individual as member of civil society was also present, while not excluding the adoption of symbolic roles when necessary and appropriate.

In modern international society, defined as being made up of modern states, the increasing tendency was for the idea of the state to be attenuated. Individuals in governments became less dominated by the symbolic state roles, and more liable to see themselves as acting in a form of civil society when dealing with peers from other states. This was essentially a change in the international social episteme and was of crucial importance in the transformation of international society. It was necessarily a product of the increasing density of social interaction between individuals across national frontiers, and could not have happened, say, in the time of Rousseau when density of international interaction was more limited, thus encouraging the ascendancy of the symbolic roles of states in individuals working for them.

Hence the difficulty found by Rousseau in reconciling the idea of federal arrangements in international society, which he thought necessary to promote international peace and security, with the idea of sovereign states. The apparent logical contradiction between the two depended in part on the greater stress on the formal role of state representatives compared with that of members of the international civil society of governments. But the development of that international civil society meant that this was no longer as real. Individuals in government had formed a different structure of links between themselves as individuals and themselves as state officers, in which the former more often prevailed over the latter. Hence the legitimacy of the sovereign state was now more often seen as conditional upon satisfying criteria which were validated in the international civil society of governments. This helped to reconcile the idea of the individuation of units, the states, with the ascendancy of the values of the collectivity, the federation.

That was not something which had happened globally, however. In many parts of the world the Emperor of China still survived and, indeed, was sometimes promoted by individual leaders who were anxious to acquire enhanced symbolic status. Indeed a major cleavage in modern international society was between those governments dominated by the ethic of intergovernmental civil society, and those which were dominated by the ethic of symbolic statism. Here was revealed yet another reason for preferring liberal pluralist societies and for promoting democracy. Such regimes were more likely to take a less primitive view of sovereignty and to be more likely to support international cooperation. At the turn of the twenty-first century the trend was towards the enhancement of the intergovernmental civil society, and that represented a change which could indeed be reasonably described as a transformation.

These changes were also fuelled by two very powerful dynamics: one was the clarification of the information sphere leading to increasing pressure to protect individuals. The greater the amount of information about such matters as human rights abuses, and the greater the confidence in its accuracy, the greater the pressure. There were two aspects to this – the penetration of news gathering and the multiplicity of separate gatherers. It was not just that CNN was there but that a whole flotilla of non-governmental organizations, and other information gatherers, were alongside or close behind: there was detail and verification. This had brought about another qualitative change. The problem hitherto had been that humans were more often confused about what was going on elsewhere; reducing that confusion meant that they were under greater pressure to act morally, as it was more difficult to resort to the strategy of denying the facts. It was not that they had been cruel and careless, but were now moral, but rather that there was now an increasing certainty about information. It was more difficult *not* to act to improve things. And paradoxically, when it became clear that there had been evil, despite knowledge and certainty, more ruthless opposing action was easier to justify.

A material change that deserved separate mention, in connection with its corresponding social episteme, was the development of a capacity to damage the environment. There was an increasing conviction that environmental damage was leading to the need for common action to protect the global environment of the earth. There were an increasing number of persuasive and well-informed people, in rich and poor countries alike, who had intimations of cataclysm. So many people had never before thought the world was in peril, could be in touch with each other through modern information technology and could identify practical measures, based on scientific insight, to begin the process of putting things right. Those who were against this view were increasingly seen as merely representatives of special interests, companies seeking to protect their pockets in the short term, or governments seeking to use the opportunity to maximize short-term reward in one form or another, or both in cahoots. The point need not really be made, but George W. Bush put himself in the company of an odd minority, albeit with power, when he decided not to go along with the Kyoto agreement. There was no certainty of outcome, but battle had been joined.

Structures and change

The above changes all tended towards the enhancement of the power to control more activities through international mechanisms – there had been changes in material circumstances, strategic behaviour and social epistemes, that tended towards the unbundling of territoriality, but, for all that, the obvious conclusion at the end of the twentieth century was that there was not yet an *uncontested* international authority in the sense proposed by Barnard: 'authority is another name for the willingness and capacity of individuals to submit to the necessities of cooperative systems'.[5] It might be, however, that there had been some movement in that direction and in the direction of an international polity in terms of Blau's argument that

> structural constraints rooted in the collectivity of subordinates, rather than instruments of power or influence wielded by the superior himself, enforce compliance with his directives. To discharge its joint obligations to the superior, the group of subordinates is under pressure to make compliance with his directives part of the common norms, which are internalized by its members, and which are socially enforced by them against potential deviants.[6]

There were, of course, very few occasions on which there was a single superior in international society: the norm was for different groups or individuals to have contested superiority in different areas of international activity. But the point is important for the development of international authority, within a collectivity of sovereign states that: authority was more to do with horizontal relationships between actors than vertical ones between inferiors and superiors. To borrow a concept again from Ruggie – it was a case of embedded multilateralism. Or in other words, hitherto only applied to the publics of stable states, international civil society was charactized by 'cross-cutting cleavages'.

These were the positive elements in the tendency to stronger forms of international cooperation. There were also negative ones. Chief among these was the structure of international society in the late twentieth century, as explained in Chapter 6. It was unlikely that the system could be led successfully by a single actor, the USA: a unipolar system was unlikely to be a supportive one. Rather the system needed a group of actors which were not grossly dissimilar in size and apparent capacity to act. The nature of the international structure meant that the internal divisions within the United States became peculiarly problematic from the point of view of international cooperation in the late twentieth century. Right-wing Republicanism was an amplified force in the absence of the Soviet Union, and, given the inability of the member states of the European Union to combine together to become more effective, particularly in the area of peace maintenance in the United Nations.

It was ironic that it would have been impossible to envisage Jesse Helms as chair of the Senate Foreign Relations Committee at the time of superpower ideological tension because the risks posed by his intransigence were acknowledged to be too great, even by the right wing of the Republican Party; but this became possible when changes in the international structure removed his primary target, and it was no longer important to insist upon the enemy which he had stressed above all others. The main loser from this was, of course, the United Nations and the value system it represented.

Globalization and regionalization

The kind of social empowerment needed for the emergence of a system of international cooperation between states was therefore not the appearance of a single international government, but rather of a habit of collective action in support of conclusions about the common good reached multilaterally. But it was hard to deny that international authority had begun to emerge. At various places in this book the intimations of this have been discussed. These include the regular search for Security Council approval for actions to maintain peace and security, even on the part of the single superpower; the increasing density of international organization and the linked development of what this author called an international civil society; the effect of this upon the way in which individuals, and increasingly governments, evaluated their own status; the increasing coincidence of interest and morality in international relations, partly caused by the CNN factor and partly by the real implications of internal disorder for order between states; and the discrediting of forms of communitarianism in favour of a cosmopolitanism dominated by individual civil and political values, and increasingly pressed by the UN and the EU.

This was not a matter of international organization overtaking the sovereign state, but of its involving and forming the universe of merit. It was also not a question of the dissolution of the state, but rather of unbundling territoriality so that the state constituted one element of the bundle. This was not a question of the sovereignty of states being lost. Other analogies were appropriate, such as the *sharing* or *pooling* of sovereignty in a multiperspectival polity.

Within this process of globalization there was also the observable process of regionalization. The material causes of this are important – analogous with the developments proposed by Ruggie, but applied to the regional level – and they were discussed in the Introduction. But the development of a regional social episteme was also a feature of this and was predictable as a consequence of the unbundling of the state. The condition of this was the dual ambition of governments to gain control over the uncertainties and disturbances resulting from the material changes, without abandoning their individuality and territoriality. The extension of competences directly to the global level was a step too far in many contexts: governments thought they were giving too much away at too great a distance. To give the power to be effective to a local agency was more acceptable as it seemed more recoverable.

It was preferable to make it a two-stage process, to extend competences to regional organizations, which could then act on behalf of the group of member states in the global organization. Regional groupings of states were more likely to be confident that they formed a community of interest, and regional centres were more accessible than global ones. Once a process of regional integration had begun the range of dynamics identified by integration theorists could apply.[7] But the key point was that in the context of globalization, there was an incentive for states to seek more effective participation in global organization, and the way to this was through regional organizations. Global organization was therefore naturally a dynamic of regionalization in the context of globalization. The more the agenda was extended in scope, so that it involved multilevel and transnational interactions, the greater the pressures on the governments to organize regionally and to obtain global representation through regional groupings. This response was, of course, uneven, and does not wholly explain regionalization. But it proposes a structural response to international organization at the regional level in the age of globalization.

This suggests that globalization led to a widening of the range of incentives on states to form regional organizations. There were incentives of a utilitarian kind, which were the more traditional kind mentioned in the Introduction. A particular goal might be easier to obtain when states in a regional organization acted together. Or one of them might prefer to seek its goals in a regional context. It might also be easier in this case to prevent something specific from happening that was judged to be undesirable. In this case regionalization had little to do with the character of the participating states, but more to do with their getting what they wanted. It did not suggest any change or alteration in the character of the international system.

But there were also pressures from globalization that were less about particular policies and more about the character of the state. They could reinforce the cohesion of existing regions or encourage further regionalization. These pressures did imply changes in the international system.

The first change was a general one and involved a change in the system in the direction of system-dominance. All states were subjected to unavoidable pressures on their sovereignty which, as argued in Chapter 1, required them to be accountable to the international community for the maintenance of acceptable standards.

The second change was that globalization now raised questions about the character of the state which were more profound than those raised before. In economic matters globalization had pushed for more openness, more transparancy and less discrimination between actors, for instance to favour insiders as against outsiders. But it also challenged traditional or indigenous forms of political and economic organization in favour of a single model, that of pluralist Western liberalism, with privatized economies and low levels of regulation. In other words it raised questions, not about specific policies and goals, but about the very nature of the state.

Two responses to this were immediately obvious. First was the response of the Western European states which had evolved more corporatist forms of government and higher amounts of welfare spending. It was predictable that those states which inclined to this model would link together to find a response to globalization which did not threaten that model. This enterprise was likely to bring together like-minded states in a common regional enterprise. Second were governments in the Far East which preferred an indigenous form of democratic compromise linked with a development process. After a period of pressure to move towards a more Western approach – orchestrated by the US, IMF and World Bank after the crises of the mid-1990s[8] – there had been a more positive assessment of the Asian model, cleansed of its less attractive aspects.[9] Again the region was likely to include states that thought alike and reckoned they were more likely to succeed by acting together. (Hence their unease about the involvement of the US in Pacific economic arrangements.) Both of these regions contained a local, regional response to a global challenge.

Globalization set up a process among the regionalizing states of seeking to demonstrate the viability of their own route to preferred values, political and economic, in the global context. In this way globalization encouraged both the development of global organizations as well as a process of regionalization, which was additional to the processes of rational choice about ends and means.

This should not be interpreted as a giving up on the process of getting states to uphold acceptable standards. Rather it posed the question of how to reconcile different forms of governance with the maintenance of such values. The envelope was being pushed in surprising ways, as it became obvious that some countries which had democratic forms had a value deficit, while others which had a democratic deficit upheld acceptable public standards. Paradoxically globalization as a process of defining and pushing acceptable standards made it easier to tolerate some falling short of the ideals of democracy.

The conclusion was that regionalization was not only happening but could also be justified as a rational way of reconciling the need for global action with the survival of states. Members of governments, who were calculating how best to adapt and survive, might be expected to conclude that working through regional organizations in the global context was the best option. Plans to reform the UN needed to take account of the virtues of regions, and should be so arranged that they were strengthened rather than weakened.

Conclusions: impediments and potentials

There was globalization, but there was regionalization. The reasons for the latter, as a response to the former, as presented in this book, can now be recapped.

- There was sometimes a need for regions to act on behalf of the global organizations because of a shortfall in the resources of the latter. There could also be regional problems which locals thought they could handle better together. There had been evidence of the regionalization of some forms of general problem, such as that of security.
- Regions emerged in response to the globalization of agendas, since, in these, specific goals were postulated and given priority over the maintenance of state autonomy. The need for local integrated programmes, relating agendas in a number of sectors together, was also conducive to regionalization. A territory had to be chosen which was optimal with regard to effectiveness in a group of linked sectors (transport, work, habitat, health maintenance, security, etc.).
- Regions were also a way in which member states could participate more effectively in other forums, including global

international organizations. They allowed appropriate and functional adjustment to globalization – not its absolute denial. They also emerged as the result of the apparent threat to preferred local forms from globalization. Globalization helped to increase sensitivity to the threat to local forms of governance or economic organization or methods.
- Regionalization was a way of ensuring the survival of the nation state, with its sovereignty altered but intact.

This brief list simply restates the conclusions of the previous chapters, but it implies the possibility of the parallel and symbiotic strengthening of two international orders, the regional one and the global one. It suggests, indeed, that each is conditional upon the attainment of the other, unless the state is to be so altered that its new forms are inconceivable. It goes without saying that there were many factors which made it necessary to postpone for a while the actual realization of this vision.

Getting sufficient resources was perhaps the most important single indication of an increasing potential for change. Money was limited, and this was itself a source of great difficulty. But the greater impediment was the perception among the main donor countries that allowing greater funding to international institutions was itself an indication of the waxing of international authority. To put the matter crudely: money was power, and placing limitations on transfers of money to international institutions, in the UN as in the EU, was a measure of national determination to hold on to power.

In 2000 a start was made with the payment by the US of the sums it owed the central UN, and the recovery of the US Administration's capacity to stay within the agreed UN budgetary rules. But the funding of many parts of the system, and many necessary activities, remained problematic. Beyond that there needed to be changes in the way the budget worked, in particular with regard to the proportion of the budget paid by the US, and the arrangements for paying it within member states. The 2000 agreement involved the US paying less, but the overall budget still needed to go up.

The argument returns to a point made frequently in this book – the need to make operations through global organizations, like the UN, a matter of routine, predictably used, and impartially deployed, with built-in endurance. In the short term there was a need to move towards calculating contributions to the UN, the Agencies and the like strictly on the basis of the ability to pay, but with an upper and lower ceiling, with recalculation being made frequently to reflect the changing circumstances of states. The system should not give a licence to states that had acquired the ability to pay more to avoid doing so, but the payment scale needed to be flatter so that the US did not have the same degree of overwhelming financial clout. There was a strong case for making payments through the routine budgets of the various national specialist departments, either directly to their opposite number in the system, or through a national fund, rather than through a specialized foreign department account.

In particular peacekeeping should be paid through the budgets of the ministries of defence, as, by the early years of the third millenium, it had come to reflect the routine of international order maintenance. It should not be paid out of special funds channelled through Foreign Offices as this reflected a false account of the relations between modern states. This was a point made by ex-Secretary-General Boutros Boutros-Ghali. The situation which applied in the late twentieth century, in which there was overdependence on the US and vulnerability to the vicissitudes of Congress–Administration politics, was highly damaging to the organization. A reduction in this dependence would be made by transferring funding to the Department of Defense budget which was much less likely to meet with Congressional scrutiny and opposition.

The positive development of a supportive social episteme had to be measured against the negative developments in what could be called the sweep of history. On the one hand there were what could be construed as the positive facts of the matter, but on the other hand there were a number of disjunctions. Of particular importance and danger was the impetus towards isolationism in the US, where there had been a refusal to accept either the agreement to set up the new International Criminal Court or the treaty banning the production and deployment of land mines, and a rearguard battle on the part of those determined to prevent the US ratification of the new Nuclear Test Ban Treaty. Once again the ambiguous consequences of the position of the US as the overwhelming power were revealed – its potential to dominate the emerging world order, and its inclination to use its power to pursue more actively, and to define more narrowly, its own interests.

In some states, though the number of these could vary very rapidly, there was an apparent preparedness for elites to pay a price on behalf of their people to maintain their own privileges and separateness. The sweep of history had moved in a surprisingly short space of time from a short spell of optimism to a pessimism about the prospect of a new world order. The trouble was that any observer had to acknowledge that the optimistic and the negative potential existed side by side, though it was unrealistic to ignore the optimistic one.

Perhaps at the end of the day all the commentator could do was identify potentials for positive development, which was the ambition of this book, and acknowledge the major problems in the way of further reform. If pressed the present writer would say that the two major impediments in the way of the further strengthening of an international authority were the rise to power of the moral-'majority'-linked anti-international right wing in the USA, and the failure of the EU to take on the role which was its for the taking. Europe's failure in the First and Second World Wars was the primary impetus for the setting up of the two global institutions in the twentieth century, the League of Nations and the UN. Continuing, though much reduced, disagreements between European states could be seen as a major problem in the way of the further strengthening of international cooperation in the United Nations in the late twentieth century. There was a dynamic of refusal here: the US right was reinforced in its disinclination to act partly because it perceived that the Europeans had not done enough.

But there was always the prospect of unintended consequences! International civil society continued to evolve and there were intense transnational coalitions between the liberal American scientific/ knowledge establishments and those in other parts of the liberal world, within which agreement about technical solutions would be facilitated, but also a less tangible inclination towards multilateralism embedded. This could constitute an epistemic community of great power, able to deal in subtle ways with those, particularly on the US right, who believed that the US could do without the world. Politicians might be inclined or disinclined to work internationally, but the prevailing mood among those who *knew* was towards more cooperation. The world's knowledge communities were inherently pro-multilateralism. To the extent that the US depended upon the cooperation of other states for the maintenance of values and possessions, the transnational coalitions would have influence in the various institutional contexts of which the US was a part.

The material circumstances which were to be found in the early twenty-first century, and the increasing strength of supportive social epistemes, together with the strategic responses hitherto, suggested that key Americans would be pushed increasingly to solve problems on a multilateral basis, but would also be ideologically conditioned to do so. To requote and adapt Barnard's comment: 'there would be an increased willingness and capacity of these individuals to submit to the necessities of common systems'.

Notes

Introduction

1 The case for this with reference to trade, investment and money and finance is examined sympathetically in Andrew Wyatt-Walter, 'Regionalism, globalization, and world economic order', in Louise Fawcett and Andrew Hurrell (eds), *Regionalism in World Politics: Regional Organization and International Order*, Oxford, Oxford University Press, 1995, pp. 74–121.
2 For a graphic account of these appalling events see 'US attacked: hijacked jets destroy Twin Towers and hit Pentagon in day of terror', *New York Times*, Wednesday, September 12, 2001, pp. A1–28.
3 David Held, Anthony McGrew, David Goldblatt and Jonathon Perraton, *Global Transformations: Politics, Economics and Culture*, Cambridge, Polity Press, 1999.
4 My views on this are set out in my *The European Union in the 1990s*, Oxford, Oxford University Press, 1996.
5 John Gerard Ruggie, *Constructing the World Polity: Essays on International Institutionalization*, London, Routledge, 1998, chapter 1 and *passim*.
6 J. J. Mearsheimer, 'The false promise of international institutions', *International Security*, 19(3): 5–49.
7 John Gerard Ruggie, *op. cit.*, p. 10.
8 Ibid., p. 193.
9 Peter Wilson, 'The myth of the "First Great Debate"', *Review of International Studies*, 24 (Special Issue), December 1998: 1–15 (quote at p. 5).
10 For a comprehensive account see David Held, Anthony McGrew, David Goldblatt and Jonathon Perraton, *Global Transformations*, Cambridge, Polity Press, 1999.
11 Ulrich Beck, *Risk Society: Towards a New Modernity*, Sage, London, 1992; John S. Dryzek, *The Politics of the Earth: Environmental Discourses*, Oxford, Oxford University Press, 1997.
12 Joan Edelman Spero, *The Politics of International Economic Relations*, 3rd edn, London, Allen & Unwin, 1985, especially chapter 7; Gautam Sen, 'UNCTAD and International Economic Reform', in Paul Taylor and A. J. R. Groom (eds), *Global Issues in the United Nations Framework*, London and Basingstoke, Macmillan, 1989.
13 Carol Cosgrove Twitchet, *A Framework for Development: The EEC and the ACP*, London, Allen & Unwin, 1981.
14 The Brandt Commission, *Common Crisis North–South: Cooperation for World Recovery*, London and Sydney, Pan Books, 1983.

15 Paul Taylor, 'Reforming the system: getting the money to talk', in Paul Taylor and A. J. R. Groom (eds), *International Institutions at Work*, London, Frances Pinter, 1988, pp. 220–35.
16 Their ideas are ably discussed in Peter Robson, *The Economics of International Integration*, London, Allen & Unwin, 1980.
17 Joseph S. Nye, 'Regional Institutions', in Cyril E. Black and Richard A. Falk (eds), *The Structure of the International Environment*, Princeton, NJ, Princeton University Press, 1972.
18 Hedley Bull, 'Civilian power Europe: a contradiction in terms?', in Loukas Tsoukalis, *The European Community: Past, Present and Future*, Oxford, Basil Blackwell, 1983, pp. 149–64; Bernard Burrows and Geoffrey Edwards, *The Defence of Western Europe*, London, Butterworth, 1982.
19 See Stanley Hoffman, 'Towards a common European foreign and security policy?', *Journal of Common Market Studies*, 38(2), June 2000: 189–98.
20 For an account of these see Sally Morphet, 'States groups at the United Nations and growth of member states at the United Nations', in Paul Taylor and A. J. R. Groom (eds), *The United Nations at the Millennium: The Principal Organs*, London, Continuum, 2000, pp. 224–70.
21 See John Zysman, 'The myth of a global economy: enduring national foundations and emerging regional realties', *New Political Economy*, 1(2) July 1996: 157–84.
22 David Held and Anthony McGrew, 'The end of the old order', *Review of International Studies*, 24 (Special Issue), December 1998: 219–43 (quote at p. 223).
23 Held and McGrew, *op cit.*, p. 223.
24 See B. Hettne and A. Inotai, *The New Regionalism*, Helsinki, 1994.
25 Georg Sorensen, 'IR theory after the Cold War', *Review of International Studies*, 24 (Special Issue), December 1998: 83–100 (especially p. 99).
26 Zysman, *op cit.*
27 Roger Masters, 'A multi-bloc model of the international system', *American Political Science Review*, 55(4) December 1961: 780–98.
28 Werner J. Feld and Robert S. Jordan with Leon Hurwitz, *International Organizations: A Comparative Approach*, 3rd edn, Westport, Praeger, 1994.
29 See the excellent introduction to the development of the security functions of the United Nations in Adam Roberts, 'The United Nations: variants of collective security', in Ngaire Woods, *Explaining International Relations Since 1945*, Oxford, Oxford University Press, 1996, pp. 283–308.
30 See Paul Taylor, *The European Union in the 1990s*, Oxford, Oxford University Press, 1996.
31 For an interpretation of Functionalism see Inis Claude Jr, *Swords into Plowshares*, 5th edn, New York, Random House, 1971.
32 See Paul Taylor, *International Organization in the Modern World*, London, Pinter, 1995.
33 Paul Taylor, 'International organization and international order', in John Baylis and Steve Smith (eds), *Globalization and International Order*, 2nd edn, Oxford, Oxford University Press, 2001.
34 Gavin Boyd *et al.* (eds), *Globalizing Europe*, Cheltenham, Edward Elgar, 2001.
35 Paul Taylor and A. J. R. Groom (eds), *The United Nations at the Millennium*, London, Continuum, 2000.

Chapter I The United Nations at the Millennium: Order and Sovereignty

1 Hedley Bull, *The Anarchical Society: A Study of World Order*, London, Macmillan/ New York, Columbia University Press, 1977.
2 For an account of the diplomacy leading up to the agreements at Dayton in 1996 see Spyros Economides and Paul Taylor, 'Former Yugoslavia', in James Mayall (ed.), *The New Interventionism, 1991–1994*, Cambridge, Cambridge University Press, 1996.
3 See George Drower, *Britain's Dependent Territories*, Dartmouth, Aldershot, 1992.
4 See Charles Beitz, *Political Theory and International Relations*, Princeton, NJ, Princeton University Press, 1979.
5 Michael Waltzer, *Just and Unjust Wars*, New York, Basic Books, 1977; and Terry Nardin, *Law, Morality and the Realities of States*, Princeton, NJ, Princeton University Press, 1983.
6 This is one of the arguments in R. J. Vincent, *Human Rights and International Relations*, Cambridge, Cambridge University Press, 1986.
7 For example see Jens Bartelson, *A Genealogy of Sovereignty*, Cambridge Studies in International Relations, Cambridge, Cambridge University Press, 1995 and Cynthia Weber, *Simulating Sovereignty: Intervention, the State and Symbolic Exchange*, Cambridge Studies in International Relations, Cambridge, Cambridge University Press, 1995.
8 Paul Taylor, *The European Union in the 1990s*, Oxford, Oxford University Press, 1996.
9 See James Mayall (ed.), *The New Interventionism*, Cambridge, Cambridge University Press, 1996.
10 The essay is entirely consistent with the arguments in defence of sovereignty which are well developed in Michael Ross Fowler and Julie Marie Bunck, *Law, Power and the Sovereign State; The Evolution and Application of the Concept of Sovereignty*, University Park, PA, Pennsylvania State University Press, 1995.
11 Alexander B. Murphy, 'The sovereign state as political-territorial ideal', in Thomas J. Biersteker and Cynthia Weber (eds), *State Sovereignty as Social Construct*, Cambridge, Cambridge University Press, 1996, pp. 81–120.
12 For an excellent examination of the concept of intervention and its variations see Oliver Ramsbotham, 'Humanitarian intervention, 1990–95: a need to reconceptualize?', *Review of International Studies*, 23 (1997): 445–68.
13 This argument is borrowed from David Malone, 'The UN Security Council in the post-Cold War world: 1987–97', *Security Dialogue*, 28 (1997): 393–408.
14 Robert McCorquodale, 'Human rights and self-determination', in Mortimer Sellers (ed.), *The New World Order*, p. 26.
15 Perez de Cuellar set up an Office for Research and the Collection of Information (ORCI) which was abolished by Boutros Boutros-Ghali, its functions being then assigned to the new Departments of Political Affairs (DPA) and of Peacekeeping (DPK). Boutros-Ghali stated 'That Department . . . is now organized to follow political developments worldwide, so that it can provide early warning of impending conflicts and analyse possibilities for preventive action' (A/50/60–S1995/1, 3 January 1995, para. 26).
16 The United Nations Registry of Conventional Arms was created by the General Assembly in December 1991. Member states were required to provide data for the

previous year on imports and exports of battle tanks, armoured combat vehicles, artillery, combat aircraft, attack helicopters, warships and missiles and missile launchers, as of 30 April 1993. See John Tessitore and Susan Woolfson (eds), *A Global Agenda: Issues before the 48th General Assembly of the United Nations*, Lanham, University Press of America, 1993, pp. 141–2.
17 See *Command and Control of United Nations Peacekeeping Operations: Report of the Secretary-General*, GA, A/49/681, 21 November 1994.
18 See Paul Taylor, 'Options for reform', in John Harriss (ed.), *The Politics of Humanitarian Intervention*, London, Pinter and Save the Children, 1995, pp. 91–144 (especially p. 96).
19 For a useful account of the problems in the way of more effective peacekeeping see Gareth Evans, *Cooperation for Peace: The Global Agenda for the 1990s and Beyond*, St Leonards, NSW, Allen & Unwin, 1993, pp. 70–80 and *passim*.
20 A similar organization was Sandlines which caused embarrassment to the British Foreign Office in 1998 because of its involvement in the war in Sierra Leone and the allegation that it had procured and supplied arms to the ousted government in defiance of UN sanctions.
21 Michael Scott Doran, 'Somebody else's civil war', *Foreign Affairs*, 81(1), January/ February 2002: 22–42.
22 According to the new Title VI of the Treaty on European Union. Andrew Duff concluded: 'For all the difficulties what emerges is a picture, in five years time, of an extensive and sophisticated web of police coordination throughout the European Union' – Andrew Duff (ed.), *The Treaty of Amsterdam: Text and Commentary*, London, Federal Trust for Education and Science, 1997, p. 42.
23 Letter from the Presidency of the EU, at the Permanent Mission of Ireland to the United Nations, to the Secretary-General, 16 October 1996, para. 21.
24 David Malone, 'Haiti and the International Community: a case study', *Survival: the IISS Quarterly*, 39 (1997): 126–46.
25 EU letter, p. 8.
26 See James Matheson, *Multiple Conditionality and the EU*, London School of Economics and Political Science, unpublished PhD Thesis, 1997.
27 Nira Wickramasinghe, 'From human rights to good governance: the aid regime in the 1990s', in Mortimer Sellers (ed.), *The New World Order*, p. 311.
28 Hinsley, *Power and the Pursuit of Peace*, Cambridge, Cambridge University Press, 1963, pp. 65–7.
29 The elements of continuity in the state system are discussed in Robert H. Jackson and Alan James, *States in a Changing World: A Contemporary Analysis*, Oxford, Clarendon Press, 1993.
30 Economides and Taylor, in Mayall (ed.), *The New Interventionism*, p. 91.
31 See the excellent discussion of the issues raised here, including recognition by the UN, in John Dugard, *Recognition and the United Nations*, Cambridge, Grotius Publications, 1987.
32 This issue is discussed by the author in his *The European Union in the 1990s*, Oxford, Oxford University Press, 1996, chapter 2.
33 The list draws on the wide range of reports on reform of the United Nations which were current in the late 1990s. Particular use was made of The Commission on Global Governance, *Our Global Neighbourhood*, Oxford, Oxford University Press, 1995; *A Report of the Independent Working Group on the Future of the United Nations*, appended to Klaus Huefner, (ed.), *Agenda for*

Notes 265

Change: New Tasks for the United Nations, Opladen, Leske+Budrich, 1995; Guido de Marco and Michael Bartolo, *A Second Generation of United Nations: for Peace and Freedom in the 21st Century*, London and New York, Kegan Paul International, 1997, especially chapter 10 and Annexe 1, *Summary of previous proposals*.

34 The Report of the Independent Working Group, reproduced in Huefner, *Agenda for Change*, calls this a Security Assessment Staff.
35 New Article F 1, Clause 2 referred to the Council's right to 'suspend certain rights ... including the voting rights' of a member state found to be in serious and persistent breach of the principles (including respect for human rights [Article F]).
36 See the excellent consideration of this question in David Held, *Democracy and the Global Order: From the Modern State to Cosmopolitan Governance*, Cambridge, Polity Press, 1995.

Chapter 2 Peacekeeping in the Age of Globalization: Kosovo and After

1 See David M. Malone and Ramesh Thakur, 'UN peacekeeping: lessons learned?', *Global Governance*, 7(1) January–March 2001: 11–18.
2 See Steven L. Burg and Paul S. Shoup, *The War in Bosnia–Herzegovina: Ethnic Conflict and International Intervention*, New York, M. E. Sharpe, 1999; Albrecht Schnabel and Ramesh Thakur (eds), *Kosovo and the Challenge of Humanitarian Intervention: selective indignation, collective action, and international citizenship*, Tokyo and New York, United Nations University Press, 2000.
3 See Alan James, *Peacekeeping in International Politics*, Basingstoke, Macmillan, 1990.
4 See Spyros Economides and Paul Taylor, 'Former Yugoslavia', in James Mayall (ed.), *The New Interventionism, 1991–94*, Cambridge, Cambridge University Press, 1996, pp. 59–93.
5 See Report on the fall of Srebenica, UN Doc. A54/549, 15 November 1999.
6 Charles King, 'Where the West went wrong', *The Times Literary Supplement*, 7 May 1999: 4.
7 See Paul Taylor and A. J. R. Groom, *The United Nations and the Gulf War: Back to the Future*, Discussion Paper no. 38, London, Royal Institute of International Affairs, 1992.
8 Statement, Friday, 19 March, 5.05 pm.
9 S/PRST/19992 and 5, 19 and 29 January.
10 Taylor and Groom, *op. cit.*
11 Interview FCO official, 24 June 1999.
12 Edward N. Luttwak, 'Letting wars burn' (cover title) or 'Give war a chance' (text title), *Foreign Affairs*, 78(4) July/August 1999: 36–44.
13 King, *op cit.*, p. 4.
14 Interview with a Canadian Foreign Ministry official, May 1999.
15 For a more extended discussion of the problems with the new peacekeeping see Paul Taylor, 'The United Nations in the 1990s: proactive cosmopolitanism and the issue of sovereignty', *Political Studies*, 47(3), Special Issue, 1999: 538–65.
16 Boutros Boutros-Ghali, *An Agenda for Peace, 1995* (2nd edn), United Nations, 1995.

17 Report of the Panel of Experts on United Nations Peace Operations, UN Doc. A/55/305–S/2000/809.21, August 2000 (the Brahimi Report).
18 Ibid., pp. viii–xv.

Chapter 3 Globalization and Regionalization among Modern States: The Case of the EU

1 A. Beattie, 'The deflationary ogre smiles', *Financial Times*, 9 April 1999.
2 The argument here relies heavily on evidence in Bernard Casey and Michael Gould, *Social Partnership and Economic Performance; The Case for Europe*, Cheltenham, Edward Elgar, 2000, pp. 15–21.
3 For a penetrating analysis of the trends in the welfare arrangements of various EU states see Colin Hay, Matthew Watson and Daniel Wincott, *Globalisation, European Integration and the Persistence of European Social Models*, Working Paper 3/99, POLSIS, University of Birmingham. Though their conclusions differ from those developed here they do agree that 'it is surely right to point to the potentially positive externalities of social democratic institutions and practices, particularly quality (as distinct from cost) competitive growth strategies and encompassing labour market institutions. Nonetheless, it is by no means unproblematic' (p. 24). And: 'The relationship between welfare states and labour markets in contemporary Europe is a complex, changing and, above all, contingent one. As such it is subject to political contestation' (p. 39).
4 *The Times*, 14 May 2000.
5 British Prime Minister, Tony Blair, was moved to an energetic criticism of the way the British press reported European issues in November 2000.
6 Paul Taylor, *The European Union in the 1990s*, Oxford, Oxford University Press, 1996.
7 See arguments of Ulrich Sedelmeier in Karlheinz Neunreither and Antje Wiener (eds), *European Integration: Institutional Dynamics and Prospects for Democracy after Amsterdam*, New York, Oxford University Press, 1999, pp. 218–37.
8 *Financial Times*, 4 October 2000.
9 See the excellent critique of the neoliberal assault on the welfare state in Giuliano Bonoli, Vic George and Peter Taylor-Gooby, *European Welfare Futures: Towards a Theory of Retrenchment*, Cambridge, Polity Press, 2000.
10 The objections to enlargement are in Paul Taylor, *op. cit.*, chapter 3.
11 See Bonoli, George and Taylor-Gooby, *op. cit.*, pp. 50–71.
12 A leading example is C. Murray, as in *Losing Ground*, New York, Basic Books, 1984 and *The Emerging British Underclass*, London, Institute of Economic Affairs, London, 1990.
13 Hamish McRae, *The Independent*, 21 September 2000.
14 Nigel Grimwade, *International Trade: New Patterns of Trade, Production and Investment*, 2nd edn, London and New York, Routledge, 2000.
15 *The Independent*, 25 September 2000.
16 *The Independent*, 21 September 2000.
17 A picture of a global financial system that, after the Mexican crisis of 1994, was increasingly out of control is effectively painted by Robert Went, *Globalization: Neoliberal Challenge, Radical Responses*, London, Pluto Press, 2000.
18 *Consumer Reports*, 65(9), September 2000, Yonkers, NY: 42–53.

19 A further illustration of US obduracy on fuel and linked environmental issues was their stance at the Environment Conference at The Hague in December 2000. The European Union negotiators were united in resisting US arguments on tradable environmental quotas and the setting up of alternative strategies to cutting fossil fuel consumption by setting up so-called sinks in the form of new afforestation.
20 *Consumer Reports*, 65(10), October 2000, Yonkers, NY: 62–4.
21 Interviewed, BBC News, 'The World at One', 28 September 2000.
22 See Julie Smith, 'Destination Unknown', *The World Today*, 56(10), October 2000: 20–2.
23 Grimwade, *op. cit.*
24 Loukas Tsoukalis, *The New European Economy Revisited*, Oxford, Oxford University Press, pp. 225–33.
25 Lorenzo Binin Smaghi and Claudio Casini, 'Monetary and fiscal policy cooperation in EMU', *Journal of Common Market Studies*, 38(3), September 2000.
26 Tsoukalis, *op. cit.*, p. 234.

Chapter 4 The Social and Economic Agenda of International Organization in the Age of Globalization

1 I am deeply indebted to a large number of officials in the UN Secretariat in New York and in a number of national UN missions for their invaluable advice on what follows.
2 See James Mayall (ed.), *The New Interventionism*, Cambridge, Cambridge University Press, 1996.
3 See Under-Secretary-General Connor's press statement of 24 January 1996.
4 See Paul Taylor, *International Organization in the Modern World: The Regional and the Global Process*, London and New York, Pinter, 1993, chapters 1 and 2.
5 Martin Hill, *The United Nations System: Coordinating Its Economic and Social Work*, Cambridge, Cambridge University Press, 1978, p. 95.
6 Report of the Secretary-General, *Renewing the United Nations: A Programme for Reform*, A/51/950 14 July 1997, pp. 25–6.
7 *Reporting to the Economic and Social Council*, prepared by Maurice Bertrand, Joint Inspection Unit, JIU/REP/84/7, Geneva, 1984, para. 35, p. 16.
8 From an anonymous internal US administrative document, headed *North/South Dialogue and UNCTAD*, dated 16 February 1984, Section 11, p. 2.
9 For an account of the problems in the system see Paul Taylor, *International Organization in the Modern World: The Regional and the Global Process*, London and New York, Pinter, 1993.
10 See John Ruggie, *Constructing the World Polity*, London and New York, Routledge, 1998, p. 21.
11 See a comment on this in Paul Taylor and A. J. R. Groom (eds), *Global Issues in the United Nations Framework*, Basingstoke, Macmillan, 1989, chapter 1.
12 This is the approach recommended by Rosemary Righter in her *Utopia Lost: The United Nations and World Order*, New York, Twentieth Century Fund Press, 1995.
13 Robert O. Keohane, *After Hegemony: Cooperation and Discord in the World Political Economy*, Princeton, NJ, Princeton University Press, 1984, p. 57.
14 Oran Young, *International Governance: Protecting the Environment in a Stateless Society*, Ithaca, NY, Cornell University Press, 1994.

15 An epistemic community is a group of people who share an area of knowledge or expertise, and who might belong to common professional associations or work together on common problems over a period of time. They may include people from a number of countries and therefore they may lead to transnational alliances. They could be called more colloquially knowledge clubs!
16 See Paul Taylor, *op. cit.*, chapter 5.
17 Set out in A/47/199 at para. 9, and frequently alluded to in the later resolutions.
18 By an official Danish mission to the UN, September 1996.
19 See Paul Taylor, 'Options for the reform of the international system for humanitarian assistance,' in John Harriss, *The Politics of Humanitarian Intervention*, London, Pinter and Save the Children, 1995.
20 Commissions were first created in the 1940s; they were only later attached explicitly to global conferences and their number then increased.
21 Economic and Social Council, General Segment, Background paper on the harmonization and coordination of the agendas and multi-year programmes of work of functional commissions of ECOSOC, E/1996/CRP.4, 10 July 1996, para. 6.
22 Ibid.
23 E/1996/CRP.4, July 1996, paras 8–10.
24 For an account of the reforms in budgetary arrangements see the author's *International Organization in the Modern World*, London, Pinter, 1993, chapter 5.
25 I am indebted for this note of caution, and for a number of other corrections in the text, to David Mallone, Canadian representative to ECOSOC, 1992–4.
26 For an account of subsidiarity see Paul Taylor, *The European Union in the 1990s*, Oxford, Oxford University Press, 1996, pp. 65–9.

Chapter 5 Development and Labour Welfare in the Age of Globalization: Aspects of the US International Economic Stance and International Organization

1 *Address of Secretary-General Kofi Annan to the World Economic Forum in Davos, Switzerland*, on 31 January 1999, Press Release SG/SM/6881, 1 February 1999.
2 Among a rapidly increasing literature a good sample would be Ethan B. Kapstein, *Sharing the Wealth: Workers and the World Economy*, New York, Norton, 1999; Robert Went, *Globalization: Neoliberal Challenge, Radical Responses*, London, Pluto Press, 2000; Naomi Klein, *No Logo*, London, HarperCollins, 2000.
3 Duncan Green and Mathew Griffith, 'Globalization and its discontents', *International Affairs*, 78(1), January 2002: 49–68 (quote from p. 68); see also Saskia Sassem, *Globalization and its Discontents*, New York, The New Press, 1998.
4 As prematurely announced by Francis Fukuyama in his *The End of History and the Last Man*, London, Penguin, 1992.
5 Economists find difficulty in agreeing on a definition of macro-management. I understand it in a rather general sense as policies which are about the overall framework of economic activity. These can be positive or negative, and be more or less political in character. The acceptance of existing arrangements can be as much a policy as the proposal to change them.
6 The case for this is persuasively argued by Richard Higgott and Nicola Phillips, 'Challenging triumphalism and convergence: the limits of global liberalization in Asia and Latin America', *Review of International Studies*, 26(3), July 2000: 359–80.

7 See Peter Malanczuk, *Akehurst's Modern Introduction to International Law* (7th rev. edn), London, Routledge, 1997, pp. 239–40.
8 Quoted in ibid., p. 239.
9 *The Independent on Sunday*, London, 7 January 2001.
10 John S. Dryzek, *The Politics of the Earth: Environmental Discourses*, Oxford, Oxford University Press, 1997, chapter 3.
11 *The Independent*, 29 March 2001.
12 As reflected in the work of Frederick L. Anderson and Donald R. Leal, *Free Market Environmentalism*, Boulder, Westview Press, 1991.
13 Thomas J. Biersteker, 'The triumph of neoclassical economics in the developing world: policy convergence and bases of governance in the international economic order', in James N. Rosenau and Ernst-Otto Czempiel, *Governance without Government: Order and Change in World Politics*, Cambridge, Cambridge University Press, 1992, pp. 102–31.
14 Richard Higgott and Nicola Phillips, *op. cit.*, p. 371.
15 See Annan, *op cit.*
16 For example, some oil companies, such as Shell, started to redefine themselves as energy companies, and to explore sources of energy other than fossil fuels.
17 See D. Rodrik, *Has Globalization Gone Too Far?*, Washington DC, Institute for International Economics, 1997.
18 Michelle Sforza-Roderick, Scott Nova and Mark Weisbrot, *Writing the Constitution of a Single Global Economy: A Concise Guide to the Multilateral Agreement on Investment Supporters' and Opponents' Views*, Preamble Center, 1997.
19 Ibid., p. 27.
20 The following is illustrative:

> Indeed, the assumptions on which the rules of WTO are based are grossly unfair and even prejudiced. Those rules also reflect an agenda that serves only to promote dominant corporatist interests that already monopolize the arena of international trade. The rules assume an equality of bargaining power between all the countries that engage in trade. They are also designed on the basis of a premise that ignores the fact that the greater percentage of global trade is controlled by powerful multinational enterprises. Within such a context, the notion of free trade on which the rules are constructed is a fallacy.

'Globalization and its impact on the full enjoyment of human rights, Preliminary Report, Sub-Commission on the Promotion and Protection of Human Rights', *UN Press Release, E/CN.4/Sub.2/2000/13*, 15 June 2000.
21 Reported in *UN Development Report*, January–February 1999.
22 *The OECD Guidelines for Multinational Enterprises*, Revision 2000, OECD, Paris, 2000.
23 See Andrew Walter, 'NGOs, business, and international investment: the Multilateral Agreement on Investment, Seattle, and beyond', *Global Governance*, 7(1) January–March 2001: 51–74.
24 Speech entitled 'Rediscovering public purpose in the global economy', Harvard University, 15 December 1998.
25 Bob Deacon, *Who Should Devise and Own the Proposed Global Social Policy Code?* Globalism and Social Policy Programme (GASPP), February 1999.
26 Higgott and Phillips, *op cit.*, p. 370.

27 Robert Holzmann, and Steen Jørgensen, *Social Risk Management: A New Conceptual Framework for Social Protection, and Beyond*, Social Protection Discussion Paper no. 0006, World Bank, February 2000.
28 Faisal Islam, 'Conflict leaves World Bank policy in disarray', *The Observer*, 4 February 2001.
29 See Naomi Klein, 'UN pact with business masks real dangers', *Toronto Star*, March 1999.
30 Statement of UNICEF Executive Director Carol Bellamy to Harvard International Development Conference on 'sharing responsibilities: public, private and civil society', Cambridge, MA, 16 April 1999.
31 Gene M. Lyons, 'Review essay: the UN and American Politics', *Global Governance*, 5(4): 497–511.
32 Diana Tussie and Ngaire Woods, 'Trade, regionalism and the threat to multilateralism', in Ngaire Woods (ed.), *The Political Economy of Globalization*, Basingstoke, Macmillan Press, 2000, pp. 54–76 (reference at p. 64).
33 Judith Miller, 'Outgoing UN Development chief berates US', *New York Times*, 1 May 1999.
34 Biersteker, in Rosenau and Czempiel, *op. cit.*, p. 106.
35 Higgott and Phillips, *op. cit.*, p. 359.
36 The following section draws on the work of Michelle Sforza-Roderick, Scott Nova and Mark Weisbrot, *Writing the Constitution of a Single Global Economy: A Concise Guide to the Multilateral Agreement on Investment: Supporters and Opponents' Views*, Preamble Center, 1997.
37 See Higgott and Phillips, *op. cit.*, p. 369.
38 Went, *op. cit.*, pp. 78–9 and *passim*.
39 See Susan Strange, *Casino Capitalism*,
40 Ibid., p. 99.
41 Ibid., p. 112.
42 Article headed 'US in no hurry over rogue tax havens', in *Business, The Observer*, London, 24 June 2001, p. 2.
43 See R. H. Jackson on quasi-states in his *Quasi-States: Sovereignty, International Relations and the Third World*, Cambridge, 1990.
44 *New Straits Times*, 10 April 2001.
45 Simon Clarke, *Keynesianism, Monetarism and the Crisis of the State*, Aldershot, Edward Elgar, 1988.
46 Torsten Persson and Guido Tabellini, 'Is inequality harmful for growth?', *American Economic Review*, 84, June 1994, discussed in Kapstein, *op. cit.*, p. 115.
47 The reader should evaluate David Dollar and Aart Kraay, 'Spreading the wealth', *Foreign Affairs*, January/February, 2002: 120–33.
48 See Rorden Wilkinson and Steve Hughes, 'Labor standards and global governance: examining the dimensions of institutional engagement', *Global Governance*, 6(2), April–June 2000: 259–77.
49 Ibid., p. 269.
50 See Went, *op. cit.*, p. 61.

Chapter 6 The Principle of Consonance in Global Organization: The Case of the United Nations

1. See Report of the Secretary-General, A/50/666/Add.4/Corr.1, 2 April 1996. For updated reports see the annual *A Global Agenda: Issues before the General Assembly of the United Nations*, published by the UN Association of the USA, New York, University Press of America.
2. Richard Langhorne, 'Full circle: new principles and old consequences in the modern diplomatic system', unpublished paper, written for the Westphalia Conference at Enschede, Netherlands, 16–19 July 1998, p. 2.
3. See the evaluation of regionalism in Lousie Fawcett and Andrew Hurell (eds), *Regionalism in World Politics*, Oxford, Oxford University Press, 1995. See also Paul Taylor, *International Organization in the Modern World*, London, Pinter, 1993, chapters 1 and 2; and the special volume on the UN and regionalism of *Review of International Studies*, 21(4) October 1995.
4. For an account of the development of the CFSP see Desmond Dinan, *Ever Closer Union? An Introduction to the European Community*, Basingstoke, Macmillan, 1994, chapter 17.
5. On the faltering record of the UN see Marc Weller, 'Undoing the global construction: the UN Security Council action on the International Criminal Court', *International Affairs*, Vol. 78, No. 4, October 2002, pp. 693–712.
6. Crispin Tickell, 'The role of the Security Council in world affairs', The Sibley Lecture 1989 delivered to the University of Georgia, Athens, GA, 2 February 1989.
7. See Paul Taylor and A. J. R. Groom, *The Gulf War*, Discussion Paper no. 38, Royal Institute of International Affairs, London, February 1992.
8. Paul Taylor, *International Organization in the Modern World*, London, Pinter, 1995, pp. 154–6.
9. Ibid., pp. 154–6.
10. Ibid., p. 138.
11. See the discussion of this tendency in ibid., chapter 5.
12. See ibid., chapter 5.
13. See A. J. R. Groom and Paul Taylor in John Trent, Alger *et al.*
14. Information to the author from an official in the FCO, May 1997.
15. Erskine Childers and Brian Urquart, 'Renewing the United Nations system: the International Civil Service', *Development Dialogue*, Hammarskjold Foundation, 1994, pp. 159–70; and their 'A world in need of leadership: tomorrow's United Nations', *Dialogue*, 1990s, pp. 23–30.

Chapter 7 Conclusions: Globalization, International Organization and Regionalization

1. John Gerard Ruggie, *Constructing the World Polity: Essays on International Institutionalization*, London and New York, Routledge, 1998, p. 193.
2. Ibid., p. 180.
3. Ibid., p. 195.
4. Paul Taylor, *The European Union in the 1990s*, Oxford, Oxford University Press, 1996.

5 C. I. Barnard, *The Functions of the Executive*, Cambridge, MA, Harvard University Press, 1938, p. 184.
6 Peter Blau, 'Critical remarks on Weber's theory of authority', *American Political Science Review*, 57(1): 312.
7 See Paul Taylor, 'The European Union in the 1990s: reassessing the bases of integration', in Ngaire Woods (ed.), *Explaining International Relations since 1945*, Oxford, Oxford University Press, 1996, pp. 283–308.
8 See Barry K. Gills, 'The crisis of postwar East Asian capitalism: American power, democracy and the vicissitudes of globalization', *Review of International Studies*, 26(3) July 2000: 381–403.
9 See chapter 5 above.

Index

a-national deracinated society 248
accountability 44, 49, 53
ACP (African, Caribbean and Pacific) countries 42
acquis communautaire 117, 119, 120
action *v.* inaction 4
actors 161, 166, 212, 246
Advisory Committee on Administrative and Budgetary Questions (ACABQ) 94
Afghanistan 57, 68
Africa 42, 80, 87, 154
African, Caribbean and Pacific (ACP) countries 42
Agenda for Peace (Boutros-Ghali) 87
Al-Capone syndrome states 217
al-Qaeda 37, 40
Albright, Madeleine 79
Algeria 217
Alliance Capitalism 116
alternative states 72
ambiguity 66
Anglo-American states 100, 109, 114, 121, 122
Angola 70
Annan, Kofi 87, 258
anti-globalization 76, 168
arms distribution/acquisition 76
arms registry 34
Austria 100
authority 252, 253

'bad' economies 125
banking 192–3
Bartinder Commission 45
becoming 54
beef, hormone-fed 176
Belgium 100
Biersteker, Thomas J. 174, 182
BMW 122
Bosnia-Herzegovina 59, 61, 68, 70, 84
Boutros-Gali, Boutros 138, 178, 179
Brahimi Report 87, 88–98

branded companies 191–2, 203
Brazil 216, 218, 219
Bretton Woods 141, 180
Britain 103, 110, 117, 132
    monetary union 142–3
    UN role 81, 215, 218, 219, 224, 235–6
    see also cautious states; Eurosceptics
Brown, Gordon 178
Brown, Mark Malloch 181
Brussels 110
budgetary process 94–5, 160, 225–7, 230
bureaucracy 136–9
Burma 217
Bush, George W. 171, 173, 193, 251
business cycles 125–7
business organizations 175, 178

Cambodia 70
Canada 215
capital, location of 120–4
capital movements 203, 205
capitalism, risks of 204
CATO institute 176
cautious states (EU) 110, 112, 115, 116
Central Europe 116, 117
cheap labour 123
China 66–7, 79, 215
Chirac, Jacques 115
Christendom 30
citizenship argument 3–4
civil order 38, 39, 48
civil society 41, 42, 79, 171
civil unrest 211
civilian protection 91
Clinton, Bill 181, 222, 225
CNN factor 57
coded language 64, 65, 66, 67
Cold War 33, 140
collective actions 220–30
collective intentionality 140
collective will 27, 78, 222

274 Index

Commissions 147, 148, 157, 159
Committee for Programme and
    Coordination 160
Common External Tariff (CET) 120
Common Foreign and Security Policy
    (CFSP) 217, 224
communitarianism 30
competences
    European Union 110, 111, 244
    global level 254
    states 46, 47–8, 53
competition 132
compliance 159, 161
confederalization 36–41
conflict, internal 75
conflict prevention 89
conflict resolution 71–2
conscience 25
consensus 56–7, 112, 118, 119, 142,
    224, 228
consonance 210–31
consumer power 196–7
core (social democratic) states (EU)
    100, 114, 116, 117, 119
    and the globalizing economies
        120–31
core–periphery relations (EU) 118
corporatism 105
Corus (steel company) 201
cosmopolitanism 31, 32, 39–40, 54
    and citizens (proposals) 50–1
    Europe and the US 128
    and sovereignty 43–8
Council (UN) 147, 149, 157
country programmes 151, 153, 154,
    155–60, 203
Country Strategy Notes 144, 153, 155,
    158, 159, 203
crime, international 37, 40
crisis response 33–6
Croatia 70
Cuba 217
cultural homogenization 8
currency value 127
Cyprus 70

Dayton agreement 61, 63, 70
de/regulation 100, 124, 169
decolonization 23–4, 30
democratization 41–3
Denmark 100, 109
Department of Peacekeeping Operations
    (DPKO) 35, 92, 93, 94, 95, 96
Department of Political Affairs (UN)
    34
Deputy-Secretary-General, office of
    151

derecognition 45
developing countries 174, 182
development 136, 153, 169–71
Development Decade agreements
    (UN) 173
development state 114
devolution 72–3
diasporas 74
differentiation (EU) 115, 116
diplomacy 24
Director-General for Development and
    International Economic
    Cooperation (DGDIEC) 141
disequilibrium 245
divine order 27, 44
domestic jurisdiction 54
donor states 234, 239
Dow Jones 126
downsizing 191
dual roles 249–50
duplication 138, 139

Eashington Consensus 175
East Asia crises 192–3
East Timor 97
Eastern Europe 116
economic activities 7
economic agenda 135–66
economic blocks 201
economic diversity (EU) 99–110
economic production zones (EPZs) 190
Economic and Social Council
    (ECOSOC) 18–19, 136, 146,
    147–8, 149, 156, 157, 159
Eliason, Jan 137, 138
employment 122, 132, 189–209
enforcement (UN Charter Ch. VII)
    57–9, 84, 89
    post-Srebrenica 61–2
enlargement (EU) 118
entrenched multilateralism 141, 159,
    252
environment issues 8, 173–4, 251
epistemic communities 197, 198, 259
ethnic cleansing 59, 62
euro 110, 124, 125, 126, 127
European Commission 112
European Court of Human Rights 52
European Court of Justice 52
European Free Trade Area 113
European Superstate 111
European Union 9, 10, 11–12, 99–134,
    140, 224
Eurosceptics 111, 112, 114, 119, 123
Executive Boards 150
Executive Committee on Peace and
    Security (ECPS) 92

Index 275

expertise 93
explicitness 83
Exxon 196

failed/failing states 28, 31–2, 140, 223
false echo 228
Far East group 12
federalism 111
Field, Frank 130
financial issues 177, 179
financial system 246
Finland 100, 215
fiscal policy reform 183
Fischer, Joshka 111, 115
flexibility 122, 131, 132
Food and Agriculture Organization (FAO) 18
foreign investment rules (MAI) 184–6
fragmentation 138
France 100, 103, 105, 215
Frechette, Louise 151
free trade 197–8
freeloading 124
frontiers 74
fuel strikes 128
funding 83, 140, 230, 257, 258
Funds and Programmes 18, 19, 148, 151–5, 156, 159

G7 meeting (Lyons 1996) 150
G77 9, 155, 160
Geneva Group 234
Germany 100, 105, 122, 129
  UN role 215, 218, 219
global agenda mechanisms 135–66
global conferences 139, 146, 153, 157, 158
global intentions 156, 157
global watch 34
globalization 1, 5, 6, 7–8, 32, 43
  and the EU 99–134
  neoliberal 168–9
  and regionalization 253–6
globalizing economies 120–31
Goldman Sachs 193
governance 141, 142, 154
governments 40, 49, 53, 81–2, 104, 105
Greece 101
Gross Domestic Product 1999 (EU) 101
Gulf war 222

Haiti 42, 78
Heavily Indebted Poor Countries (HIPC) 172
Helms, Jesse 137, 252

history 258
Hobson, John 191
holism 177, 179, 209
Holzmann, Robert 178, 179
human rights 26, 78, 83, 211, 250
humanitarian assistance 35, 66
humanitarian goals 60, 62, 64
Hussein, Saddam 40, 59

imports/exports 176
income differentials 198
India 216
inequalities 245
information gathering 34–5, 38, 83, 250–1
information management 92
information technology 96, 211
injunctions on behaviour 142
insiders 73–4
institutional development 49–50
Integrated Mission Task Forces (IMTFs) 95–6, 145, 158
integration (EU) 113, 114–15, 117, 118
intelligence services 34
interdependence 76
international civil society 83, 246–51
  counterterrorism 80
  emergence 30
  governments 81–2
  members of governments 248–9
  and the UN 233, 240
international community 48
international cooperation 179, 247, 252
International Criminal Court 42
international forces 72, 213
International Labour Organization (ILO) 18, 171, 200
International Monetary Fund (IMF) 125, 141, 175, 179
international organization 5, 14–20, 41–3
  evolutionary proposals 48–51
international will 27
intervention 26, 30, 42, 45, 67, 83
investment (EU) 108–9
investment funds (EU) 124–8
investment regions 204, 205
Iran 217, 222, 223
Iraq 217, 220, 222, 223
Ireland 100
Islamic world 37
isolationism 258
Italy 100, 105, 117

Japan 215, 219
justice 25

Kant, Immanuel 25, 44
King, Betty 175
Korea 59
Kosovo 15, 55, 56–82
Kuwait 24
Kyoto agreement 173, 251

labour 122, 132, 189–207
laws 180–1, 188–9
leadership 232, 234, 239
League of Nations 16, 33
legal regulation 207
liberal pluralism 41, 255
liberalization 183
Libya 217
licensing 26, 44–5, 53
Lomé Conventions 42
lourdeur 119, 222
low social wage strategies 123, 132
Luttwak, Edward 69, 84, 85
Luxembourg 53, 100

Magnet, Myron 173
Malaysia 189, 199, 217
managerial approach 140
marginalization 118
Marks and Spencer 201
material environment 242, 243–6
media 221
medievalism 73
mercenaries 36
MERCOSUR 218
Mexico 193
Microsoft 190
milieu goals 10
military issues 76, 84, 92
Mill, John Stuart 75
Milosevic, Slobodan 59, 61, 62, 63
mission guidance/leadership 92–3
mistrust 139
Mogadishu 77
monetary union 142–3
moral dimension 3–5, 7, 23–5, 28, 81–2, 206, 221
motor car analogy 247
multicentrality 240
Multilateral Agreement on Investment (MAI) 171, 174, 176, 183–9
multilateral companies 174–5
multilateral diplomacy 142, 143
multinational companies 193, 196, 202
multiperspectival polity 244, 253
multiple conditionality 42
Murdoch, Rupert 112
Mussa, Michael 125

NASDAQ 126

national constitutions 110
National Insurance system 129
national interest 23–5
national security 36–41
NATO (North Atlantic Treaty Organization) 56–63
neoliberalism 3
  alliances 174
  and development practice 169–71
  employment 189–209
  European Union 114, 125, 126, 127, 128
  United States 171–2
neorealism 2–3
Netherlands 100, 101, 215
neutrality 29
new dissatisfied powers 217
New International Economic Order 9
New Labour 175, 219
Nigeria 216
non-governmental organizations (NGOs) 80, 85, 144, 174, 197
norm maintenance 220
North American Free Trade Area 12
North–South issues 175–6, 193
Norton, Gale 173
Norway 215

Olasky, Marvin 173
O'Neill, Paul 194
OPEC 203
opt-out argument/counter-argument 69–77, 80
order, sovereignty and 21, 25
Organization for Economic Cooperation and Development (OECD) 178
outsourcing 191

P5 arrangement 222–3
pacific engagement 32
pacts 105
Panel on United Nations Peace Operations 88
peacebuilding 89, 90
peacekeeping
  evolution 28–32, 35
  funding 258
  Kosovo and after 55–98
  millennium reforms 82–6
  opt-out argument, arguments against 69–77, 80
  principles 90
pension costs 128
peripheral states (EU) 115, 119
police forces 38, 39, 74
policy disagreement (EU) 120–4
political diversity (EU) 110–20

Index 277

political/economic élites 195–6
Population Conferences 157
Portugal 101, 103
privacy, right to 28, 30
private profit 193–4
privatization 129, 130
protectionism 176
public sector 124
Purchasing Power Parities (PPP) 101, 103

Quebec 53

rapid deployment 93
reformist states 215–16
refugee centres 84
regime theory 141
regionalization 5, 9–14, 240–1, 253–6
  and globalization 253–6
regulation 207
regulatory reform 103
relocation, social costs of 204
Republicans 76, 79, 171, 193
resources 83, 97, 245
responsibility 46–7, 110, 124
retirement 129, 130
Right to Development 170, 171
right to judge 31
risk factor 7–8, 208
rogue governments 40
Rousseau, Jean-Jacques 250
Rover car company 122
Rubin, Robert 193
Ruggie, John 242, 243, 252
rules 142
rules of engagement 91
Russia 64–6, 68, 211, 224–5
Rwanda 84

safe areas 61, 85
Sarajevo 84
self-determination 31
self-fulfilling prophecy 142, 166
September 11, 2001 36–8, 69, 71
Serbia 60, 62
settlement frameworks 71–2, 81
single currency 143
Single European Act 217
social agenda 135–66
social charge liability 205–7
Social Charter (Maastricht) 123
social democracy 101, 105, 121–2, 125, 127
social democratic (core) states (EU) 100, 114, 116, 117, 119
social empowerment 242, 253
social epistemes 242, 245, 247, 253, 258

social practice, code of 178, 199
social protection, *see* welfare provision
social regulation 207
Social Security Fund (US) 128–9
Somalia 70, 85
sources 20
sovereignty 39
  changing meaning 25–8, 257
  and cosmopolitanism 43–8
  dialectal quality 52
  European Union 110, 111
  evolution 48–51, 83
  and intervention 45
  order and 21, 25
  and unbundling 253
Soviet Union 210
Spain 101, 103
Spanish Civil War 75
specialist forces 38
Specialized Agencies 18
  country programmes 155, 156, 159
  institutional relationships 19, 137, 179
Speth, Gus 41, 181
'start-up kits' 94
state-building 72–3
statehood 23, 24, 40, 44
states 27–8, 29–31, 48, 254, 256
status quo powers 215
Stiglitz, Joseph 174
strategic analysis 92
strategic behaviour 242
subsidiarity 165
Sudan 217
supply centres 83
supranational management principles 140, 232–3
Sweden 100, 105, 215
system-dominance 255
system-loading claimants 216–17
system-reinforcing problem-solving states 215

Taliban 57, 58
Task Forces 95–6, 145, 158
tax havens 194
taxation 102, 120–1, 132
terrorism 8, 37, 39, 43, 58
Thatcher, Margaret 42, 111
theory 2–3
theory of states 243
Thomson, John 222, 223
Tickell, Crispin 223
Tobin tax 203
Track II process 151–5
trade barriers 176
trade fairs 245

trade issues 177
trade unions 199
trans-state territoriality 74
transnational forces 72, 213
transnational society of groups 248
travel and communication 7
Treaties of Westphalia 211
Treaty of Amsterdam 115, 116, 118
Treaty of Maastricht 140, 217
Treaty of Nice 115, 116, 118
Treaty of Rome 111
troop levels 91
Turner, Ted 181

unanimity 112
unbundling 244, 253
unilateralism 173
United Nations
 failures 223–4
 functions and institutional locations 79–80, 86
 general policy recommendations 227
 high office in 81
 membership 214–20
 overall structure 230–8
 post-Cold War agenda 33–51
 post-Kosovo 69–82
 procedural principles 231
 reforms 212
 specialized character of institutions 231
 system 14–20, 21, 35
United Nations Charter 15, 18, 33
 chapter VII 57–9, 61–2, 84
 chapter VIII 67, 68
United Nations Children's Fund (UNICEF) 42, 154
United Nations Development Assistance Frameworks (UNDAFs) 151, 153, 154, 155–60, 203
United Nations Development Group (UDG) 152
United Nations Development Programme (UNDP)
 Capital Development fund 146
 cooperation with businesses 179
 Resident Coordinator 144, 145, 158
 Speth, Gus 41, 152
United Nations General Assembly 16–17, 18, 147, 149, 227–8, 229
United Nations Headquarters 92, 95, 146

United Nations Relief and Work Administration (UNRWA) 84
United Nations Secretariat 17–18, 34, 236–8
United Nations Secretary-General 17, 33, 35
United Nations Security Council 16, 33, 42
 collective will 78–9
 enlargement 232
 reforms 85, 219
 relationship with US 68
 resolutions 58, 62, 63–4, 65, 67, 68, 143
United Nations standby arrangements system (UNSAS) 93
United States
 abroad 180–2
 Afghanistan 57–8
 and the European Union 113, 125–9
 international cooperation 252
 intervention 71, 86
 laws 180–1
 neoliberal policy 171–2
 political culture 172–4
 republicanism 259
 and the Right to Development 170–1
 special responsibilities 76–7
 UN role 215, 220, 257
upward mobility 198–9
USSR 215

war crimes 64
wealth, distribution of 172, 195
welfare provision
 European Union 105, 106–7, 110, 123
 and MAI 187
 US policy 173
welfare state 30
Westphalian system 43, 44
willing states (EU) 118, 119
Working Groups 147
World Bank 141, 175, 178, 179
World Economic Forum Conference 178
World Health Organization (WHO) 18, 172
world order 212, 213
World Trade Organization (WTO) 47, 176, 177, 199

Yemen 217
Yugoslavia 45, 60–3, 84